# THE LEGENDS OF
# LEICESTER CITY

# THE LEGENDS OF
# LEICESTER CITY

DAVE BRACEGIRDLE

PUBLISHING

First published in Great Britain in 2010 by
The Derby Books Publishing Company Limited
Breedon House, 3 The Parker Centre, Derby, DE21 4SZ.

ISBN 978-1-85983-760-3

Printed and bound by OZ Graf, Poland.

# CONTENTS

# ACKNOWLEDGEMENTS

There have been so many people involved in putting *The Legends of Leicester City* together, and I hope the final outcome will make them all feel that their efforts have been worthwhile.

First and foremost, I must publically acknowledge the tremendous assistance given by Alan Bennett. Helping former Foxes to remain in touch has become something of a full-time occupation for Alan – and without his vast collection of addresses and contact numbers this project would have been much more difficult to complete.

Virtually everyone reading this piece will be familiar with the impact Alan Birchenall has had since moving to Leicester – not just on the football club, but also on the community. Unsurprisingly, he's been hugely supportive as the book has taken shape and I make no apologies for the number of mentions he gets over the course of the next few pages. Most who have come into contact with 'The Birch' have a story to tell – and several have done so!

In no particular order I'd also like to thank many others who have been instrumental in giving either their time, a phone number or an opinion when asked. They include Phil Adlam, Carly Bassett, Darren Bentley, Rachel Cluley, Mike Donovan, Claire Huggins, Sarah Meakin, Geoff Peters and Steve Wilson.

Closer to home, many hours of domestic chores have been lost whilst I've been slaving over the laptop, so a heart-felt thank you to Karen for her support.

As I've discovered over the past few months, the Foxes story has never been dull – there have been as many downs as ups for the club, but through them all the most stoical bunch of supporters in the land have always pulled together and enjoyed them as one.

Putting *The Legends of Leicester City* together has been a real labour of love because it's afforded me the opportunity of being able to speak to some of the warmest, most passionate football folk around.

It also brought great sadness. Bobby Smith was interviewed in August 2009, some six months before his untimely passing. The content of that interview has been used for Bobby's tribute on page 174.

Finally, to all of the Legends – thank you for your time and for allowing me to share your memories. I hope I've been able to accurately portray your story!

**Dave Bracegirdle**

June 2010

# MICKY ADAMS

*Born:*          8 November 1961, Sheffield, Yorkshire.

## Leicester City record:
*Manager:*        April 2002–October 2004.

*Played for:*     Gillingham, Coventry City, Leeds United, Southampton, Stoke City (loan), Fulham, Swansea City, Brentford.

*Also managed:*   Fulham, Swansea, Brentford, Brighton and Hove Albion, Coventry City, Port Vale.

There is no doubt that the only place for a successful English football club to be is in the Premiership. With the game not just a sport but also a highly competitive and lucrative business, the high finances involved mean it is paramount for clubs to be playing at that level.

As such, the competition to play in the top division becomes more competitive each year. The last manager to guide Leicester City into the 'promised land' was Micky Adams, who took the Foxes up at the end of the 2002–03 season. Given that the club were in administration at the time and banned from entering into the transfer market, the achievement remains even more remarkable.

Micky had moved to Leicester in October 2001, initially serving as assistant manager under Dave Bassett. Comments – for which he later apologised – suggested that Micky had wanted the manager's position for the following campaign; however, his appointment came about fairly soon with the senior man moving 'upstairs' to become the club's director of football.

A turbulent period for the club was about to become worse – much worse. On the playing front City were in a period of transition, and the cold hard statistics were that they were not good enough to stay up.

Only two of the last 24 League matches were won – the second of which came on the final afternoon of the season against Spurs, on the day that tears were shed, not only for the impending relegation but also because it signified the closure of Filbert Street.

Life at the new Walkers Stadium threatened to be de-railed due to financial constraints. Promised television money was not forthcoming due to the collapse of ITV Digital, the heavy price for the new arena and a large wage bill all but crippled the aspirations of the manager and the resultant move into administration saw a ban imposed on any dealings in the transfer market.

Despite all of these handicaps, Micky fought fire in a manner which would have made 'Red Adair' envious. Clinging to the coat-tails of an impressive Portsmouth side all season, the Foxes secured 92 points on their way to automatic promotion.

Following a successful takeover by the consortium led by Gary Lineker, the club came out of their period of administration and Micky was able to replenish his squad and stabilise first-team affairs in time for an assault on the Premiership.

If life among the elite was not difficult enough anyway for a newly-promoted side, there was a further period of strife which made the news headlines all around the world. During a mid-season training break to the La Manga resort in southern Spain, several members of City's first-team squad were falsely alleged to have been involved in incidents of a serious sexual nature with three African women.

Enquiries focused upon three of the City players – Paul Dickov, Keith Gillespie and Frank Sinclair – and they were all imprisoned for a week. Throughout the ordeal Micky maintained the innocence of his staff, and his beliefs were truly vindicated when all charges were eventually dropped.

Despite the inevitable trauma that the case had caused for all involved, the dignified and compassionate manner

*No amount of preparation could have prepared Micky for the turmoil he would experience during his Leicester City days*

in which the manager had dealt with the considerable distress endeared him to many. Micky and his players became much closer after all they had been through.

It had been far from a conventional period in charge for Micky, however, and the poor start to the 2004–05 contributed to his decision to resign from his post.

Micky was soon back in the game with a two-year stint in charge of Coventry City. He briefly joined Colchester United as assistant to Geraint Williams, but, eager to return to management, he returned to Brighton (having been there prior to joining Leicester City), but he was soon back in the Midlands, taking over at Port Vale in June 2009 and leading the Valiants to a 10th-place finish in his first season.

Sheffield-born Micky's own playing career had begun at Gillingham, where he made over 100 first-team appearances – starting as a left-winger before being converted into a full-back. Further lengthy spells at Coventry City, Leeds United and Southampton were the significant ports of call during a consistent, if unspectacular, playing career.

Short player-manager appointments at Fulham and Swansea City and then a brief stint at Brentford enabled him to cut his teeth as a manager, but no amount of preparation could have prepared Micky for the turmoil he would experience during his Leicester City days – and the job he did there under difficult circumstances should not easily be forgotten.

# HUGHIE ADCOCK

*Born:*         10 April 1903, Coalville, Leicestershire.

*Died:*         16 October 1975, Coalville, Leicestershire.

## Leicester City record:

*Appearances:*    League 434, FA Cup 26.

*Goals:*    League 51, FA Cup 1.

*Debut:*    25 August 1923 v Hull City (a) drew 1–1.

*Also played for:*    Coalville Town, Loughborough Corinthians, Bristol Rovers, Folkestone, England (5 caps).

Hughie Adcock was one of the most dynamic of Leicester City's early wingers, possessing great pace and trickery and becoming a stalwart of the side that so nearly brought the League title to Filbert Street in 1929. During more than a decade of loyal service to the Foxes he compiled over 450 appearances and gained international recognition.

Having picked up a County Cup-winners' medal in 1922 with Central Alliance side Loughborough Corinthians, Hughie was on the radar of his local Football League club and was watched with increasing regularity before making the move to Filbert Street early in 1923.

He had to wait awhile for his introduction into the first team, but it duly arrived at the start of the following season, debuting away at Hull on the same day that Arthur Chandler was also blooded into the side. A couple of days later – on his home bow – Hughie scored his first senior goal in a 5–0 drubbing of Stoke City.

Scoring was a bonus, but Hughie became more valuable as a supply line. With goal-grabbers like Chandler and Johnny Duncan in the side, they were good times to be a wide player and City's outside-right would regularly earn the plaudits for slipping past his full-back and setting up a succession of simple chances.

City had finished 12th in Hughie's first year at the club but were celebrating 12 months on as Peter Hodge's side clinched the Division Two title, finishing a couple of points clear of Manchester United. The backbone of the success was an unbeaten run of 18 matches (14 wins, four draws) between 6 December and 30 March. This was among a host of new club records set that season, including the most wins (24), most goals (90) and most points (59). (Remember it was still two points for a win in those days.)

Hughie was an ever-present throughout both 1926–27 and 1927–28 and missed only a couple of games the following season as City finished as League runners-up, their best-ever placing. In all, he played in a consecutive 119 League matches – another milestone in the club's history.

# City's outside-right would regularly earn the plaudits for slipping past his full-back and setting up a succession of simple chances.

Big games were becoming more commonplace for City and, statistically, there were none bigger than a fifth-round FA Cup tie at home to Spurs on 18 February 1928 as a Filbert Street record attendance of 47,298, aided by the recent opening of the new Double Decker Stand, crammed in to see it. The result went against the Foxes that day but later in the same calendar year Hughie played his part on a happier occasion – the day of City's record 10–0 battering of Portsmouth.

During 1929 Hughie finally caught the eye of the national selectors and won England recognition – his five full caps coming in the space of six months. His debut, in Paris on 9 May, resulted in a 4–1 win over the French. In three of the matches he played alongside his cousin, Birmingham City's Joe Bradford, with Leicester teammate Ernie Hine also playing in a couple.

Considering that England won four of the games and that he scored in his final appearance, a 6–0 victory against Wales, Hughie was perhaps a little unlucky not to be selected again; although in both 1929 and 1930 he was also picked to play in representative matches for the Football League.

At club level Leicester's fortunes were heading south. After their runners'-up finish of 1928–29 it became a continual battle to avoid the drop over the next few seasons. Spirits were momentarily lifted in the spring of 1934 when the club reached its first-ever FA Cup semi-final. Hughie had played his part in each of the previous rounds but was unable to inspire his teammates as Portsmouth gained a measure of revenge for that 10-goal mauling six years earlier by winning the last-four clash at St Andrew's.

City's manager that day, Peter Hodge, then tragically died during the close season – Hughie was one of the pall-bearers at his funeral. The loss had a knock-on effect to performances and Leicester finally succumbed to relegation in 1935.

By now 32 and losing some of his blistering pace, Hughie was one of the players put up for sale and he moved to Bristol Rovers for £150. Ironically, his debut was against a Notts County side featuring debutant Arthur Chandler – another player let go by City.

After hanging up his playing boots Hughie maintained his love of the game and became a trainer for many years in the Leicestershire Senior League, looking after both Whitwick Colliery and Coalville Town, while working until retirement as a maintenance engineer.

Born in Coalville, he had lived there most of his life and also died there in 1975.

# JOHNNY ANDERSON

| | |
|---|---|
| *Born:* | 8 December 1929, Barrhead, Renfrewshire, Scotland. |
| *Died:* | 22 August 2001, Leicester. |

**Leicester City record:**

| | |
|---|---|
| *Appearances:* | League 261, FA Cup 16. |
| *Debut:* | 6 April 1949 v Barnsley (a) lost 1–3. |
| *Also played for:* | St Charles (Paisley), Arthurlie, Peterborough United, Nuneaton Borough, Bedworth Town, Scotland (1 cap). |

At a club which has prided itself on the quality of its goalkeepers, Johnny Anderson can quite rightly hold comparison with the very best. He served City with huge distinction throughout the 1950s, making a total of 277 first-team appearances after first being brought to Filbert Street by manager John Duncan in the FA Cup Final season of 1948–49.

The Scot began his career in Paisley and then moved to Arthurlie – another Glasgow-based non-League side – and his early promise was rewarded with selection for his country in a Junior international against the Republic of Ireland at Hampden Park.

Regularly watched by the Leicester scouts, he was just 19 when he arrived in the East Midlands and, as third choice 'keeper on City's books, he knew he would have to bide his time before being handed an opportunity. In pretty unusual circumstances, though, he featured before the end of his first season at the club.

With the current first choice, Gordon Bradley, out of the side through injury, Ian McGraw – recently signed from Arbroath – had begun to put in some sterling performances between the sticks, notably in the FA Cup semi-final win over Portsmouth. Tragically, however, in a League match

*He served City with huge distinction throughout the 1950s, making a total of 277 first-team appearances after first being brought to Filbert Street by manager John Duncan in the FA Cup Final season of 1948–49.*

against Grimsby Town a week later, Ian fractured a finger which eventually developed complications and, distressingly, had to be amputated.

With that as an unfortunate backdrop, Johnny was plunged into the side for his Division Two debut – lining up against Barnsley at Oakwell. Despite the FA Cup run, only two of the previous 13 League matches had been won – so it was perhaps not surprising, nor reflective of the new goalkeeper's performance, that the Yorkshire side ran out 3–1 winners.

Bradley's return to the side relegated Johnny to the back-up role, but gradually over the next two years his opportunities became more and more frequent. By 1951–52 the number-one position was his, and so it remained for the next six or seven years.

Although considered to be slightly shorter than the perceived norm for a 'keeper, Johnny was fit, agile and an outstanding shot-stopper. He was considered to be 'proactive' rather than 'reactive', with his ability to anticipate imminent danger saving his side on many occasions.

The undoubted highlights of his time with the Foxes were the victorious Division Two Championship campaigns. Johnny was an ever-present in the first of them, in 1953–54, playing in all 42 games in the League programme and making another eight appearances as City almost advanced to the Cup semi-finals, before being denied by Preston North End in a sixth-round second replay!

City had taken that title by the slenderest of margins, pipping Everton on goal average only. The Foxes had scored 97 and conceded 60, while the Toffees' tally had been 92/58.

Right at the end of the season, on 25 May 1954, Johnny's consistency was rewarded with a call-up to win his first and only full international cap, keeping goal for Scotland in a 2–1 victory over Finland in Helsinki.

This performance confirmed the judgement of the selectors and he was immediately announced in the squad for the 1954 World Cup Finals, to be held in Switzerland. In a scenario that is hard to envisage in the modern game Scotland chose to travel with just 13 of the selected party – the rest, including Johnny, remaining at home on standby. Regrettably, he was not called upon again!

Back at club level City were relegated in their first year back in the top flight, but they took just two seasons to win another Second Division title, this time more convincingly – finishing seven points clear of nearest rivals Nottingham Forest.

Johnny's association with the Filberts ended in the summer of 1960 when he joined Peterborough United, who were just about to embark on their new adventure of life in the Football League. He remained on the periphery of the first-team squad, however, and played in just one League Cup tie; although he did briefly assume the mantle of caretaker manager on a couple of occasions as the Posh changed managers twice within the space of 16 months.

Moving into the non-League game, Johnny played briefly at both Nuneaton Borough and then Bedworth Town before hanging up his boots to set up a painting and decorating business in Leicester, where he lived until his death in 2001, aged 71.

# COLIN APPLETON

*Born:*          7 March 1936, Scarborough, Yorkshire.

## Leicester City record:

*Appearances:*    League 277, FA Cup 32, League Cup 20, Other 4.

*Goals:*           League 19, FA Cup 0, League Cup 2, Other 1.

*Debut:*           4 September 1954 v Manchester City (h) lost 0–2.

*Also played for:*  Charlton Athletic, Barrow, Scarborough.

*Managed:*       Scarborough, Hull City, Swansea City, Exeter City.

It is fitting that the first Leicester City captain to be able to hold a major trophy aloft was loyal club servant Colin Appleton, who was then able to parade the 1964 League Cup at his own testimonial match a few days later. The success was an appropriate reward for the tough-tackling wing-half, who had already suffered the blow of playing in two losing FA Cup Finals – one of them as skipper.

The Yorkshireman had arrived at Filbert Street a decade earlier, thanks to a sharp tip-off from a former Fox: 'Reg Halton, who'd only recently left Leicester as a player, had taken over at Scarborough and gave me an opportunity with my local side.'

The youngster made rapid progress and began to attract the attention of a well-known figure in the North East. 'George Hardwick, the former Middlesbrough and England left-back, was manager of Oldham and came and spoke to my dad about taking me there, but Reg arranged for me to go to Leicester for a trial instead.'

The appeal of joining the Foxes was not solely for footballing reasons, however: 'My dad had always insisted that I got myself a career to fall back on, and I'd started an apprenticeship as a joiner. One of the Leicester directors arranged that I could continue this with a local company – I think they were called Chittam and Co.'

Still aged only 18 when he made his League debut, Colin recalls with affection one of the great characters from that first City line up. 'Jack Froggatt played in that match – he was an extraordinary player, good enough to be capped by England at both centre-half and on the left wing. Our training often consisted of just doing a few laps of the pitch – Jack would always be a couple of laps behind everybody else, but he more than made up for it when he took to the field on Saturday.'

When he reached 21 Colin did his National Service with the Royal Leicestershire Regiment and was able to play in the British Army side alongside some future household names: 'There were guys like Dave Whelan, Gerry Hitchens, Cliff Jones, Bobby Charlton, Bill Curry and John White.' (Just a few years later Jones and White for Spurs and Charlton for Manchester United would play against Colin in Wembley Cup Finals.)

*'the introduction of the 4–4–2 system meant that I played alongside the centre-half more then. I think I had enough natural ability to be able to settle anywhere, but I just loved playing football.'*

Considered by many astute judges to be worthy of international recognition, Colin did earn a place on the 1961 FA Tour of New Zealand and Hong Kong. 'Tom Finney was in charge of us, and Bobby Moore was also in the team.'

That tour came shortly after City had lost to Spurs in the Cup Final. Two years later they returned to the Twin Towers to face Manchester United and Colin had taken over as club captain. He admits to being so proud at leading the team out that he nearly forgot a key part of the job. 'Prince Phillip was the Royal guest, and he almost had to remind me that it was part of my duty to present the rest of the team to him! As we were walking down the line he observed that the lads gave off rather a strong smell of horse liniment!'

City went into that game full of confidence and with high expectations, but it did not turn out that way, as Colin recalls. 'United had had a poor season, and most people predicted that we would win, but they had some very good players that we knew would rise to the occasion. We had to be at our very best to beat them but, for whatever reason, we just weren't.'

Styles of play evolved as Colin progressed through his career, and players had to be adaptable. 'When I began I was the left-half in the old WM formation,' he explains, 'but the introduction of the 4–4–2 system meant that I played alongside the centre-half more then. I think I had enough natural ability to be able to settle anywhere, but I just loved playing football.'

In 1964 Colin skippered the side to their two-legged League Cup Final triumph against Stoke City, and he scored a year later in the losing Final against Chelsea. His occasional forays upfield did bring a steady quota of goals, with a particular favourite coming against Manchester United at home. 'A cross was cleared out of the box – I was 25 yards out, and all the defence rushed out towards me – perhaps I over-hit my first touch, but it enabled me to just run through the back line and was then able to push it past 'keeper Harry Gregg.'

Persistent knee injuries, initially sustained against Arsenal, then began to take its toll, and after 333 first-team outings for the Foxes, via a brief stint at Charlton Athletic, Colin returned to Scarborough where he at last tasted Wembley success in the FA Challenge Trophy.

Truly worthy of an elevated place in the club's history, Colin believes that continuity was the key to City enjoying a small amount of success during his time there. 'Between 1961 and 1964 we hardly changed the team,' he explains. And he has some advice for today's young footballers: 'Try to keep it in perspective – football is important, but it is just a game after all.'

# GORDON BANKS

*Born:*          30 December 1938, Sheffield.

## Leicester City record:

*Appearances:*    League 293, FA Cup 34, League Cup 25, Other 4.
*Debut:*          9 September 1959 v Blackpool (h) drew 1–1.
*Also played for:* Millspaugh Steelworks, Rawmarsh Welfare, Chesterfield, Stoke
                  City, Hellenic, Fort Lauderdale Strikers (USA), St Patrick's
                  Athletic (Rep of Ireland), England (73 caps).

Leicester City's contribution to England's 1966 World Cup success was to provide the national team with their agile and popular goalkeeper Gordon Banks. On that sunny and emotional July afternoon the country rejoiced as Alf Ramsey's side picked up the Jules Rimet Trophy – and Gordon at last picked up a Wembley winners' medal after twice losing there for City in FA Cup Finals. He says 'Against Spurs in 1961 we did really well, and had it not been for Len's [Chalmers] injury I think we might have beaten them. As it was, there were no subs allowed then so we had to play with 10 men really from about the 25th minute.'

Two years later it was a similar story against Manchester United. 'The 1963 Final was a big disappointment to us all, particularly me because I dropped a cross right at David Herd's feet for one of the goals. We were favourites that day but didn't play our usual game – we didn't get tight and gave them too much room. If you do that to good players they will hurt you.'

Gordon's grounding in League football had come at Chesterfield, whom he had joined as a youngster after playing in local colliery football in the Sheffield area. After completing his National Service, he made just 23 appearances for the Spireites before the opportunity came to move to Filbert Street in the summer of 1959.

He admits to being a little shocked when he reported for pre-season training at his new club. 'We had to report for our pre-season photos, and I was amazed to see five goalkeeping jerseys hung up on the pegs in the dressing room – there were so many I wondered if Leicester played in green. My immediate thoughts were to question why they'd signed me, and I was starting to wish I hadn't signed.'

Gordon's anxiety was soon put at rest, however: 'At the start of the season I was picked to play in the reserves, so I thought I couldn't be too far off the first team – then Dave McLaren got injured and I played a couple of matches.'

McLaren returned to the side when he resumed fitness but then conceded 14 goals in just five games, so Gordon was put back in and given a run in the side.

'I thought this is my chance and now I must take it,' he explains. Take it he surely did, going on to make over 350 first-team appearances for Leicester, as well as establishing himself as the best 'keeper around.

'My positional play was my best asset – I liked to make it difficult for the shooter – I liked to close down the angle without getting too close. In training I would always put in a lot of work on my agility and reflex work.'

'Banksy' also placed a lot of emphasis on communicating with his defenders. 'A lot of modern 'keepers yell when the ball has flown over the crossbar, but you've got to be organising them whilst the game is in motion. I considered it a vital part of my game to properly organise my defence.'

April 1963 was a significant month for Gordon. It was then that he was selected for England for the first time – against Scotland – and also shut out Liverpool in the FA

*'It was one-way traffic – they were all over us, and I was just so busy. Stringy [Mike Stringfellow] scored for us after about 20 minutes with a great header, then it was bombardment all the way, so to finish up with a clean sheet I was so thrilled.'*

Cup semi-final, an afternoon that offers warm memories: 'That was the best club game I ever played in during my career,' he says. 'It was one-way traffic – they were all over us, and I was just so busy. Stringy [Mike Stringfellow] scored for us after about 20 minutes with a great header, then it was bombardment all the way, so to finish up with a clean sheet I was so thrilled.'

City's fast-growing reputation as Cup specialists was enhanced with back-to-back League Cup Finals – Gordon keeping goal in the victory over Stoke City in 1964 and the defeat at the ultimate stage to Chelsea a year later.

All was well with club and country until the emergence of another new goalkeeping talent began to spark rumours that Gordon was about to leave. 'I read that Peter Shilton was being quoted as saying that if he did not get first-team football he'd leave. I thought it laughable as he had only just turned pro – but I knew he was going to be good from the sessions I'd done with him. Nothing was said at the time of those quotes but one day Matt Gillies [manager] was at the training ground – which was unusual in itself – and he shouted me over and asked me if I'd heard and what did I think about leaving? I said if that's all you think of me then I'll go, so I was transfer-listed and Stoke City came in for me.'

Gordon would go on to make the most famous save of all time – to deny Pelé in the 1970 World Cup competition – before his career at the highest level was tragically ended in October 1972 when he lost an eye in a road accident.

Reflecting on his time with Leicester, Gordon retains many happy memories. 'They were great days – we had a lovely set of lads who all got on well and to play in two FA Cup Finals so early in my career was an experience I'll never forget.'

# ALAN BIRCHENALL

| | |
|---|---|
| *Born:* | 22 August 1945, East Ham, London. |

## Leicester City record:

| | |
|---|---|
| *Appearances:* | League 163, FA Cup 14, League Cup 6. |
| *Goals:* | League 12, FA Cup 1, League Cup 1. |
| *Debut:* | 2 October 1971 v Crystal Palace (h) drew 0–0. |
| *Also played for:* | Thornewood Thistle, Sheffield United, Chelsea, Crystal Palace, Notts County, San Jose Earthquakes, Memphis Rogues (both USA), Blackburn Rovers, Luton Town, Hereford United, Trowbridge. |
| *Managed:* | Trowbridge. |

Not since Dick Whittington became Lord Mayor of London has an 'outsider' been embraced in the way that Leicester has 'adopted' Alan Birchenall. To all and sundry he is 'Mr Leicester City', and in February 2009 he was given the Honorary Freedom of the City. 'I couldn't believe it,' reflects Alan. 'I always thought you had to be born in a place to get that sort of honour.'

His association with the Foxes began in 1971 when manager Jimmy Bloomfield signed him from Chelsea – to become part of the most talked-about side in City's history. 'Martin O'Neill always kept reminding me that Bloomfield's side never won bugger all – but it was different then. Our criteria was to try and stay up, and if we could entertain as well, then all the better. We wanted to win, of course, but it was difficult to challenge the big boys, so the alternative was to stay up and play entertaining football.'

That philosophy held true for the team – and the individual. 'I played something like 500 games in my career and can honestly say I never came off without having had a smile or a chuckle, whether it be with one of your own side, the opposition or the ref. Don't get me wrong, I was deadly serious about my football – I had a family and a mortgage – but you could still do it with a smile on your face.'

Asked to sum up his standing in the game, Birch reflects, 'I was a good player, though not a great player – perhaps I was in the top 100 of the day – but I was surely in the top five for putting a smile on people's faces.'

Alan had played as a striker at his previous clubs but dropped back into midfield at City. 'I'd got fed up of being kicked and asked Jimmy to move me back into a holding position – sort of an early Neil Lennon,' he laughs.

Scorer of some stunning goals, Alan recalls a home match from 1973, along with the pet name for his favoured left foot. 'When they talk about my best goal, the Leeds United one usually gets a mention. Attacking the Filbert Street End, 30 yards out, Mike Stringfellow rolled it to me, and I cracked it into the top corner with "The Claw".'

In an otherwise meaningless last day of the season encounter at Bramall Lane in April 1975, Alan and Sheffield United's Tony Currie created a moment that reverberated around the world. 'T.C. and I had become mates before then – I'd left Sheffield United, and they signed him to replace me. It was a red hot day and we both went for a ball – neither of us could tackle – I think I did a forward roll, and we both just ended up sat there looking at each other. I said, "Give us a kiss" and that's what happened. A photographer with a zoom lens captured the moment and it went all over the world – I think he won the European Sports Photograph of the Year award, but there were repercussions, questions were asked in the Houses of Parliament and we both had letters from gay magazines and that sort of thing!'

Since hanging up his boots Alan has enjoyed a lengthy association with The Foxes, taking on a variety of hosting and public relations positions, as well as becoming the 'voice of the club' as the on-pitch announcer at all home games – and latterly earning the official title of Club Ambassador.

His years of service have brought him into contact with literally hundreds of City players, but he struggles to pick out his favourites. 'I can honestly say whether they've been good, bad or indifferent as players, 99.9 per cent of them have been brilliant with me – whenever I've wanted a hand to make a presentation or needed anything signing they've all been happy to help out.'

For the past 30 years it has been a feature that before the final home game of the season Birch will complete a 90-minute run around the pitch – all in aid of charity. 'At the start I wanted to do something different – I'm not into jumping out of aeroplanes or anything like that, so we gave the run a go and I now think it's pretty unique. I think we've raised almost £750,000 for good causes in the Leicestershire area. Plus when Keith Weller needed specialist treatment we managed to come up with the £75,000 for that.'

In 2002 he was awarded the MBE. 'I heard the announcement on Radio Leicester – and they said it was for my charity work – NOT my football. It was like they were confirming that I wasn't that good a player! I was extremely proud to receive it nevertheless!'

There was more recognition with his Freedom of the City Award; although long-time friend and former teammate Steve Kember observed, 'He's had the Freedom for 40 years because he's never bought a drink here yet!'

Though that is far from the truth, it is the sort of sentiment that Alan enjoyed, a spontaneous moment designed to create a laugh – something he has excelled at for a great number of years.

*'I was a good player, though not a great player – perhaps I was in the top 100 of the day – but I was surely in the top five for putting a smile on people's faces.'*

# ADAM BLACK

*Born:*        18 February 1898, Denny, Stirlingshire.

*Died:*        30 August 1981, Leicester.

## Leicester City record:

*Appearances:*    League 528, FA Cup 29.

*Goals:*        League 4, FA Cup 0.

*Debut:*        24 January 1920 v Hull City (h) won 3–2.

*Also played for:*  Bathgate.

Although second only to Graham Cross in the total number of first-team appearances he made for City, Scottish full-back Adam Black actually holds the record for the most Football League outings for the club, playing in 30 more matches than the cricketing half-back of the 1960s and 70s.

Adam was just 21 years of age when he arrived in the East Midlands, but already he had led an eventful life, including serving in the Great War with the Argyll and Sutherland Highlanders, with whom he was the proud recipient of the Distinguished Conduct Medal. In peacetime he joined Scottish Central League side Bathgate, picking up a Scottish Cup-qualifying winners' medal with them.

Over 300 miles away, football was being given a new lease of life in Leicester, coinciding with its return to 'city' status after an absence of 700 years. Pre-war, the Leicester Fosse side had struggled to survive, both on and off the field. Huge debts were accrued and a final finishing position of 19th in the Division Two table meant that re-election had to be sought. Although they comfortably received enough votes to survive, football was suspended due to the hostilities and a 0–2 defeat at Clapton Orient on 24 April 1915 proved to be the final League match for Fosse.

Re-formed as Leicester City, life began with a new playing strip of blue-and-white stripes and a new manager, former Raith Rovers and Stoke boss Peter Hodge. In assembling a squad capable of remaining competitive throughout the campaign, Hodge travelled near and far and glowing reports alerted him to Adam's athleticism and versatility.

The young Scot was brought to Filbert Street and made his League debut at left-back in a 3–2 home victory over Hull City in January 1920. Over the course of the next couple of seasons he switched from left to right – and vice versa – with great regularity, proving himself to be equally adept on either flank.

Along with goalkeeper George Hebden he was an ever-present during the 1922–23 season, the first of four occasions when Adam achieved that feat (he only just missed one game in each of another three seasons), but his biggest ambition – and that of the side – was to earn promotion, and that eventually came at the end of the 1924–25 term, winning the title by two clear points from runners-up Manchester United.

During that season Adam appeared on the goalscoring charts for the first time, and his maiden League goal came at home against Sheffield Wednesday on 7 February 1925, on the occasion of his 150th Division Two appearance for the Foxes.

Despite the presence on the park of those two insatiable goal-getters John Duncan and Arthur Chandler, Adam was promoted to penalty taker and struck home the goal with such conviction that later in the game when City were awarded another spot-kick he converted that one as well, doubling his career tally in one afternoon! Incidentally, the match was won 6–1, with Duncan and Chandler also each scoring a couple – it is not recorded if either man regretted spurning the chance of yet another career hat-trick!

*Over the course of the next couple of seasons he switched from left to right – and vice versa – with great regularity, proving himself to be equally adept on either flank.*

Another penalty-kick that year, against Crystal Palace, was to be Adam's last score for eight years until he netted against Sunderland in April 1933 – his fourth and final goal and only one scored from open play.

Having gained promotion, City made an impact on the top flight, recording their highest League placing in the club's history. Under new boss Willie Orr they came third in Division One at the end of the 1927–28 season, three points behind Huddersfield Town and five behind champions Everton.

The momentum remained and they went even closer a year later, coming second just a point behind Sheffield Wednesday. Like the Owls, City remained undefeated at home, and they notched an incredible 96 goals in the League.

On 6 January 1934, away at Manchester City, Adam played his 500th League match for Leicester City – Arthur Maw scoring the Foxes goal in a 1–1 draw. Just over a calendar year later, and in his 16th season at Filbert Street, Adam played his 528th and final League appearance, away at Sunderland on 9 February 1935, a game in which City lost 2–0.

Apart from his substantial League haul, Adam also played in a total of 29 FA Cup ties, with the 1934 semi-final defeat to Portsmouth providing an almost fairytale curtain-call on the full-back's career.

After hanging up his boots Adam remained in Leicester, where he ran a newsagents shop for many years, while continuing to follow the fortunes of his former club.

While Adam remained totally loyal to his one League club, his brother Johnny was on the other end of the scale, representing Sunderland, Nelson, Accrington Stanley, Chesterfield, Luton Town and Bristol Rovers during his career.

Adam was 83 years old when he passed away in Leicester in 1981. As a lasting tribute to their record holder, the Adam Black Suite can be located as a matchday hospitality venue on the second floor of City's Walkers Stadium

# JIMMY BLOOMFIELD

| | |
|---|---|
| *Born:* | 15 April 1934, Kensington, London. |
| *Died:* | 3 April 1983, Chingford, Essex. |

## Leicester City record:

| | |
|---|---|
| *Manager:* | July 1971–May 1977. |
| *Played for:* | Hayes, Brentford, Arsenal, Birmingham City, West Ham United, Plymouth Argyle, Leyton Orient. |
| *Also managed:* | Leyton Orient. |

Football management is a precarious occupation. Nearly all who enter into it know that time is at a premium and sooner or later, for whatever reason, they will be moving on to pastures new.

The most that they can hope for is to leave a club on good terms and in better shape than they found it, but Jimmy Bloomfield did much more than that. For six years he nurtured a Leicester City side that reminded us of the true meaning of football – that it forms part of the entertainment industry and is designed to give us a welcome and uplifting distraction from the hum-drum of everyday life.

London-born James Henry Bloomfield enjoyed a fruitful playing career which brought him domestic and European medals, as well as gaining international recognition. He started at one of the capital's leading non-League clubs, Hayes, before moving on to begin his professional career in October 1952 with a move to Brentford, a Second Division club at the time.

Two years later, following the Bees' relegation, Jimmy joined Arsenal, with a fee of £8,000 securing his services. Playing either as an out-and-out striker or dropping back to inside-forward, he was renowned for his energetic running and accurate distribution, qualities that brought him selection for the England Under-23 side as well as an appearance for the Football League XI. He was a member of the hastily-formed London XI which not only entered but also went on to reach the Final of the inaugural Inter-Cities Fairs Cup in 1958 before falling to Barcelona.

*Jimmy knew that all good sides were built on a solid foundation*

During his six-year stay at Highbury, Jimmy made 210 League appearances for the Gunners, scoring 54 times. He then joined Birmingham City, where he reached another Fairs Cup Final – this time losing to Roma – but he tasted victory in the 1963 League Cup, scoring for Blues in their two-legged Final victory over near-neighbours Aston Villa.

A second short stint with Brentford, followed by spells with West Ham United, Plymouth Argyle and Leyton Orient, took Jimmy's number of career League games to a total of 499 – during which he scored a healthy 95 goals.

While winding down his playing days with the O's, his opportunity came to turn his hand to management, and there was almost immediate success when his new side took the Third Division title in 1969–70, only Jimmy's second full season in charge.

A year later he was lured to Filbert Street, where City were preparing for life back in the top flight without the manager who had led them there, Frank O'Farrell having being lured away to Manchester United. The City board appointed Jimmy as his replacement and, uniquely, his first match in charge saw the club lift some silverware following a Charity Shield triumph over Liverpool.

Jon Sammels, from Arsenal, was the new manager's first signing, and he was soon followed by two more recruits from London – Chelsea's Keith Weller and Alan Birchenall of Crystal Palace. The Scottish twang, that had been so predominant in the City dressing room for many years, had given way to this new Cockney explosion, and there were more to come with the likes of Dennis Rofe, Steve Earle and Steve Kember joining the group.

It was no coincidence that Jimmy's side was packed with players who liked to express themselves. Frank Worthington, brought in from Huddersfield Town, and Lennie Glover, another Londoner, who had been at the club since 1967, were others who were tagged as being 'flair players', but above all else, they could play – they were fine footballers.

There was a great camaraderie among the squad – it was clear they all got on together and all enjoyed each other's company. This was not a fortunate coincidence, as Jimmy had blended together guys who shared his footballing philosophy, those who wanted to be expressive and who wanted to entertain.

His beliefs were not totally reckless, however. Jimmy knew that all good sides were built on a solid foundation, and with either Shilton or Wallington in goal – and defenders of the calibre of Whitworth, Nish, Rofe, Cross, Sjoberg and Munro to call upon – he knew that they would allow the creativity in the side to flourish.

Jimmy had the temerity to meddle with tradition as well, changing the club's playing strip to all-white rather than blue for the 1972–73 season; however, one year later it was changed back!

There could no finer testimony to his style of play than to reflect, almost 40 years on, that City supporters still look back on the Bloomfield era with great fondness. Maybe Jimmy's side was not quite the finished article, and maybe they did not win the League title, but they came almighty close to reaching the FA Cup Final in 1974 – losing to Liverpool in a semi-final replay.

Most observers feel that City would have beaten either of the two other semi-finalists that year, Newcastle United or Burnley, and how they would have loved to see the 'entertainers' grace the Wembley stage.

At the end of the 1976–77 season (during which City had finished 11th in the First Division), Jimmy resigned and returned to Orient, whom he took to another FA Cup semi-final – but ill-health and a disagreement with the chairman prompted him to leave in 1981. Two years later, while working as a part-time scout for Luton Town, Jimmy died from cancer at the age of 49.

Ultimately, Jimmy's legacy was to leave a lasting memory of the way the game should be played.

# LEN CHALMERS

*Born:*          4 September 1936, Corby, Northamptonshire.

## Leicester City record:
*Appearances:*   League 171, FA Cup 20, League Cup 9, Other 4.
*Goals:*         League 4, FA Cup 0, League Cup 0, Other 0.
*Debut:*         26 April 1958 v Birmingham City (a) won 1–0.
*Also played for:* Corby Town, Notts County, Dunstable Town.
*Managed:*       Dunstable Town.

Despite clocking up more than 200 first-team appearances for Leicester City, right-back Len Chalmers is probably best known for picking up an injury which severely restricted his participation in the biggest game of his career – the 1961 FA Cup Final.

The game was only around 20 minutes old when Lennie went into a challenge with the Tottenham Hotspur player Les Allen and was left in a crumpled heap with a leg injury. In pain and hobbling, the City player should have gone off for treatment and not taken any further part in the game, but in the age before substitutions were allowed this was seen as a last resort. Bravely – but without any significant purpose – Lennie hobbled out to the left wing, where he remained a hindrance, perhaps to his own side as much as to the opposition.

Gillies re-shuffled his pack in an attempt to minimise the numerical disadvantage City were clearly under – even though 11 men still remained on the park. Frank McLintock, arguably the most creative player and certainly one of the fittest, was removed from his central role to cover at right-back, while goalscoring opportunities became even less likely with Ken Keyworth being withdrawn into midfield.

That Spurs' two late goals clinched the Cup is no longer of consequence to City fans – but the bigger picture would point to a case of 'what if Lennie hadn't been injured?' Would the full-strength Foxes have gone on to win their first FA Cup Final? After all, they had beaten the same opponents in a White Hart Lane League match just a few weeks earlier, or would Spurs still have gone on to become the first side in the 20th century to record the League and Cup double regardless?

Lennie had originally joined City as a junior, having started his football with his home-town club, Corby Town. He had to bide his time playing as a wing-half for the reserves in the Football Combination side but was made to wait for a first-team opportunity.

When it came, his debut could hardly have been in more dramatic circumstances. City had to go to St Andrew's on the final day of the season knowing that only victory over Birmingham City would guarantee top-fight survival for another campaign.

Manager David Halliday, under the most severe pressure, gambled spectacularly – and threw a six! He made five changes to his under-performing outfit and gave Lennie his first start. The youngster showed he could cope under the most intense pressure and played splendidly, proving he had the right temperament for the big occasion.

The manager's other big call was to leave out top scorer and crowd favourite Arthur Rowley and recall Ian McNeill from a two-month sabbatical in the reserves, and the striker popped in the crucial goal which ensured First Division survival.

By the start of the 1959–60 season, and with Matt Gillies now in charge, Lennie had switched from wing-half to the right full-back position he would occupy for the rest of his career. His consistent performances and resolute approach had been rewarded with the club captaincy (although this was for one season only), and he had also been handed the added responsibility of taking penalties – three of Lennie's four goals for City came from the spot, the exception coming in a home win over Sheffield United.

The following year, in an omen that the competition was not ever going to be kind to Len, his own-goal in the sixth round of the FA Cup against Wolves marked the end of a City Cup dream that would go even further in 1960–61, only for the dreaded 'Wembley hoodoo' to strike their number two.

Although the full-back was noted for his crisp and accurate tackling, and he had the pace to match any winger around, his nickname of 'Chopper Chalmers' was more an alliteration than a reflection on his method of dealing with opponents, á la Ron 'Chopper' Harris!

After more than 10 years on City's books Lennie joined Notts County, initially taking over the captaincy and making 35 League appearances in the 1966–67 season, but then he took more of a back seat and became a part-time professional in order that he could pursue business interests outside the game.

He played in another 15 games for the Magpies before accepting a player-manager role at non-League Dunstable Town. Later Lennie moved down under to coach the Sydney-based Melita Tigers, before returning to his Northamptonshire roots.

*'he had the pace to match any winger around, his nickname of 'Chopper Chalmers' was more an alliteration than a reflection on his method of dealing with opponents'*

# ARTHUR CHANDLER

*Born:*        27 November 1895, Paddington, London.

*Died:*        18 June 1984, Leicester.

## Leicester City record:

*Appearances:*    League 393, FA Cup 26.

*Goals:*        League 259, FA Cup 14.

*Debut:*        25 August 1923 v Hull City (a) drew 1–1.

*Also played for:*  West London Schoolboys, Handley Page, Hampstead Town, Queen's Park Rangers, Notts County.

Leicester City's highest-aggregate goalscorer of all time is Arthur Clarence Hillier Chandler, a London-born son of a cycling champion and brother of Sidney Chandler, a League footballer with Aston Villa, Preston North End and Reading.

In 12 seasons with the Foxes Arthur smashed in a phenomenal 259 League goals, eight more than closest rival Arthur Rowley; although the latter could claim to have scored his tally at a much better goals-to-game ratio.

'Channy' arrived at Filbert Street in the summer of 1923, signed on a hunch from QPR by manager Peter Hodge. Considering that the new acquisition was well into his 28th year and had managed only 18 first-team goals to that point, it stands alongside any transfer ever made in terms of value.

His goal-scoring exploits apart, Arthur remained remarkably fit, and he happily stayed injury-free for most of his career. He was an ever-present in each of his first two seasons with the club, notching 24 goals in 1923–24 and 32 the following term, playing a major hand in City's Second Division title success.

Aside from the volume of goals Arthur scored, there was the inevitability that he would get them in multiples. Throughout his haul of City goals were 17 instances of hat-tricks or better – another record that will be difficult for future generations to overhaul.

Among his collection were three separate occasions when he netted five goals in a match, and, even more spectacularly, he became only the second Fox, after John Duncan four years earlier, to hit six goals in a League game. That came on 20 October 1928 during the Foxes' 10–0 whitewashing of Portsmouth in a Division One match, the club's largest-ever winning margin.

In the most one-sided of contests City were 5–0 up by the break, with Arthur having claimed a hat-trick inside the space of 14 minutes. Whether the 'swan' story has become a little embellished over the years is hard to substantiate, but it has long been reported that when the striker scored his fifth (City's seventh) five swans flew over the ground, as if in tribute. Shortly afterwards a sixth straggler appeared overhead. The crowd called for another goal and 'Channy' duly obliged!

Arthur was, by nature, of a cheerful disposition – he always saw the good in people and was one of the most popular players at the club. Although only 5'8" tall, his predatory instincts made up for his lack of height. Powerfully built and difficult to dispossess, he was ruthless anywhere within sight of goal.

That he failed to gain full England honours is a slight on the selectors rather than on Arthur. He came close though, three times playing in the annual trial match – once for the North against the South and twice for The Rest against England. On each occasion he scored, making it even more remarkable that he did not win a full cap. He also represented the Football League in a 1927 fixture against the Scottish League, which was conveniently played at Filbert Street.

*Arthur smashed in a phenomenal 259 League goals, eight more than closest rival Arthur Rowley*

In 1929 'Channy' was selected to go on an FA Tour to South Africa and again he shone, netting 33 times in 16 games.

Arthur's total haul of goals included a record 173 at Filbert Street – another record, although his 100 away from home was topped by Rowley's 102. Nevertheless, his final haul of 273 first-team goals will never be bettered. His total would undoubtedly have been much greater but for a reluctance to take penalty-kicks. Arthur only took one for City, against Chelsea in 1924 – and the 'keeper saved it!

His final game for the Foxes came on 22 April 1935 in a home game against Grimsby Town. Regrettably he did not register that day – in a drawn 2–2 encounter – but at 39 years 114 days he set the mark as the oldest outfield player to appear for City. Goalkeeper Joe Calvert, a dozen or so years later, became the only 40-year-old to play in a first-team fixture for the club.

Incredibly, 'Channy' was able to postpone his immediate retirement by accepting an offer to join Notts County where he notched up another eight goals in 13 League outings.

He then returned to Filbert Street where he remained part of the backroom team for many years. The club afforded him a testimonial match in December 1961 when over 13,000 fans turned up to pay tribute and watch a thrilling match between a City side and an Arthur Chandler XI.

A truly incredible goalscorer, and a thoroughly nice gentleman, Arthur was 88 when he passed away in 1984. He would have been humbled by the club naming a hospitality suite after him at the Walkers Stadium.

# ALBERT CHEESEBROUGH

*Born:*            17 January 1935, Burnley, Lancashire.

**Leicester City record:**

*Appearances:*     League 122, FA Cup 11, League Cup 4, Other 1.
*Goals:*           League 40, FA Cup 2, League Cup 1, Other 0.
*Debut:*           22 August 1959 v West Ham United (a) lost 0–3.
*Also played for:*  Burnley, Port Vale, Mansfield Town.

One of City's 1961 FA Cup finalists was the popular Lancastrian Albert Cheesebrough, who clocked up a total of 138 first-team appearances during a pivotal four-year period for the club which saw them reach Wembley twice and make their bow in the new League Cup competition.

Albert had begun his career at home-town club Burnley and played in more than a century of top-flight matches for them, as well as making one appearance for England's Under-23 side, against France. The first impact he made on Leicester's supporters was a depressing one, however, because he scored a hat-trick for the Clarets in a 7–3 mauling against City at Turf Moor in November 1957.

Speaking in April 2009, Albert recalled how his subsequent move to Filbert Street came about. 'Burnley were my club as I'd grown up there and supported them as a youngster, but manager Harry Potts took me to one side at the end of the 1958–59 season and said that I no longer fitted in with his ideas, but he did tell me that a club in the East Midlands fancied me, so I spoke to Matt Gillies and made the move.'

For a fee of just under £20,000 Albert joined the Foxes to bolster their left flank. He could play as an out-and-out winger or in an inside-forward position. Wherever he was asked to perform, though, he displayed a keen eye for goal.

'Scoring goals was always a very pleasant surprise for me. It wasn't my main job within the team but I was very fortunate to score as many as I did.'

Albert scored 17 goals in his first season at Filbert Street and a dozen the year after; although

> **'Scoring goals was always a very pleasant surprise for me. It wasn't my main job within the team but I was very fortunate to score as many as I did.'**

he had lost his place towards the end of the season. Ken Keyworth was given the number-10 shirt, and Gordon Willis was playing at outside-left.

In one of those twists that invariably seem to occur ahead of most FA Cup Finals one player's injury opens the door for another: 'Gordon was injured in the first semi-final meeting against Sheffield United, and that allowed me back in for both the replays and then the Final itself.'

Burnley had won the League Championship the year earlier, and any regrets Albert may have had about leaving his boyhood club were instantly evaporated with the realisation that he would be playing in an FA Cup Final against a side destined to do the double. 'Tottenham Hotspur were a very good side at that time,' recalls Albert. 'Defensively they made it very hard for us at Wembley, but we lost Len Chalmers through injury, so I think we acquitted ourselves as well as we could have done with just 10 men.'

Albert's medal remains a treasured possession, as do the memories of the return home. 'It really was a proud moment for us all to see the crowds outside the town hall when we came back for a civic reception. They were fantastic with their applause and seemed to really appreciate what we'd done.'

Earlier in that same season the inaugural League Cup competition had begun, and Albert not only played in City's first match – a 4–0 home win over Mansfield Town – but he contributed a goal alongside Jimmy Walsh's hat-trick.

When asked to assess his own worth to the team Albert is swiftly to the point. 'My pace, that was a major part of my game. If you are quicker than the next guy it always helps!'

Sadly, his explosive bursts down the City flank were curtailed by an injury at Birmingham City late in the 1962–63 season which not only necessitated a cartilage operation but also marked his Foxes swansong and ruled him out of any possible late selection for the club's second FA Cup Final appearance in three years.

Albert was a Wembley onlooker as his side succumbed to Manchester United beneath the Twin Towers. 'I was only on the fringes of the team at that time anyway and was never going to be selected even if fit,' he says. 'But I went to Wembley and enjoyed being part of the day, but ultimately our performance wasn't good enough to beat them.'

Moves to Port Vale and Mansfield materialised for Albert, but having lost some of his pace due to the injury he was already planning for life after football. 'I'd married a butcher's daughter, and during my time at Port Vale I'd been shown the ropes and began to learn something about the business. My old Burnley captain Tommy Cummings persuaded me to join Mansfield, but I broke my leg against Lincoln and I decided that was it.'

Albert moved to Southport to set up his new business and remained there, contented, until his retirement. Even from afar he has always retained a soft spot for Leicester: 'I'm absolutely made up that the club seem to be on their way back to better times. Every week I have a telephone chinwag with my good friend Maurice Whitby about the club's fortunes. I knew they needed to go straight back up after dropping into the First Division, and I was delighted they did!'

# STEVE CLARIDGE

| Born: | 10 April 1966, Portsmouth, Hampshire. |
|---|---|

**Leicester City record:**

| | |
|---|---|
| *Appearances:* | League 63, FA Cup 4, League Cup 8, Other 5. |
| *Goals:* | League 17, FA Cup 1, League Cup 2, Other 2. |
| *Debut:* | 3 March 1996 v Ipswich Town (a) lost 2–4. |
| *Also played for:* | Fareham Town, Bournemouth, Weymouth, Crystal Palace, Aldershot, Cambridge United, Luton Town, Birmingham City, Portsmouth, Wolverhampton Wanderers, Millwall, Brighton and Hove Albion, Brentford, Wycombe Wanderers, Gillingham, Bradford City, Walsall (loan), Worthing, Harrow Borough. |
| *Managed:* | Portsmouth, Weymouth, Millwall. |

If, as a striker, you are only going to be remembered by fans of your club for just two of the goals you scored, then you might as well make them important ones. In the annals of Leicester City's history there have been very few more significant ones than Steve Claridge's Play-off decider in 1996 and the League Cup winner a year later.

Steve has been a 'wandering minstrel' thoughout his footballing career – the oft-used cliché 'more clubs than Jack Nicklaus' could certainly be applied to him as he represented 15 different League clubs, some on more than one occasion, plus a number of non-League sides as well.

For all of his travels, his period at Leicester City was undeniably the most successful of his career and catapulted him – and the club – into the big time, but he admits he was not in either the best of form or health when he signed for the Foxes. 'I'd been very ill just before then as a thyroid gland had packed up, and I'd also not scored for a while. Martin O'Neill made no secret of his desire to sign me, though, and Birmingham pretty much said I ought to go – but I didn't need telling, I knew for myself that Leicester were a good club with good fans.'

City had been going through something of a rough passage and their Play-off hopes were receding. Top of the table in late October, they had dropped to ninth by early April when they travelled to the Valley to face Charlton, and Steve came up with a priceless winner.

'That goal was probably my most important for the club, not just because it was my first but because of the circumstances. We simply couldn't afford not to win. I got the ball on the edge of the box and Chris Whyte, a former teammate, came to close me down. I dropped my shoulder, went past him and curled it right-footed past the 'keeper.'

The goal broke a 15-game drought for Steve (eight at St Andrew's and seven for City): 'It was the longest spell of my career without scoring and it really was the last-chance saloon for us, but we delivered the goods when we had to. That match had come on the back of a defeat against Sheffield United which had seen the fans protest after the game.'

Steve finished the season with a glut of goals – five in eight games – but it looked as if Crystal Palace were going to break City hearts when they took the lead in the Play-off Final. Steve viewed it differently, though: 'Even when we went one down at no stage did I think we'd lose – we didn't panic and it wasn't because we were dominating the game – I just knew we were a good team and would get the result we needed.'

Garry Parker's equaliser looked to have earned a draw, and the dreaded penalty shoot-out was moments away when the manager replaced 'keeper Kevin Poole with the much taller Zeljko Kalac in readiness for spot-kicks.

The next few moments changed the course of City's history. 'I got fouled in the build up,' says Steve, 'and told Parks to wait before he took the free-kick and let me get up there – but he hit it early as I was still making my way forward. The ball was headed out and from the edge of the box I hit it sweet as a nut past Nigel Martyn.'

Steve's joyous celebrations were more than matched by the Blue Army. 'As I was leaving the ground there were still thousands of fans drinking and enjoying themselves and singing "Super Stevie Claridge!"'

There was more success for the Foxes 11 months later. After Emile Heskey had scored a late equaliser in the League Cup Final at Wembley, it was time for Steve to deliver another late show-stopper in the replay. 'It was very reminiscent to the Wembley goal in its execution. It was a long ball forward headed down, and I just got a clean connection and hit it low and hard on target.'

*'As I was leaving the ground there were still thousands of fans drinking and enjoying themselves and singing "Super Stevie Claridge!"'*

Often tagged in the press as being something of a 'scruffy' player due to his penchant for having his socks rolled halfway down and shin-pads showing, he admits people's perceptions of him are far from the truth. 'For around 10 years I struggled with that viewpoint. My teammates and the fans knew that I put in the work-rate – and always gave 100 per cent commitment – but that can sometimes overshadow the fact you can still be a good player as well. Bang it up to me and I'll bring it down and play. I tried to remain as fit as I could and never sold anybody short.'

In terms of the importance of Steve's goals, no one at Leicester will ever feel he short-changed them.

# TONY COTTEE

*Born:*          11 July 1965, West Ham, London.

**Leicester City record:**

*Appearances:*     League 85, FA Cup 5, League Cup 9, Other 1.

*Goals:*          League 27, FA Cup 2, League Cup 5, Other 0.

*Debut:*          27 August 1997 v Arsenal (h) drew 3–3.

*Also played for:*  West Ham United, Everton, Selangor (Malaysia), Birmingham City (loan), Norwich City, Barnet, Millwall, England (7 caps).

*Managed:*        Barnet.

It is fair to say that Martin O'Neill did not always look towards the Far East when he was hoping to bolster his squad, but it was a good day's work for the City boss when he persuaded Tony Cottee to return to the Premiership. The former England international repaid his new 'gaffer' with a sequence of match-winning strikes, including all three in the 1999 League Cup semi-final against Sunderland.

During his 10-month stint in Malaysia Tony's goals had helped his club, Selangor, to win the equivalent of the English Charity Shield and also their domestic League Cup Final, but he is grateful to an old teammate that his footballing 'exile' was not even longer: 'Steve Walford knew my dad and asked how I was getting on. "He's not happy – can't wait to come home," was the reply. My dad told me about the conversation, but I didn't think anything of it.'

Walford was a member of City's coaching staff and had tipped the manager off about Tony's availability, and very soon afterwards a deal was done. The new arrival's debut was a classic encounter, but he remembers that his own role in it was mainly as a peace-keeper. 'I came on as sub for a 15-minute cameo in the famous 3–3 match against Arsenal, where Denis Bergkamp scored a fantastic hat-trick for them. I didn't contribute a great deal until the very end when Steve Walsh and Ian Wright had a bit of a tear-up, and I had to get between them and have a few strong words!'

Within just a few weeks of becoming a Fox, TC was pulling on a different blue shirt – that of Birmingham City. 'Martin identified that I wasn't as fit or as sharp as I might have been after my spell in Malaysia so he sent me there on loan.'

*'In 14 years of trying I'd never scored a goal at Old Trafford, but Garry Parker put a ball over the top, a defender misjudged the bounce and I was able to volley it past Peter Schmeichel for the only goal of the game.'*

Back at Filbert Street, Tony was given an early incentive to prove himself. 'I was selected for a reserve game against Notts County, and Martin told me that if I played well I'd be back in the firsts. I had a good game and scored – and the manager was true to his word.' The next League game was away against Manchester United, a place where Tony had a score to settle. 'In 14 years of trying I'd never scored a goal at Old Trafford, but Garry Parker put a ball over the top, a defender misjudged the bounce and I was able to volley it past Peter Schmeichel for the only goal of the game. Whenever I meet any Leicester fans that's the game and goal they most remember me for!'

There were two other major grounds that TC had not registered at during all of his years of top-flight scoring: Elland Road and Anfield. During his Leicester service he managed to score at both, and each time, as at Old Trafford, in a winning cause!

The 1998–99 season was a memorable one for the striker, for as well as top scoring for City, he also collected the Supporters' Player of the Year Award. The only blemish was the disappointment of losing to Spurs in the League Cup Final, especially after he had helped to secure a place there by scoring all of the goals in the 3–2 aggregate win over Sunderland in the semis. His first goal in the 2–1 win at the Stadium of Light remains one of his favourites. 'Frank Sinclair put a cross in, I ran to the near post and scored with the outside of my left foot,' he explains. 'It was a goal where I just about got everything right and one I look back on with a great deal of satisfaction.'

Just a few days after their Wembley showdown the same two sides met again at White Hart Lane in the League. City gained a token of revenge by winning 2–0, with Tony's second-half strike bringing up a personal milestone. 'It was my 200th League goal. Emile Heskey crossed from the right, and I just toe-poked it in.'

The following season, 1999–2000, Tony endured a troubled campaign with a persistent calf injury, but yet again he emerged as the club's leading marksman but admits he owed his place in the Wembley line up due to the enforced absence of an in-form striker. 'I was probably fortunate that Stan Collymore was Cup-tied,' he says.

Victory over Tranmere Rovers gave Tony a League Cup-winners' medal to add to the seven England caps he had claimed earlier in his career.

In a very different way, Tony's departure from Leicester was almost as unique as his arrival. Having played for City at the start of the 2000–01 campaign, he also represented Norwich City, Barnet and Millwall within a few months – achieving the rare distinction of playing in all four divisions in the same season.

Had the Leicester board of directors considered differently, then Tony might well have extended his career in the East Midlands. 'When Martin left, Steve Walsh and myself were interested in becoming joint-managers. Although they said they were surprised at how well we'd done during the interview, I think they'd already made their mind up to appoint Peter Taylor!'

Tony has successfully made the transition into the world of broadcasting and is a very popular match summariser and expert analyser on Sky Sports.

# GRAHAM CROSS

*Born:*          15 November 1943, Leicester.

## Leicester City record:

*Appearances:*   League 498, FA Cup 59, League Cup 40, Other 2.
*Goals:*         League 29, FA Cup 6, League Cup 2, Other 0.
*Debut:*         29 April 1961 v Birmingham City (h) won 3–2.
*Also played for:* Chesterfield (loan), Brighton and Hove Albion, Preston North End,
                 Enderby Town, Lincoln City, Leicestershire County Cricket Club.

Leicester City's record appearance holder is Graham Cross, who, from making his debut as a 17-year-old inside-forward to an acrimonious disagreement with his manager 15 years later, played in a total of 599 first-team matches.

Surely one more would have been a more fitting figure to end on? 'I'd have loved to have reached 600,' says Graham. 'I wasn't aware, though, of how many games I had played until I was told some time later, but I would have loved to have reached that milestone.'

There were plenty of opportunities for Graham to continue playing for the Foxes as well. 'I'd carried on playing cricket for Leicestershire throughout July 1975 when I should have been back in pre-season training with the Foxes.' (Graham was a hugely talented cricket all-rounder who helped Leicestershire to win the County Championship that summer.)

'The club suspended me for a fortnight, and then Jimmy Bloomfield wouldn't pick me. It was a waste of a season, although I played in a couple of matches and a few reserve games. I became fairly bitter towards the end, which was a sad way really for me to end my career there.'

Around 14 years earlier Bloomfield had featured in Graham's first match as well: 'He played on the opposing side when I made my debut, and I scored a simple tap-in as we beat Birmingham City 3–2. It was the week before the FA Cup Final, and the manager decided to rest a few players.'

Graham's progression into the first-team ranks included a couple of European matches the following season, most notably away at Atletico Madrid, a fixture which coincided with his 18th birthday. 'I was asked to go out and do a job at centre-half. It was a wonderful experience and an awesome stadium. I'd never seen or heard anything like it – it really was a volatile atmosphere.'

Although City bowed out of the competition that night, Graham's performance in a pressure-cooker environment had impressed all onlookers, and his elevation to first-team regular was almost complete.

With football firmly in the ascendancy and cricket having to fit around it, Graham played in the majority of the matches in the 1962–63 season and was an automatic selection as City reached the Cup Final yet again, on the back of a match he describes as 'The Battle of the Alamo'.

'We played Liverpool in the semi at Hillsborough and went ahead through Stringy [Mike Stringfellow] after about 20 minutes. They threw everything at us but Banksy [goalkeeper Gordon Banks] played out of his skin that day.'

And so to Wembley, where yet again the Foxes underperformed and had to be content with losers' medals. There was success to celebrate the following season, though, as City won their first League Cup, overcoming Stoke City in the two-legged Final.

'We won it relatively easily, but the League Cup wasn't taken too seriously by a lot of the big clubs and didn't have either the prestige or the European qualification it would later have.'

Nevertheless, City were keen to retain their hold on the Cup and were only denied in the Final the following year, losing 3–2 to Chelsea at Stamford Bridge and being frustrated in the goalless draw which was played out in the return.

Graham was being increasingly used in a variety of positions, sometimes switching in the middle of matches. 'Myself and Frank McLintock were often asked to change roles during games, with us being switched from inside-forward to wing-half or vice versa. This was a tactic devised by our coach Bert Johnson, who thought it would work and confuse the opposition, and for a while it did!'

Often popping up with a crucial goal, Graham registered a unique hat-trick in a 2–1 home win against Nottingham Forest in April 1966. 'I'd netted twice for us and then conceded an own-goal when the ball came back off a post, hit me and went in. I thought I should have had the match ball, but they wouldn't give it to me!'

At the end of the 1968–69 season City were relegated, but not before they had again reached the FA Cup Final, with Graham again playing his part in a losing cause – this time against Manchester City.

'We created plenty of chances but couldn't take any of them and were unlucky with the one we conceded. Mike Summerbee got past Alan Woollett and cut the ball back, and I just couldn't get my toe to it – if only I hadn't cut my toenails that day! But it reached Neil Young, who drove it into the net.'

Modestly, the man who has played more matches for City than anyone else plays down his own ability. 'I wasn't the greatest player in any aspect of the game really, but I always gave 120 per cent,' he says. 'You can't really ask for any more than someone who gives it everything, every time they play!'

Exactly Graham – and thank you!

> **'You can't really ask for any more than someone who gives it everything, every time they play!'**

# BRIAN DEANE

*Born:*　　　　　7 February 1968, Leeds, Yorkshire.

## Leicester City record:

*Appearances:*　League 52, FA Cup 2, League Cup 2.
*Goals:*　　　　League 19, FA Cup 0, League Cup 0.
*Debut:*　　　　8 December 2001 v Southampton (h) lost 0–4.
*Also played for:*　Doncaster Rovers, Sheffield United, Leeds United, Benfica (Portugal), Middlesbrough, West Ham United, Sunderland, Perth Glory (Australia), England (3 caps).

For a short period of time it seemed that the only player who was ever going to score a League goal at the Walkers Stadium was Brian Deane. The former England international scored the first three goals at Leicester City's plush new home when it opened in 2002.

The first actual game played there was a pre-season friendly between the Foxes and Athletic Bilbao of Spain – and it was the Basques' midfielder Roberto Martinez Ripodas (Tiko) who scored the inaugural goal at the Stadium. Jordan Stewart replied for Leicester in a one-all draw.

Just six days later, on 10 August 2002, Watford provided the first League opposition that City would face at the Walkers, and it took until two minutes after the interval for the breakthrough goal to arrive. As Brian recalls, there was a lot of tension around the Stadium that day. 'I think it was important for the team to make a statement. 'Here we are – in our new home – and we want to be successful'. The first goal just settled everybody's nerves – a cross came in from the right, the defenders went to sleep a little bit and I just headed it into the top corner.'

Brian's second goal of the afternoon followed shortly afterwards to seal an historic first victory. A couple of weeks later, playing against Reading, the big striker scored an early opener, and it was only when Paul Dickov converted a penalty-kick that the PA announcer could shout out a name other than Brian's as being a Walkers goalscorer.

Leeds-born, Brian had played in over 500 League games before his move to Leicester and played three times for his country, as well as spending a year in Portugal with Benfica when he was signed from Middlesbrough by Dave Bassett, his former boss when they were both at Sheffield United.

'I went to Leicester primarily to play first-team football. When I moved there they were already up against it towards the bottom of the Premiership table, and it was always going to be a struggle to stay up. It was a case of hoping that if the worst scenario happened then I felt there were enough quality players around that would hopefully stay to ensure that we made a strong challenge for promotion at the first attempt.'

Brian's debut was a reflection of how difficult City were finding it in the top flight — coming on as a late substitute for Ade Akinbiyi in a 4–0 home reversal to Southampton. He did score the following week, though, on his full debut against Leeds, and he added five more goals in the forlorn battle to avoid the drop. Aside from the disappointing spectre of relegation, the City fans also had to say farewell to Filbert Street — their headquarters for more than a century. 'It was clearly an emotional time leaving Filbert Street', recalls Brian. 'Obviously I was a relative newcomer to the club, but I could see it clearly meant so much to a lot of people. I have to say from a personal point of view I was sorry to see the old ground close because I'd also enjoyed success there because I'd played for Sheffield United the day we won 5–2 to win promotion to the top flight. I always enjoyed the way the crowd seemed to be right on top of you — there was always a really good atmosphere there, and it always seemed as if there were a lot more people in the ground than there actually was.'

As Brian had hoped when he arrived to join the Foxes, City had been able to hang on to a good number of experienced players which helped them in their quest for an immediate 'bounce-back' to the top tier. 'All along we felt that we were strong enough to go up. Mickey Adams had taken over and it helped that he was able to put out a team that had a lot of natural leaders out there on the park — players like Matty Elliott, Gerry Taggart, Muzzy Izzett, Ian Walker, Paul Dickov and myself — it was like we had a lot of captains on the field, and everybody pulled together.'

*'All along we felt that we were strong enough to go up. Mickey Adams had taken over and it helped that he was able to put out a team that had a lot of natural leaders out there on the park... ...it was like we had a lot of captains on the field, and everybody pulled together.'*

Brian's aerial ability and prowess inside the box often counted to his detriment. 'When you're a 6ft 3in striker it's easy to get pigeon-holed unfairly as being just a big, physical target-man. Towards the end of my career, it's true, I became more of a box player but I'd always been used to playing wide or part of a three-pronged attack, and I always did a lot of my best work outside the area.'

It was from a deeper position that Brian scored his favourite Foxes goal, however: 'Our very last match in the Premiership — away at Everton — it was a really good team move, and I hit it right-footed into the top corner from about 20 yards out.'

Earlier in his career — on 15 August 1992 playing for Sheffield United against Manchester United at Bramall Lane — Brian Deane scored the first-ever goal in the newly-formed Premiership, and 10 years later he also took his place in history as the man who scored the first League goal at the Walkers Stadium.

# GEORGE DEWIS

*Born:*          22 January 1913, Burbage, Leicestershire.

*Died:*          23 October 1994, Hinckley, Leicestershire.

## Leicester City record:

*Appearances:*   League 116, FA Cup 13, Other (wartime) 81.

*Goals:*         League 45, FA Cup 6, Other (wartime) 62.

*Debut:*         9 December 1933 v West Bromwich Albion (h) lost 0–1.

*Also played for:* Stoke Golding, Nuneaton Town, Yeovil Town.

Lauded as being 'one of the biggest influences on their careers' by former Leicester City greats Peter Shilton and Gary Lineker, George Dewis had a coaching style that, while based on simplicity, was hugely popular with his players and benefited City enormously as dozens of his protégés graduated through into the club's first-team ranks.

It was not just as a vital cog in the Belvoir Drive backroom team that George deserves to be remembered in City's annals of history. As a player he was a predatory centre-forward who, despite losing the best years of his League career to World War Two, totalled more than a century of goals for the club in all matches played, and he is one of only seven men to achieve that landmark.

He had joined City after learning his art playing under the club's former inside-forward George Carr at Nuneaton Town. Within a couple of weeks of joining Leicester he had been thrust into First Division action, although in a losing cause at home to West Brom. His second outing a week later at Birmingham City brought joy and disappointment, and his first goal for the club counted for nothing when the match was abandoned after 65 minutes due to thick fog.

Despite his athletic build, raw strength and good aerial ability, he remained on the fringes of the squad for several seasons, although he was still able to maintain a healthy goal ratio whenever he was called upon to perform.

He made just eight appearances in the promotion-winning team of 1937, 16 a year later and 29 in the 1938–39 campaign, which saw him collect 10 goals in the League and another couple in the Cup, his healthiest return up to that point.

In 1939 George scored City's first goal in the 2–0 away win at West Ham – the last fixture the club played before the outbreak of hostilities caused the League programme to be cancelled.

During the war George served in the Army and played football for Northern Command. Apart from assorted 'guest' appearances for Chesterfield, Leeds United, Sheffield United and Yeovil Town, he was also able to turn out fairly frequently for his true love – Leicester City. In

81 wartime games for the Foxes he recorded a staggering tally of 62 goals, which included hat-tricks against West Brom, Chesterfield and Sheffield Wednesday, plus a four-goal haul in a 9–1 romp over Notts County in October 1943.

He also scored three times on Christmas Day 1940, although they came in two separate matches against the same club. After scoring both of the Foxes' goals in a 5–2 defeat in a game which kicked-off at 10.45 at Northampton Town, he then scored again in the 3pm return – this time City won 7–2!

These two matches came in the middle of a scoring spree which brought George 15 goals, with him scoring in 10 successive fixtures.

When League football resumed in 1946–47 he continued to plunder opposition defences and scored an aggregate of 19 goals for the club that season – one more than Jack Lee. George's total included yet another hat-trick, this time against Millwall.

*He also scored three times on Christmas Day 1940, although they came in two separate matches against the same club. After scoring both of the Foxes' goals in a 5–2 defeat in a game which kicked-off at 10.45 at Northampton Town, he then scored again in the 3pm return – this time City won 7–2!*

At 36 years of age he was out of the squad by the time of the 1949 FA Cup run but continued playing, with a short stint at non-League Yeovil before returning to join Leicester's backroom staff – initially as assistant coach, then working with the youth and reserve teams.

Many of the great players that have passed through the clubs doors have heaped the highest amount of praise possible on George for his patience and understanding, as much as for his coaching methods.

Peter Shilton, in particular, benefited from hours of extra training with him and paid his former mentor a huge number of compliments in his autobiography. 'I can't overstate the influence George Dewis had on me, not only as a goalkeeper but as a person. He took me under his wing, spent countless hours with me and what he taught me about goalkeeping, football and life in general was to prove invaluable.'

The former England 'keeper also revealed that Gary Lineker shared similar thoughts. 'When I was away with England Gary would always say that George had instilled in him the importance of keeping your shots low and on target. Obvious things really, but when you had someone working constantly on the basics with you, it eventually paid dividends.'

Later George took over as City's kit-man before retiring in 1983, having given the club half a century of dedicated service. His incredible loyalty and whole-hearted commitment may never be seen again.

George Dewis – a true Leicester City Legend.

# PAUL DICKOV

*Born:*            1 November 1972, Glasgow, Scotland.

**Leicester City Record:**

*Appearances:*     League 110, FA Cup 7, League Cup 7, Other 1.

*Goals:*           League 34, FA Cup 3, League Cup 3, Other 0.

*Debut:*           23 February 2002 v Derby County (h) lost 0–3.

*Also played for:* Arsenal, Luton Town (loan), Brighton and Hove Albion (loan), Manchester City, Blackburn Rovers, Crystal Palace (loan), Blackpool (loan), Derby County (loan), Leeds United, Scotland (10 caps).

*Managed:*         Oldham Athletic.

Football supporters love nothing more than to watch a player who clearly cares about the club he represents as much as they do. When that player has the knack of combining a healthy work-rate with a steady quota of important goals then he comes close to approaching iconic status with his fans.

Paul Dickov was vital to Leicester City's promotion hopes in 2002–03, and his 17 League goals helped the club to a runners'-up berth behind Portsmouth and an instant return to the Premiership.

The striker was an outstanding schoolboy player and represented Scotland in the 1989 FIFA Under-16 World Championships, where they reached the Final. His eye-catching performances brought a host of admirers, but it was Arsenal who stepped in to sign the youngster.

Although the North London club provided a perfect 'finishing school' for Paul, first-team opportunities were rare. He did, however, pocket some serious silverware with a winners' medal, gained as a non-playing substitute in the 1994 European Cup-Winners' Cup triumph over Parma.

A move to Manchester City brought regular matches and plenty of goals, none more important than one at Wembley Stadium in a Play-off Final against Gillingham. The beaten 'keeper was Vince Bartram, the best man at Paul's wedding!

In February 2002 he joined a Leicester City side that was struggling against relegation from the Premiership, and despite him hitting four goals in a dozen appearances he could not avert the slide. It was not just the drop that forced a few tears, however, as on the final afternoon of the season (11 May 2002) the club ended its 111-year residency at Filbert Street with a home game against Spurs.

The visitors went ahead before Paul scored the penultimate goal at the old ground – firing a sweetly-timed right footer beyond former City 'keeper Kasey Keller. Matthew Piper's only first-team goal for the Foxes soon followed – cementing him in the club's annals of fame for all time.

# *He was either 'the Wasp' or 'the Pest' depending on who you spoke to, but both accurately summed up what opposing centre-halves thought of him.*

No sooner had the club bade farewell to their former home than they were inviting guests over for the house-warming at the splendid new Walkers Stadium.

After Brian Deane had scored two goals against Watford in the first match at the new ground, and then added the opener in the next match against Reading, Paul slotted a penalty beyond 'keeper Phil Whitehead to become the second Fox to open his tally there.

That was the start of a campaign that saw him reach 20 goals for the first time – two in the FA Cup, one in the League Cup and 17 in the League as City claimed promotion, finishing just behind Portsmouth. Paul's haul included a hat-trick at home to Wimbledon in February 2003, with a couple of the goals coming from the penalty spot. Voted the club's Player of the Year by the City fans, he also made it into the PFA Team of the Season. He also earned a recall to the Scottish international side, having been first capped while at Manchester City.

Paul's style of play had earned him a couple of very appropriate nicknames – he was either 'the Wasp' or 'the Pest' depending on who you spoke to, but both accurately summed up what opposing centre-halves thought of him. At 5ft 6in he was never going to outjump a big stopper, but he would certainly not give them a minute's peace while the ball was on the ground, and his harrying and workman-like attitude provided the perfect incentive to energise tiring colleagues.

Back in the 'big time', 'Dicko' scored 11 Premiership goals in 2003–04, but his season was totally – and unfairly – wrecked while at a training camp in La Manga in March. Paul, plus two of his City teammates, Frank Sinclair and Keith Gillespie, were wrongly accused of sexually assaulting three African women, and the players were held in a Spanish prison for a week. All charges were dropped, but understandably Paul said: 'it was the darkest period of my career'.

Blackburn Rovers signed 'the Wasp' in June 2004 – but via a very circuitous route, which also saw him score a last-minute winner against the Foxes while on loan at Blackpool in February 2008. He returned to the Walkers four years later.

On snapping up the impish striker, manager Nigel Pearson told the City website: 'Paul has all the attributes you require to succeed as a footballer. He has tremendous spirit and I am delighted to have been able to bring him here. He is the sort of player who never believes the team is beaten. He breeds fear into defences and I am sure he will be a tremendous asset for us. He will give us everything and I am sure he will be a big favourite with the fans here once again.'

Making his second debut in a 2–0 home win over the MK Dons on 9 August 2008, Paul became the first Fox to play for the club in three different Divisions – his role in the ensuing title-winning campaign has hopefully ensured that no one will ever achieve that feat again!

# DEREK DOUGAN

*Born:* 20 January 1939, Belfast, Northern Ireland.

*Died:* 24 June 2007, Wolverhampton.

## Leicester City record:

*Appearances:* League 68, FA Cup 5, League Cup 3.

*Goals:* League 35, FA Cup 1, League Cup 5.

*Debut:* 21 August 1965 v Liverpool (h) lost 1–3.

*Also played for:* Distillery (Northern Ireland), Portsmouth, Blackburn Rovers, Aston Villa, Peterborough United, Wolverhampton Wanderers, Los Angeles Wolves , Kansas City Spurs (both USA), Shamrock Rovers (Republic of Ireland), Kettering Town, Northern Ireland (43 caps).

Derek Dougan was not at Leicester City for long, and he then went on to become one of Wolverhampton Wanderers' finest-ever players, but he should be held in high esteem for his achievements at Filbert Street. Indeed, until Matty Fryatt repeated the feat 42 years later, 'The Doog' (as he was known) was the last City player to score 20 goals for the club before Christmas.

He was 26 by the time he signed for the Foxes, having gained early success with Distillery, helping them to an Irish Cup win in 1956, when he was just 17 years of age. Derek's potential was obvious, and Portsmouth backed their judgement with a £4,000 cheque to secure the services of the lanky centre-forward.

Inside a couple of years he was on the move again, and this time the fee was £15,000 as Derek moved to the North West to join Blackburn Rovers. His two goals in the FA Cup semi-final win over Sheffield Wednesday at Maine Road secured his place in the side for the 1960 Wembley showpiece, but it was to be a losing Final for Derek, ironically against Wolves, the club where he would later enjoy great success.

Further moves to Aston Villa and Peterborough United emphasised Derek's wanderlust personality – a freedom of spirit that was not afraid to move on impulse and try something new. On reflection he was perhaps always seeking the right club at the right time – and he eventually found it – after a goal-laden two years with City!

Although Derek had become established as an almost permanent fixture in the Northern Ireland international set-up (his first cap had come way back in 1958 during the World Cup Finals in Sweden), the jury were still out on whether his early promise was ever going to be totally fulfilled. The role of club joker and an ability to remain somewhat parallel to the party line had been features of his career to that point, but a spell at Third Division Peterborough had perhaps provided the necessary focus to get him back on track.

Certainly the move to Leicester benefitted all parties. Manager Matt Gillies had spent just over £20,000 on 'The Doog' and a similar figure on Dunfermline's nippy winger, Jackie Sinclair. The two made their City bow on the same day and formed an instantly successful partnership.

Finishing 18th the year before, the Foxes improved dramatically with a seventh-place finish in the top flight, thanks in no small measure to the goals of the front two – Dougan scored 20 and Sinclair 24 (although the Scot did play in half a dozen more matches and was the club's penalty-taker).

In Gordon Banks, England's recent World Cup-winning goalkeeper, City had a household name at one end of the field, but in the early stages

*It was odds-on that Derek would get those 20 goals before Christmas – a stat somewhat akin to a cricketer scoring 1,000 runs before the end of May. The landmark duly arrived on 3 December*

of the 1966–67 season they had the hottest property in the land playing up-front. Despite losing 3–2 to Liverpool at Anfield on the opening day, Derek scored both of City's goals to begin a scoring sequence that tallied 13 goals in the 10 matches which were played during August and September.

If Derek's undoubted forte was his strength in the air, he also had an excellent touch on the ground and possessed a lethal shot when given the opportunity. None knew that better than Aston Villa, one of his former clubs, who were given a real battering at Filbert Street. Dougan scored three of the goals in the 5–0 demolition – his only Foxes hat-trick – and so desperate were Villa to keep track of the 'big man' that legend has it that one marker even followed him around the back of the goal while they were waiting for a corner to be taken!

Having made such a hot start to the campaign, it was odds-on that Derek would get those 20 goals before Christmas – a stat somewhat akin to a cricketer scoring 1,000 runs before the end of May. The landmark duly arrived on 3 December in a home win over Stoke City, which was only his 22nd game of the season.

All strikers go through peaks and troughs, however, and somewhat bizarrely Derek then added just one more goal – a home winner against Arsenal – from his next 13 outings. That proved to be his final strike in a City shirt because Dougan's seemingly irrepressible urge to move every couple of years coincided with Leicester accepting a £50,000 bid from Wolves for his signature. The fans were not happy, with manager Matt Gillies bearing the brunt of their frustration. A season that promised much better ended with City eighth in the table.

Derek spent the next nine years at Molyneux, bagging 95 goals in 258 appearances. He became part of their folklore before ending his career with a brief fling in the United States. He played in a match for a Shamrock Rovers XI against world champions Brazil designed to help the peace process in Northern Ireland, before having a short stint as player-manager at non-League Kettering Town.

Forthright, colourful and always entertaining, Derek Dougan was a football man through and through. He later served as both chief executive and chairman of Wolves before he tragically died of a heart attack in 2007.

# JOHN DUNCAN

*Born:* 14 February 1896, Lochgelly, Fife.

*Died:* 14 March 1966, Leicester.

## Leicester City record:

*Appearances:* League 279, FA Cup 16.

*Goals:* League 88, FA Cup 7.

*Debut:* 26 August 1922 v Stockport County (a) won 5–4.

*Also played for:* Denbeath Star, Lochgelly United, Raith Rovers, Scotland (1 cap).

*Managed:* Leicester City (March 1946–October 1949).

Johnny Duncan earns his place among the Leicester City greats for his achievements, both as a free-scoring inside-forward and as an inspirational manager, whose finest hour was leading the Foxes to their first Wembley FA Cup Final.

'It's not what you know but who you know' would aptly describe Johnny's route to Filbert Street. Peter Hodge, the Leicester boss, had been Johnny's 'gaffer' at Raith Rovers and kept an eye on his old club after his move to the East Midlands. Johnny, his brother Tom and striker George Waite all moved south together to provide some Kirkcaldy kindred spirit inside the home dressing room, and this would explain why Johnny's nickname 'Tokey' also travelled with him.

His debut could hardly have been more compelling, two goals in a thrilling 5–4 away victory at Stockport County. That first season at Filbert Street unfortunately ended in the cruellest of misfortune. Having played in all the matches to that point, the injured Johnny had to sit out the closing fixture – a 0–2 defeat at Bury which meant that the Foxes missed out on promotion to the top tier on goal difference to West Ham, who themselves were runners-up to champions Notts County. Although there was plenty of remorse, it was truthfully pointed out that the Hammers had a reasonable argument for going up, as they had won 6–0 on their visit to Leicester in February.

Despite the introduction of Arthur Chandler into the side, the expected push did not materialise the following season, but 1924–25 proved to be a golden campaign for the Foxes. Johnny replaced Mick O'Brien, the Irish international, as club captain and oversaw the winning of the Division Two title, won in something of a scoring-frenzy with the 42 matches producing 90 goals for and just 32 against.

Of those 90, Johnny, in the number-eight jersey, scored 30 from 40 League appearances, yet he still finished a couple behind the ever-present Chandler. Despite not picking up the accolade of being the leading scorer, the Scot certainly had a Christmas Day to remember, breaking the club record for most goals in a match by scoring six in a 7–0 home romp over Port Vale.

Onlookers at some of City's early First Division performances must have included the Scotland selectors because they selected Johnny for the national side, and he was among the scorers in a 3–0 victory over the Welsh in Cardiff. Somewhat astonishingly, it turned out to be his only cap, but their loss was clearly Leicester's gain.

He was an ever-present throughout the 1926–27 season, but a dislocated elbow and broken arm forced him to miss much of the following League programme. Over the course of the next few years City were one of the dominant forces in the land, twice finishing in the top three positions, with Johnny's performances pivotal.

In the summer of 1930 things came to a head between Johnny and the Leicester City board when it was revealed that he had contravened club policy by taking over the licence of a public house – the Turk's Head on Welford Road. Amid much acrimony, and a failed bid from Northampton Town to sign him, Johnny decided that enough was enough and announced his retirement from the game in order to pursue his new business venture. The pub became, as you would expect, a favourite port of call for all City fans eager to chew the fat with one of their former idols.

Not for one fleeting second did Johnny's affection for the club begin to wane, however, and he became one of the inaugural committee members of the supporters' club when it was formed in August 1940.

Earlier that year 'Tokey's brother Tom had passed away, leaving a daughter Elsie, who later married City player Don Revie.

In March 1946, with League football about to resume after the war years, Johnny succeeded Tom Bromilow as City's manager. The side were firmly ensconced in the Second Division and, in truth, no trees were pulled up with either performance or position in the League, but in his third season in charge the Foxes advanced to Wembley for their first FA Cup Final.

There was no prouder man in the land than Johnny Duncan as he walked out with his Wolves counterpart Stan Cullis. As huge underdogs it was not a surprise that Leicester went down on the day, but the fact that they almost dropped out of the division at the end of the season deeply concerned the manager. Principled – and disappointed that he could not steady the flagging fortunes – Johnny resigned from his post, amid strong rumours that he had 'lost the confidence of his dressing room'.

The Scot died in 1966 but will always be remembered as a man who cared deeply about Leicester City Football Club and was an integral part of their successes both as player and manager.

*Over the course of the next few years City were one of the dominant forces in the land, twice finishing in the top three positions, with Johnny's performances pivotal.*

# MATT ELLIOTT

Born:                    1 November 1968, Roehampton, Greater London.

## Leicester City record:
Appearances:      League 245, FA Cup 19, League Cup 22, Other 4.
Goals:                League 27, FA Cup 3, League Cup 3, Other 0.
Debut:                18 January 1997 v Wimbledon (h) won 1–0.
Also played for:   Epsom and Ewell, Charlton Athletic, Torquay United, Scunthorpe United, Oxford United, Ipswich Town (loan), Scotland (18 caps).

Most young footballers have one recurring ambition – to play at Wembley Stadium. Probing even deeper, you may get them to admit to a secret wish to either lead a side out at the 'Venue of Legends', or maybe even to score a winning goal there.

For Matt Elliott, all his dreams came true on Sunday 27 February 2000 when he skippered Leicester City to League Cup glory with a 2–1 victory over Tranmere Rovers – and the 6ft 3in centre-half headed both of the Foxes' goals. There was a huge similarity with each, in that both came from Steve Guppy corners. For the first, after 29 minutes, he pulled out towards the penalty spot and with neck muscles bulging he leapt to perfectly time a bullet beyond 'keeper Joe Murphy and in off the underside of the crossbar.

Nine minutes from time – and shortly after the side from the Wirral had equalised – came another Guppy left-footed corner. This time Matt, at the far post, shrugged off a lame challenge from a defender and guided the ball inside the unguarded upright.

With understandable pride he then led his jubilant teammates up to the Royal Box to collect and hoist aloft the winners' silverware. To make the day even more complete, along with his medallion, City's captain was also deservedly named as the Man of the Match and was awarded the Sir Alan Hardaker Trophy, emulating Steve Walsh's achievement for the Foxes three years earlier.

The fact that City were at Wembley anyway was in no small part down to Matt. After being held at home to a goalless draw in the first leg of the semi-final against Aston Villa, they ventured to the return with their numbers depleted. Boss Martin O'Neill elected to use Matt as a makeshift striker, and the hunch reaped huge dividends as Matt nodded in a Robbie Savage cross, just before the break, to settle the tie.

Whatever his dreams, scoring a Wembley winner must have seemed a long way off for Matt as he began his career in the Isthmian League with Epsom and Ewell. Charlton Athletic gave him his first senior contract, but after just one Cup outing for the Addicks he was sold to Torquay United.

Further moves to Scunthorpe United and Oxford United spread over the next six or seven years gave him a solid grounding, but by the time he had reached 28 years of age all he had got to show for his experience was one promotion campaign.

In January 1997 manager O'Neill paid out a club record £1.6 million to bring Matt to Leicester, and although he played in most of the remaining Premiership matches, his early-season exploits at the Manor Ground had cup-tied him and he was therefore unable to participate in City's League Cup glory.

Immensely powerful both on the ground and in the air, Matt presented a physically imposing challenge — even for the very best — and his whole-hearted commitment endeared him to the Blue Army. His affable nature earned him a

*Matt was an obvious choice to take over as club skipper, and he responded by triumphantly leading his team to their win over Tranmere beneath the Twin Towers. It was the third time that the Foxes had won the League Cup and the last Final to be held at the old Wembley Stadium.*

nickname of 'the Honey Monster', but he also became used to some good-natured shouts of 'Jock', after Craig Brown called him up for the full Scottish squad on learning that Matt had a grandparent from north of the border. In all, he played in 18 internationals, scoring once, and was part of the World Cup squad in France 1998.

In 1999 he played in City's losing League Cup Final side against Spurs, but his time came 12 months later. An astute reader of the game, as well as a natural leader, Matt was an obvious choice to take over as club skipper, and he responded by triumphantly leading his team to their win over Tranmere beneath the Twin Towers. It was the third time that the Foxes had won the League Cup and the last Final to be held at the old Wembley Stadium.

Over the course of the next couple of seasons life did not always run smoothly for Leicester City, but even during the darkest days of administration they were nobly led on the field by their determined number 18.

Being named as captain for the club's final match at Filbert Street and their first at the Walkers Stadium were also notable additions to the Elliott CV, but a constant battle against knee injuries was finally lost, and despite a brief loan stint at Ipswich Town he retired from the game — having amassed a career total of over 700 appearances.

Matt spent the 2008–09 season as assistant manger at Hednesford United before stepping down to concentrate on his business pursuits, although he soon returned to the game, taking up a similar position at Midland Alliance side, Oadby Town.

# RODNEY FERN

*Born:*          13 December 1948, Burton-on-Trent, Staffordshire.

## Leicester City record:

*Appearances:*   League 152, FA Cup 23, League Cup 12.

*Goals:*         League 32, FA Cup 5, League Cup 3.

*Debut:*         3 February 1968 v Leeds United (h) won 1–0.

*Also played for:* Measham, Luton Town, Coventry City (loan), Chesterfield, Rotherham United.

Rodney Fern was something of a cult figure during his days at Filbert Street, as much for his appearance as for his telling contributions and vital goals: 'Many people remember me for the sideburns as much as anything,' recalls Rod. 'It was a fashion at the time, and I just thought they looked good!'

Equally as comfortable on the flank or playing straight through the middle, Rod joined the Foxes from Measham Miners' Welfare and was fortunate to get an encouraging pep talk each day on his way to work. 'Derek Hines used to give me a lift to training, and he kept telling me that I'd be the next youngster to break through into the first team.'

Manager Matt Gillies clearly agreed with the forecast, although he was not around to see Rod make his debut. 'Matt was off convalescing after an illness when Bert Johnson, the coach, threw me in against Leeds United. After only about 15 seconds I was kicked up in the air by Norman Hunter, but then Stringy [Mike Stringfellow] headed in a free-kick and that settled me down. We won it 1–0 against a side that had previously won about six on the trot.'

A few days later Rod was given a taste of FA Cup action, and his first senior goal helped inspire the Foxes to a magnificent comeback win over Manchester City. 'We were 2–0 down in a replay at home, and about 30 seconds before half-time I scored from the edge of the box, with a left footer that flew into the roof of the net.'

The FA Cup, of course, gave City a roller-coaster ride all the way to the Twin Towers at the end of the 1968–69 season. Having scored in the third round against Barnsley, Rod scored with a back-post header to oust Mansfield Town in the sixth-round clash at Field Mill.

After disposing of West Brom in the semis, Rod and his teammates walked out to face Manchester City in the Wembley showpiece. 'It was undoubtedly the biggest day of my footballing life. It's true what people say – it did seem to pass by very quickly, but we had our chances and just sadly didn't take them.'

City did not have time to dwell on their disappointment, however, as the focus quickly turned back to League matters and the struggle to avoid an unwanted relegation. 'We still had five matches to play after the Cup Final, and it proved too much as we went down after needing to beat Manchester United in the last match to have any hope. George Best, though, was brilliant that day and scored a very special goal past "Shilts".'

Hopes of an immediate return were raised on the opening day of the new campaign with Birmingham City comprehensively beaten. Rod was first to get on the scoresheet with a stunning overhead-kick. 'Lennie Glover put over the cross, and I was about 10–12 yards out and just took off and hit it sweetly into the roof of the net.'

On 12 November 1969, away at Bolton's Burnden Park, Rod hit the only hat-trick of his Foxes career. 'Charlie Hurley was marking me that day – the ex-Sunderland player. He was a huge man and wasn't very happy about me giving him the run-around.' Despite scoring all of City's goals in their 3–2 victory, Rodney has one slight regret. 'Sadly I didn't get to keep the matchball afterwards – for some reason I don't think they wanted me to have it!'

After just missing out on promotion in 1969–70 City made sure the following season, with many seasoned observers feeling that Rodney's finest-ever game came away at Luton. 'It was over the Easter period and they had a decent side, with guys like Malcolm McDonald and Chris Nicholl in their line up. We went one down and then I just had one of those days – everything I tried came off and we took them apart 3–1 in the end.'

Another splendid FA Cup run was controversially halted in a sixth-round replay against Arsenal, but only after Rod had a score ruled out. 'The ref said he'd chalked it off for pushing a defender, but I honestly didn't touch him,' he says.

After proudly collecting a Division Two Championship medal and then playing one more season of top-flight football, Rod moved to Luton, who had clearly been impressed by his virtuoso performance against them 14 months earlier.

# 'It's true what people say – it did seem to pass by very quickly, but we had our chances and just sadly didn't take them.'

'I didn't really want to leave, but I was a bit naïve as it was my first move. In truth it was a wasted two years and I couldn't wait to move back nearer home.'

He was top scorer in three of his four years at Chesterfield then closed down his time in the Football League with a stint at Rotherham, where he was able to enjoy something of a swan-song to his career. 'We won the Division Three Championship and turned over a lot of top clubs in the Cup competitions. I scored four times in a match against Chelsea and then upset the Leicester fans by scoring home and away against them in the League Cup. Nevertheless I'll always maintain a soft spot for City, I've got some great memories and had some great times there.'

# BILLY FRAME

*Born:*        7 May 1912, Carluke, Lanarkshire.
*Died:*        9 September 1992, Nottingham.

## Leicester City record:

*Appearances:*    League 220, FA Cup 19, Other (wartime) 220.
*Debut:*        6 October 1934 v Tottenham Hotspur (a) drew 2–2.
*Also played for:*  Shawfield Juniors, Rugby Town.

The record books show that William Lammie Frame played in 220 League matches for City – an impressive enough total on its own but made even more worthy when you add in a similar number of wartime appearances that he participated in for the club.

Billy was playing in Scottish Junior club football in Glasgow before being snapped up by City along with his teammate Johnny Grogan, who himself went on to make 46 League appearances for the Foxes.

Slotting in at his accustomed right-back, Billy's debut would have traumatised lesser men, as he conceded an own-goal in a 2–2 draw against Spurs at White Hart Lane. He settled into his new life in the East Midlands and became an automatic selection almost immediately.

Early in the 1936–37 season City changed managers, with Arthur Lochhead making way for Frank Womack. Despite this apparent upheaval it developed into a fine campaign for the Foxes, and they entered their final match – at home to Spurs – knowing that a win would secure the Division Two Championship shield. A 4–1 victory brought Billy the only major medal of his playing career.

By way of celebration the entire City squad left for a tour of Eastern Europe, which included games in Rumania, Hungary, Yugoslavia and Czechoslovakia.

A creditable 16th position enabled City to survive their first season back in the top tier, but the following campaign brought little comfort. The squad was barely able to cope with the demands at this level, and the impending likelihood of war threw the darkest of veils over everyday life.

Only two wins out of the first 12 fixtures told its own story. On 1 October 1938 City suffered a wretched 8–2 mauling at Leeds United. There were slightly extenuating circumstances, however, as 'keeper Sandy McLaren was injured early in the contest and unable to continue. Both Billy and Fred Sharman took a turn in goal, but the final outcome is testimony to their success in the role!

Relegation back to Division Two came as a blessed relief for City and their followers, although they suspected that football would be at the back of everyone's minds for the foreseeable future.

Once the Football League programme had been abandoned in the autumn of 1939, City found themselves in the Midland Division. Billy was available to play in most of the fixtures, and among the 'guest' players he was able to take to the field alongside was Tommy Lawton, later to become England's centre-forward.

During 1940–41 Billy was a member of the side that won the Midland Cup Final, defeating Walsall to take the silverware. That same season City also came perilously close to advancing to a Wembley Cup Final for the first time, reaching the semi-finals of the Wartime Cup before bowing out to a strong Arsenal team which included England skipper Eddie Hapgood and the cricketing brothers Denis and Leslie Compton in their ranks.

Playing ahead of Billy on the Leicester right was another player destined to have a huge future in the game. Later to win over 100 caps for England as a centre-half was Billy Wright, the Wolverhampton Wanderers star, who 'guested' for City for a couple of seasons.

With 220 appearances spread over seven years, Frame played in more wartime matches for City than any other player, and fittingly he was able to resume his League career when the programme recommenced on 31 August 1946; although the omens were not too promising when Manchester City left Filbert Street as 3–0 victors on the opening day.

*During 1940–41 Billy was a member of the side that won the Midland Cup Final, defeating Walsall to take the silverware. That same season City also came perilously close to advancing to a Wembley Cup Final for the first time, reaching the semi-finals of the Wartime Cup before bowing out to a strong Arsenal team which included England skipper Eddie Hapgood and the cricketing brothers Denis and Leslie Compton in their ranks.*

Billy's 200th League appearance for the club came on 13 November 1948 in a 4–2 home victory over Nottingham Forest, a match in which Don Revie registered his only City hat-trick.

That same season Leicester City's shirt was adorned with a club crest for the first time, and fittingly it was worn at Wembley after the club had progressed through to reach their first FA Cup Final. Sadly for Billy, his role became one of onlooker after he had been badly injured and was forced to miss the second half of the season.

A week after the Cup Final loss to Wolves, City travelled to Cardiff City needing a point to avoid the drop, and the experienced Billy was able to return – in place of Cup Final right-back Ted Jelly – to help the team to the one-all draw they needed to stay up.

Billy played only a bit-part role during the following season before being allowed to see out his playing career with Rugby Town after a free transfer.

Later Billy became a licensee, running the Griffin Inn in Leicester, where he would spend many a happy hour regaling the customers with tales of his 16 years at Filbert Street but never once being able to explain just why he had never managed to score a single goal for the club!

# MATTY FRYATT

*Born:*        5 March 1986, Nuneaton, Warwickshire.

**Leicester City record:** (to the end of season 2009–10).
*Appearances:*    League 156 FA Cup 7 League Cup 7 Other 5.
*Goals:*        League 49 FA Cup 5 League Cup 2 Other 2.
*Debut:*        14 January 2006 v Sheffield Wednesday (a) lost 1–2.
*Also played for:*  Walsall, Carlisle United (loan).

For many years no footballer wanted to be allocated a number outside the traditional one to 11, but in recent years all sorts of squad numbering has become fashionable, and the 'Leicester City Number-12 shirt' has become synonymous with one of the hottest strikers ever to play for the club.

Having taken a couple of seasons to get into his stride at Leicester, Matty Fryatt has now established himself as one of the most lethal predators in the country.

Displaying a real poacher's instinct for being in the right place at the right time, he enjoyed a record-breaking season in 2008–09, when the former Walsall hot-shot struck 32 times – 27 of which were in the League – as City clinched the Division One title and a return to the Championship.

Apart from an enforced lay-off, after sustaining a broken jaw in a League match against Doncaster Rovers, Matty again remained prolific throughout the following season. His 13th goal of the campaign – against Cardiff City in the Play-off semi-final second leg – ensured he finished as the club's top scorer for a second consecutive season.

Matty had graduated through the junior ranks at Walsall before going on to score 30 goals for the Saddlers, from 78 outings. His first senior goal, though, had come after he had been allowed out on loan to gain some experience. Playing for Carlisle United, he scored the winner in a 2–1 home triumph over Boston United.

*'against Crewe Alexandra, he took his tally to 32 – the best by a City player for more than 50 years'*

After returning to his parent club, Matty was handed the opportunity of a prolonged spell in the first team, and he responded by becoming the club's top scorer in each of the next two seasons. In 2004–05 he netted on 15 occasions – with a memorable hat-trick, his first in the League, coming in a 4–3 win over Huddersfield Town.

Early international recognition came his way with a call up for the England Under-19s side, and he responded with a hat-trick for them (against Serbia and Montenegro) in the 2005 European Championships at that level.

Thirteen goals from 25 League and Cup games during the first part of 2005–06 confirmed that Matty was not going to be a 'flash in the pan', and it was inevitable that the opportunity would materialise to play at a higher level, and one of Craig Levein's final acts as Leicester City manager was to convince the young striker that his future lay at the Walkers Stadium.

Matty signed for Leicester City during the January 2006 transfer window and made his debut as a late replacement for Joe Hamill in a 2–1 reverse at Sheffield Wednesday. It was enough to earn him a start the following week against Cardiff City, and he crowned his first Walkers Stadium match with a goal.

Playing against Preston North End on 15 April 2006, the striker scored after just nine seconds – the quickest ever City goal. Coincidentally he had also held that record at his previous club, with another nine-second effort!

Struggling with ankle and toe problems early in his Foxes career, the anticipated bucketful of goals did not initially arrive, although he did convert a high-profile winner against Aston Villa in a League Cup tie at Villa Park in September 2007. Latching on to a pass from James Chambers, he fired past 'keeper Stuart Taylor from a narrow angle.

During what was an uncertain period he had to wait two months for his next goal, but even when it came, at Bristol City, there was a bitter-sweet irony, as he received the first red card of his career shortly afterwards.

The 2007–08 campaign ended disappointingly in relegation but Matty remained a Fox – and a Fox with a mission – to score the goals that would secure a swift return to the Championship. Two goals on the opening day of the new season boosted his confidence – and two more in the next home match – sent it sky-rocketing as Matty embarked on a campaign that was to see him become the first City player since Derek Dougan in 1966 to score 20 goals before Christmas.

His tally had been bolstered by back-to-back hat-tricks, with all of the goals coming in Walkers Stadium wins over Dagenham and Redbridge in the FA Cup competition and Southend United in the League – it was the first time a Fox had done that since Arthur Chandler had achieved the feat 83 years earlier.

Matty emphasised his commitment to City by signing a new three-and-a-half-year contract during December 2008 and celebrated by being named the League One Player of that Month.

Goals continued to flow, as City roared away from the chasing pack, and his 20th League goal of the season came in a 4–1 win at his old club, Walsall. Fittingly, considering how big his impact on the season had been, Matty scored both goals – his personal 30th and 31st – at Southend United on the day the club promotion was secured as champions.

On the final day of the season, against Crewe Alexandra, he took his tally to 32 – the best by a City player for more than 50 years. Arthur Rowley had bagged 44 goals in 1956–57 – and his League return of 27 pipped the 26 scored by Gary Lineker in 1984–85, the previous best since Arthur's feat.

In his own unflappable style, Matty Fryatt has made goalscoring look easy since arriving in LE2 – and the Blue Army hope he will continue to do so for many more years to come!

# DAVIE GIBSON

*Born:*　　　　　23 September 1938, Winchburgh, West Lothian.

## Leicester City record:

*Appearances:*　　League 280, FA Cup 29, League Cup 30.
*Goals:*　　　　　League 41, FA Cup 5, League Cup 7.
*Debut:*　　　　　3 February 1962 v Fulham (h) won 4–1.
*Also played for:*　Livingston United, Hibernian, Aston Villa, Exeter City, Scotland (7 caps).

Davie Gibson was a wonderfully gifted inside-forward who played in four domestic Cup Finals for City after first making an impression in his homeland. He was born in Winchburgh, just outside Edinburgh, 'Willie Thornton, the old Rangers and Scotland player, lived on the same street and Bobby Moncur, later to star for Newcastle, came from the next village.' Davie began in Junior football with Livingston before making the grade at Hibs.

After six years at Easter Road he journeyed south to join City for a fee of around £40,000 in January 1962. 'Football is all about highs and lows', he says. 'The first of my highs was signing for City – it was the start of nine wonderful seasons I spent at Filbert Street.'

By contrast, most of the 'lows' he experienced involved one or other of the teams from a city in the North West. 'We lost the 1963 FA Cup Final to Manchester United, the 1969 FA Cup Final to Manchester City and were then relegated shortly afterwards when we lost to Manchester United – so you can understand why I don't have a soft spot for that city!'

Davie looks back with pride on his first full season with the Foxes. 'I remember we had a really good run at one point of seven or eight wins on the trot, and for a while it looked as if we might be on for the double, but looking back we then lost form towards the end of the campaign – I think we lost four on the trot so went into the FA Cup Final lacking our usual confidence.'

City's defeat in that match still clearly hurts. 'Manchester United had just escaped relegation and blossomed on the day, but they had good players; the likes of Law, Charlton and Crerand were always going to play well on the big occasion. You wonder afterwards "were we that bad because they were good – or were they that good because we were that bad?" It was probably my worst-ever game – it just didn't happen – we'd had a good season, but it felt like failure because we wanted to win the FA Cup for our terrific fans.'

That campaign contained plenty of other highlights for the elegant midfielder, including a call-up for his national side. 'I scored an important goal against Liverpool at Anfield and Ian McColl, the Scotland manager, was there watching, and I got called-up for my first international shortly afterwards. It wasn't a blockbuster of a goal, I just slid it past Tommy Lawrence, but it was important for me for what happened afterwards.'

He also recalls playing in one of the most exciting matches of his career in that same season. 'It was the League game against Manchester United at Filbert Street, when we beat them 4–3, with both Ken Keyworth and Denis Law scoring hat-tricks.'

There was some tangible reward at last for City with the League Cup triumph in 1964. Davie managed to score in both legs of the Final, helping his side to a 4–3 aggregate victory over Stoke City. 'I remember the goal in the second leg at Filbert Street very well as I didn't score too many with my head. Howard Riley put over a corner – he didn't hit them gently – and I made a near-post run and went to flick the ball, but it cannoned off my head at great pace and flew into the net.'

He played in the losing Final, against Chelsea, the following season and suffered another setback in 1969. 'I was invited to go and speak at Manchester City's 40th anniversary dinner of their FA Cup Final win against us, and all the way through the dinner they showed the film of the match. Seeing it again reminded me of the good chances we had that day, but in the end we were only beaten by something of a wonder goal. I thought Peter Shilton made a magnificent effort to get to it though. When I stood up to speak I said, "I guess I'm the only person in here who didn't want to watch that again!"'

Davie admits to being a little uncomfortable with being termed a 'Leicester Legend': 'I honestly believe that word is thrown around too easily in today's football world. Personally I feel it disrespectful to players like Stanley Matthews, Tom Finney, Bobby Charlton and Jimmy Greaves, the true Legends of our football world.'

'I was fortunate though to play with some great players during my time at Leicester – Gordon Banks, Peter Shilton, Peter Rodrigues, Derek Dougan and the most inspirational player of my time there, Frank McLintock. I was also grateful that in Matt Gillies, the manager, and Bert Johnson, the coach, we had two of the finest footballing gentlemen you could ever hope to play for.'

'I thoroughly enjoyed my time at Leicester City, and hopefully I left the supporters with some happy memories, and I'm quite happy to be remembered, as they say in Scotland, "He wisnae a bad wee player!"'

> *'I was fortunate though to play with some great players during my time at Leicester – Gordon Banks, Peter Shilton, Peter Rodrigues, Derek Dougan and the most inspirational player of my time there, Frank McLintock.*

# MATT GILLIES

*Born:*           12 August 1921, Loganlea, West Lothian.
*Died:*           24 December 1998, Nottingham.

## Leicester City record:

*Appearances:*    League 103, FA Cup 8.
*Debut:*          26 January 1952 v Doncaster Rovers (h) won 2–1.
*Manager:*        November 1958–November 1968.
*Also played for:* Motherwell, Bolton Wanderers.
*Also managed:*   Nottingham Forest.

If the 1960s was a golden decade for English football, it was also a period in the game's history when Scottish managers came to the fore. Matt Busby and Jock Stein led their sides to European Cup success, while Bill Shankly was kick-starting Liverpool's era of dominance.

Another Scot, Matthew Muirhead Gillies, although less celebrated, could arguably be said to have achieved even greater success considering the resources at his disposal. 'Little, unfancied, Leicester City' reached four domestic Cup Finals in the space of five years, heights and achievements that had seemed totally unrealistic before Matt's appointment.

As with so many young men of his generation, Matt's life was shaped by the outbreak of World War Two. Before it, he had been on Motherwell's books as a player, but he was also studying for a career in medicine. Called upon to serve, he had joined the RAF where he became a navigator in Bomber Command. His various postings around the UK enabled him to fit in the occasional football match, and he 'guested' for clubs such as Arsenal, QPR, Chelsea and Chester, as well as Bolton Wanderers, who he agreed to sign for professionally in peacetime.

Playing at either right-half or centre-half, he became a pivotal fixture in the Trotters' line up and also assumed the mantle of club captain, before signing for Leicester City in January 1952.

He wore the number-five jersey throughout the Second Division Championship season of 1954 and then wound down his playing days a year or so later before accepting a place on the club's coaching staff.

On 4 November 1958, following four successive defeats, manager David Halliday resigned. Two days later Matt was installed as caretaker boss, a post he held until 28 January 1959 when the position was made permanent. His shrewdest acquisition came during the next close-season when he persuaded Bert Johnson – a wartime friend and ex-Cup Final winner with Charlton Athletic – to join as chief scout, coach and confidante. Together the pairing would transform City's fortunes – bringing emerging talent like McLintock, Banks and Gibson to the club – and radically altered the mentality of those already on the books.

*Reaching the 1961 FA Cup Final was a sign that the club was evolving; although Matt's 11th-hour decision to leave out top scorer Ken Leek has never been fully understood. Reduced to 10 men for most of that match, due to Lennie Chalmers' injury, City were considered unlucky.*

Reaching the 1961 FA Cup Final was a sign that the club was evolving; although Matt's 11th-hour decision to leave out top scorer Ken Leek has never been fully understood. Reduced to 10 men for most of that match, due to Lennie Chalmers' injury, City were considered unlucky.

With Spurs doing the double that season, City were admitted into the Cup-Winners' Cup, their first foray into European competition and another significant stride forward for the club.

If they were unfortunate in 1961 then the same level of understanding could not be used two years later when an under-par performance in the 1963 FA Cup Final left Matt both bewildered and bemused.

Success did come at last to City, however, with the League Cup triumph over Stoke City in 1964. It was the first major domestic honour that the club had won. Failure to defend the trophy after losing in the Final to Chelsea a year later was seen as a minor blip. League placings had been consistently good, although fourth place in 1962–63 was the highest that they finished.

The manager proved himself to be an astute operator in the transfer market – his decision to allow England goalkeeper Gordon Banks to leave was not universally understood at the time but the excellence of his replacement, Peter Shilton, fully justified it.

While he continued to nurture young talent, Matt was also not afraid to spend when he had to, and a British transfer record of £150,000 was paid to Fulham to bring striker Allan Clarke to the club.

Never one to prejudge anyone or anything, it was perfectly understandable as to why Matt was briefly appointed to become a Justice of the Peace; although the pressure of management slowly began to take its toll on him, and he was absent from the club for a lengthy period in early 1968 due to a stress-related illness.

City's poor start to the next campaign brought things to a head. Matt was principled and steadfastly loyal, and the board of directors knew that, so when they sacked Bert Johnson from his position there was only ever going to be one outcome – Matt, standing by his trusty ally, resigned from the post he had held for almost exactly 10 years.

Few would have been surprised if he had left the game for good, but he quickly re-surfaced at Nottingham Forest; though his four-year tenure at the City Ground was one of constant struggle.

By a huge contrast, Matt's reign at Leicester City marked a significant period in the club's history – one in which they proved they could compete against the very best and, ultimately, one in which they won a major trophy for the first time.

# LEN GLOVER

*Born:*                31 January 1944, Kennington, London.

## Leicester City record:

*Appearances:*         League 252, FA Cup 36, League Cup 17.
*Goals:*               League 38, FA Cup 8, League Cup 2.
*Debut:*               18 November 1967 v Arsenal (h) drew 2–2.
*Also played for:*     Charlton Athletic, Tampa Bay Rowdies (USA), Kettering Town,
                       Earl Shilton Albion, Harlow Town.
*Managed:*             Earl Shilton Albion, Harlow Town.

Whether it is done through express pace or artful trickery, there are few more engaging sights for a football fan than to see a winger getting the better of an opposing full-back. The spectacle of seeing a team game being narrowed down to one-on-one combat with the dices loaded in favour of the attacker is sure to make the pulse rate quicken in even the most cynical observer.

Very few have illuminated Filbert Street over the years in the way that Lennie Glover did, and when fully fit and at his confident best he was worth the admission price on his own.

Manager Matt Gillies parted with £80,000 to sign Len from Charlton Athletic, a record fee at the time for a wide player. His first part-season was dogged by injuries and gave little indication of what was to come as he only made a dozen appearances and scored just once – at home to Wolverhampton Wanderers.

The 1968–69 campaign was a real mixed bag of a season for Leicester City and their supporters. The League form was decidedly ordinary and relegation ensued, but in the FA Cup competition the Foxes advanced to Wembley Stadium for their third Final of the decade and fourth overall.

Leicester were indebted to Lennie's goals to steer them through the troublesome waters of the opening couple of rounds. He netted the goal which earned a replay against Barnsley and scored again in the 2–1 replay win at home, then he hit the solitary goal which defeated Millwall in round four.

Lennie struggled with a groin injury during the semi-final beating of West Bromwich Albion, and it was touch and go whether he would make it for the big day. He somehow came through a midweek practice match against Brentford to confirm his fitness, but his influence against Manchester City at Wembley was minimal and he clearly looked some way short of his best.

In the two seasons of Second Division football that followed, Lennie teased and tormented opposition defences and provided countless number of assists for grateful teammates.

Capturing the Division Two title was manager Frank O'Farrell's parting gift to the club before he moved to Manchester United, but the new boss, Jimmy Bloomfield, started his own reign with a high-profile victory as City captured the Charity Shield for the first time.

Bloomfield's philosophies fitted in nicely with Len's own feeling of how the game should be played, and the acquisition of the likes of Frank Worthington, Keith Weller and Alan Birchenall provided other like-minded individuals – still desperate to win football matches but looking to entertain as they did so.

As he did with so many of his best mates, 'Birch' came up with a nickname for Len. '"Fido", because he was always going to "take the dog for a walk"'!

At his precocious best there was a clamour – and not just from City fans – for the England management to have a look at this naturally gifted rarity – a left-sided winger. But how close he came to a call-up is anyone's guess. In a different era or with a different boss, who knows?

Lennie scored a couple of goals in the early stages of the 1973–74 FA Cup competition – as he had done five years earlier – and the omens were good that another trip to Wembley would be achievable, but the semi-final draw was unkind and pitted the Foxes against Liverpool, undeniably one of the best in the land.

After a goalless draw at Old Trafford the replay seemed to be swinging towards those in blue after Lennie had pounced to score an equaliser. Although the Merseysiders were then put 'under the cosh' for a while, City could not take advantage and were finally undone by two late goals.

Another bad run of injuries dogged Lennie's final couple of seasons at Filbert Street; although he did take his number of League appearances for City past the 250 mark. He then went to try his luck in America, playing in the 'showbiz league' with the likes of Pele, Moore, Best and Beckenbauer.

After returning home, Lennie caused a 'kerfuffle' at the FA when his eligibility to play for non-League Kettering Town in a victorious Cup tie against Tilbury was officially queried. The governing body ordered a re-match and this time the result was reversed!

Lennie then took up a position as a publican but returned to the game as manager of Harlow Town and – even at 50 years of age – pulled on the boots one more time to become the oldest player to appear in the Diadora League.

At his best, Lennie Glover was one of the most exciting players ever to wear the 'City blue', and one journalist of the day summed him up thus: 'He had the pace of a Ferrari and the footwork of a Covent Garden Principal.'

*'At his best, Lennie Glover was one of the most exciting players ever to wear the 'City blue', and one journalist of the day summed him up thus: 'He had the pace of a Ferrari and the footwork of a Covent Garden Principal.'*

# JIMMY GOODFELLOW

*Born:*          30 July 1938, Edinburgh, Scotland.

## Leicester City record:

*Appearances:*   League 98, FA Cup 9, League Cup 14.
*Goals:*           League 26, FA Cup 3, League Cup 7.
*Debut:*           7 September 1963 v Stoke City (a) drew 3–3.
*Also played for:*  Third Lanark, Mansfield Town, Weymouth, Durban City (South Africa), Nuneaton Borough, AP Leamington.

Although he always had to fight for an extended run in the Leicester City team, Jimmy Goodfellow will, for all time, be remembered as being the club's first-ever substitute once the rules had been amended to allow replacements.

That statistical oddity aside, Jimmy gave City a solid five years of service, which included one stand-out campaign where he was leading marksman and also scored in a domestic Cup Final.

Jimmy had been a leading light at struggling Scottish League club Third Lanark at the start of his career and had shown sufficient promise to be selected in a trial fixture, representing the Scottish League against the full Scotland side in 1962. (An opponent that day was City's Frank McLintock!)

'Thirds' then ran into a serious financial plight which necessitated an unprecedented clear-out of talent, and Matt Gillies swooped to claim the striker on a free transfer.

His debut was eventful enough, a 3–3 draw at Stoke City, and it was on the occasion of his fifth League outing, versus Ipswich Town away, that Jimmy claimed his opening goal for the club in a match that finished 1–1.

Solely on the fringes of the squad when City won the 1964 League Cup, Jimmy was keen to make an impression the following year and did so in impressive style. He top-scored, with a total of 17 goals in all competitions – a haul which included his only Foxes hat-trick in a 5–1 home trouncing of Fulham. In the FA Cup he netted twice against Plymouth Argyle to help his side into the sixth round, where they lost to Liverpool, and he did his bit, with some important goals, to try and maintain a grip on the League Cup.

The holders' march to a second successive Final in that competition (and fourth domestic Final in four years) saw them see off Peterborough United (with a goal from Jimmy), Grimsby Town, Crystal Palace (with the Scot scoring both goals in a 2–0 replay win), Coventry City (who were vanquished 8–1 away from home) and then Plymouth Argyle in the semis.

The first leg of the Final, against Chelsea, was played at Stamford Bridge, and after 75 minutes of the contest Jimmy rounded off a fine, flowing move to level the match at 2–2. Eddie McCreadie

*For that opening-day fixture against Liverpool, Jimmy was named as City's first-ever 'Number 12', and towards the end of a contest that had already turned 3–1 in favour of the Merseysiders he was introduced at the expense of Graham Cross.*

then scored a wonderful solo goal for the home side to win the leg and eventually the tie, which finished 3–2 on aggregate.

Tough, pacy and with a poacher's eye for goal, Jimmy was beginning to make his mark in the First Division; although he would not have been too keen to be left out of the starting XI for the first game of the 1965–66 season – at home to Liverpool on 21 August.

Clubs had been campaigning for many years for substitutes to be allowed, and City had been keen supporters of the move for some time (remembering how Len Chalmers' injury in the 1961 FA Cup Final had rendered them helpless).

For that opening-day fixture against Liverpool, Jimmy was named as City's first-ever 'Number 12', and towards the end of a contest that had already turned 3–1 in favour of the Merseysiders he was introduced at the expense of Graham Cross.

Perhaps stung by that omission – and keen to regain the number-eight shirt instead (Derek Dougan wore number nine that season) – Jimmy got back into the side and fired home eight goals in a dozen outings. The goals dried up, however, and he only added one more in the League before the end of the season.

City fans perhaps best remember Jimmy for one glorious goal he scored in a 3–0 home thumping of near-neighbours Nottingham Forest, powering a header past the diving 'keeper Peter Grummitt from the edge of the box.

Jimmy's opportunities became more and more infrequent, and in March 1968 he signed for Mansfield Town, where he played in their FA Cup giant-killing run a year later. After claiming the scalp of a star-studded West Ham United side, they were finally halted at the sixth-round stage by his former club – City winning 1–0 at Field Mill.

After three years with the Stags Jimmy moved into the non-League game and also spent a brief stint in South Africa. Upon retiring from the game altogether he remained in the Leicester area, working as an electrician.

Immensely popular with the Filbert Street fans, Jimmy will remain in that small band of players who have scored for the club in a major Final, but his will be the only name on the list for trivia buffs when asked to name City's first-ever 'Super-sub'!

# SIMON GRAYSON

*Born:*          16 December 1969, Ripon, Yorkshire.

## Leicester City record:

*Appearances:*   League 188, FA Cup 9, League Cup 18, Other 15.
*Goals:*         League 4, FA Cup 0, League Cup 2, Other 0.
*Debut:*         14 March 1992 v Ipswich Town (a) drew 0–0.
*Also played for:* Leeds United, Aston Villa, Blackburn Rovers, Sheffield Wednesday
                 (loan), Stockport County (loan), Notts County (loan), Bradford
                 City (loan), Blackpool.
*Managed:*       Blackpool, Leeds United.

Although Leicester City have had their fair share of big days out at Wembley over the years, it was not until their seventh major visit – in the 1994 Play-off Final – that they tasted success, and the winning skipper that day was right-back Simon Grayson.

Simon had joined City in March 1992 from Leeds United for just £50,000 and played a major part in helping his new side cement their promotion push. 'Moving to Leicester was what I needed at that stage of my career, and in the space of a few short weeks I'd gone from playing in front of just a few hundred fans for Leeds reserves to playing first-team football and then going out in front of 90,000 at Wembley in the Play-off Final.'

Blackburn Rovers spoilt that day for Simon and the rest of the Foxes contingent, but the experience is still vivid. 'I'd played at Wembley before for Leeds in the Mercantile Credit tournament, but this was a much bigger occasion. I remember it being a red hot day, and it was unbelievable to see all the Leicester fans there. It was just so disappointing for them that the result didn't go our way.'

Twelve months on and City were again through to the nail-biting season-ending finale, although Simon was a Wembley spectator this time. 'I missed the match against Swindon – the few weeks before that Play-off Final were the only time really during my time at Leicester when I'd not played regularly. I'd had a few niggling injuries, been ill for a short while and also picked up a suspension. I was in the 18 or 20 that travelled and sat watching on the bench in my suit. Again it was heart-breaking to go so close and still lose.'

A year later and it was a similar scenario as City qualified for their third Play-off Final in succession, with their traditional East Midlands rivals providing the opposition. 'For the Derby match I was made captain. I'd played in virtually all of the games that season and had been awarded the Player of the Year, but I just didn't have a clue that I would be captain until the day of the game when the team was read out. I was immensely proud to do it, particularly at the end when I was able to turn and lift the trophy. I just wish now I hadn't spoilt it by wearing a silly hat!'

Simon (nicknamed 'Larry' for obvious reasons) knew what it meant to the fans. 'The supporters had suffered a lot of anguish in the two preceding years, and it was nice for them to be able to enjoy that moment.'

The end-of-season showdown was fast becoming a routine occurrence for the Filberts, and after an immediate relegation from the top flight they were back there to contest the 1996 Final against Crystal Palace. 'That match was evenly poised, and it looked like it was heading for penalties when Steve Claridge "shinned" a volley into the top corner. I was delighted because I didn't really fancy the prospect of having to take a penalty!'

City were soon back at the national stadium after reaching the 1997 League Cup Final, gained after squeezing past Wimbledon in the semi-finals. But they only got there on an away goal, which had been scored by Simon. 'I was playing left-back that day, and we were trailing 1–0, after a goalless draw at home,' he says. 'I made my way into the box for a free-kick. Garry Parker took it, I went up for the header, and when I opened my eyes the ball was in the back of the net! It was perhaps the most important goal of my career, and it was a great feeling to know it had taken us into a Cup Final.'

An Emile Heskey goal cancelled out Middlesbrough's opener, so the match ended in a bit of a damp squib with another meeting necessary to produce a winner. 'Of course, it was something of an anticlimax to walk off the Wembley turf still not knowing if we'd won or not – it was a good decision to stop having replays after that. At Hillsborough it was another close match, and again it was Claridge who came up with a late winner for us.'

The victory was sweet reward for Simon, who had again been the club's Player of the Year and whose versatility had been invaluable to help the City cause – nominally a right-back, he had also turned out in the centre of defence, at left-back and in midfield.

'I'd like to think people would say I was hard-working and honest. I've always tried to give 100 per cent in training and would do the same in whatever position I was asked to play in. I believe you should enjoy your football – it's a career that passes you by so quickly.'

Simon moved on to Aston Villa after a success-filled five years at Filbert Street, highlighted by the honour of being the club's first Wembley winning captain.

## 'I made my way into the box for a free-kick. Garry Parker took it, I went up for the header, and when I opened my eyes the ball was in the back of the net!'

# MAL GRIFFITHS

*Born:*        8 March 1919, Merthyr Tydfil, Wales.

*Died:*        5 April 1969, Wigston, Leicestershire.

## Leicester City record:

*Appearances:*   League 373, FA Cup 36, Other (wartime) 11.

*Goals:*        League 66, FA Cup 10, Other (wartime) 3.

*Debut:*        24 September 1938 v Bolton Wanderers (h) drew 0–0.

*Also played for:*   Merthyr Tydfil, Arsenal, Margate (loan), Burton Albion, Wales (11 caps).

Welsh international Malwyn Griffiths will forever be remembered as the man who scored City's first goal at Wembley Stadium. Sadly, it came in a losing cause, in the 3–1 FA Cup Final defeat to Wolverhampton Wanderers in 1949.

Mal was a terrific servant for the Foxes, turning out in over 400 matches either side of the war, having joined from Arsenal in September 1938.

He made his debut at Filbert Street against Bolton, and his first goal arrived a couple of weeks later in another home draw against Liverpool. His tally during that initial (almost-complete) season was five goals from 35 League and Cup outings.

Although Mal's performances were encouraging, he had joined a club in a perilous financial state, with little money to invest in new players and a squad unable to compete with the rest of the top flight. City finished bottom of the pile, but there were more serious concerns as the spectre of conflict preoccupied all and sundry with Europe preparing for battle.

The 1939–40 season began – naïvely in many people's opinion – and Leicester opened up with a home win over Man City and then a loss at Birmingham. On 2 September 1939 City travelled to West Ham for their third match of the campaign and recorded a 2–0 victory. George Dewis got the opener and Mal added a second. It turned out to be a goal and a result that would be expunged from the record books, however, as, that same day, conscription was announced for all men between 18 and 41 years of age. The squad travelled back home in a black-out, and war was declared the following day.

Mal was conscripted to join the Welsh Regiment but was able to turn out in wartime friendlies for a number of clubs during the next five years, including Cardiff, Aldershot, Fulham, Bournemouth, Chelsea, Brighton and Southampton, as well as playing a handful of games for the Foxes.

Once peace had returned and football was about to resume in earnest, City manager Johnny Duncan despatched a director to Wales to persuade Mal to return to Filbert Street where, fittingly, he was in the side for the opening fixture of the new era.

Bar the very occasional absence through injury, Mal became the proud wearer of City's blue number-seven jersey for the next decade.

A little bit of Foxes history was made when he was selected for his first full international appearance in April 1947, playing for Wales against Ireland in Belfast. In doing so he had become the first Leicester player to be capped since the war.

Although things were gradually getting themselves back on a sounder footing, City merely produced a couple of respectable ninth-placed finishes, so it was somewhat of a surprise when the Second Division side embarked on their 1948–49 FA Cup journey to 'the promised land'.

In 11 previous FA Cup ties, spread over almost as many years, Mal had scored just once. During that remarkable sequence of games which took City to the Twin Towers, however, he netted goals in every round except the semi.

Three matches were needed to dispose of Birmingham City in round three. Mal had scored in the second match, a home 1–1 draw. He scored in the 2–0 win over Preston then added three of the 10 goals needed to get past Luton Town. In an astonishing game at Kenilworth Road the winger added to Jack Lee's four-goal haul in a 5–5 thriller.

There was no let up in the excitement as City edged the replay 5–3, with Mal getting a couple. He scored again in round six against Brentford but missed the full set by not scoring in the Highbury win against Portsmouth.

League form had deserted the Foxes, however, and they found themselves in the lower echelons of the second tier as they lined up at the national stadium on 30 April 1949 to face hugely favoured First Division opponents, Wolves.

The men from Molyneux made light work of the opening period, forging a two-goal advantage. Leicester needed a quick response if it was not to become a mismatch of a Final, and they got it almost instantly. Two minutes after the re-start City's Ken Chisholm drove the ball towards goal. Wolves 'keeper Bert Williams could only parry it away, and Mal was on hand to fire home and re-kindle hopes of a shock win.

City were rejuvenated and momentarily thought they had equalised until Chisholm's next effort was ruled out for offside. Sadly for Foxes and neutrals alike there was to be no fairytale conclusion as the top-flight side added a third.

Disappointing as it undoubtedly was for City, their season was not yet over. Relegation still had to be faced and conquered. A point was needed at Cardiff City and a late equaliser from Jack Lee ensured safety – perhaps made sweeter as it condemned Nottingham Forest to the drop.

Mal's consistency was a feature over the next few seasons, culminating in him enjoying a personal best goal tally of 11 League goals during the 1953–54 Second Division Championship season, which included his only City hat-trick in a home win over Stoke City.

After he had ended his playing days Mal became mine-host at the Queens Head in Wigston Magna before dying tragically early, at just 50 years of age.

*'Bar the very occasional absence through injury, Mal became the proud wearer of City's blue number-seven jersey for the next decade.'*

# JOEY GUDJONSSON

*Born:*           25 May 1980, Akranes, Iceland.

## Leicester City record:
*Appearances:*    League 77, FA Cup 7, League Cup 5.
*Goals:*          League 10, FA Cup 1, League Cup 2.
*Debut:*          11 August 2004 v Derby County (a) won 2–1.
*Also played for:*    IA Akranes (Iceland), Racing Genk (Belgium), MVV Maastricht (loan – Netherlands), RKC Waalwijk (Netherlands), Real Betis (Spain), Aston Villa (loan), Wolves (loan), AZ Alkmaar (Netherlands), Burnley, Huddersfield Town, Iceland (28 caps).

Icelandic international Joey Gudjonsson spent just two seasons with the Foxes but made an extraordinary impact – principally with his long-range shooting – and left his mark by scoring one of the most stunning goals in the club's history.

Johannes Karl Gudjonsson comes from one of his country's most reputable footballing families. His father, Gudjon Thordason, has become well-known as a manager in Britain, taking charge of Stoke City, Notts County, Barnsley and Crewe Alexandra, while brothers Bjarni, Doddi and Bjorn Bergmann Sigurdsson have all played the game professionally.

The diminutive midfielder (5ft 8in tall) had already honed his skills in Belgium, the Netherlands, Spain and his home country prior to arriving in the Premiership, joining Aston Villa on loan in 2003. He played 11 times for them before joining Wolves for the entire 2003–04 season, again with the agreement of his parent club Real Betis.

It was during this campaign that Joey first played against City, participating in a match that still holds pain for the many Foxes present, a 4–3 defeat at Molyneux – but only after a brace of goals from Les Ferdinand and another from Riccardo Scimeca had given the visitors a seemingly impregnable 3–0 half-time advantage.

'That was perhaps one of the most extraordinary games I've ever played in', recalls Joey. 'Certainly it was the biggest comeback – it was an important match as well because both sides were locked together in a relegation battle.'

Both sides eventually succumbed to the drop, but it was to the East Midlands rather than the Black Country that Joey decided to move permanently, believing that the Foxes were better equipped to give him a return to the top fight he desperately wanted to play in.

A tough and tenacious tackler, an accurate passer of the ball and with a penchant for an explosive crack at goal, he joined Micky Adams' side in the summer of 2004 and made his debut against traditional foes, coming on as a late substitute for Lilian Nalis in an away match against Derby County. Within two minutes Trevor Benjamin had scored a winner for City. 'I can't really remember too much about it', he laughs. 'It must have been a beautiful pass to set him up for the goal!'

The new addition was already beginning to forge a reputation for some speculative pot-shots when he hit the mark in dramatic style in an FA Cup replay at Blackpool. 'It was a really windy night, and I remember winning the ball just over the halfway line and decided to go for it from about 40 yards out. The wind was in my back so once I hit it I knew there was no chance of the 'keeper saving it.'

The Walkers Stadium had witnessed some extraordinary goals in its first few years after opening – and even a 'keeper had got on the scoresheet in 2004. Preston's Andy Lonergan had propelled a long left-footer downfield which bounced spectacularly over Kevin Pressman, his opposite number in the Foxes goal.

Nevertheless, goals from inside your own half remain rare – hence the delight at seeing, for example, David Beckham's sweetly-executed strike for Manchester United against Wimbledon in 1996, or Pele's 'oh-so-close' failed attempt in the 1970 World Cup Finals. A similar once-in-a-decade moment occurred at the Walkers on 4 March 2006. Playing against Hull City in a Championship clash, and with the score level at 1–1, Joey, facing the Spion Kop End, collected the ball in the 64th minute with opposition goalkeeper Boaz Myhill half the length of the field away.

*'I saw him off his line – yes. He was stood on the edge of the box, and I just decided to go for it. I hit it quite sweetly as well with good pace on it. To be honest when I hit it I knew straight away it had a good chance of going in, and obviously I was delighted when it did.'*

In such a moment, crowd thoughts are bound to vary – was what happened next fully intended? Joey confirms his thought process: 'I saw him off his line – yes. He was stood on the edge of the box, and I just decided to go for it. I hit it quite sweetly as well with good pace on it. To be honest when I hit it I knew straight away it had a good chance of going in, and obviously I was delighted when it did.'

Perhaps predictably, the goal was replayed time and time again in the weeks that followed and again, equally predictably, it won countless awards as Goal of the Week, Goal of the Month and ultimately Goal of the Season.

If anything could have elevated Joey's cult following at the Walkers it was that goal, and it helped him clinch both the Supporters' and the Players' Player of the Year Awards – yet the fans' favourite was already committed to leaving the club to join AZ Alkmaar.

'There was a lot of uncertainty going on at the club at the time, and my contract was running out. The club didn't want to give me a new contract, and then Rob Kelly took over as manager, and he wanted to give me a contract, but by then I had already agreed to sign for the Dutch club.'

Joey soon returned to England, signing for Burnley, and in May 2009 he appeared for them at Wembley Stadium as the Clarets won the Play-off Final to return to the top flight for the first time in 33 years.

# EMILE HESKEY

*Born:*               11 January 1978, Leicester.

**Leicester City record:**
*Appearances:*    League 154, FA Cup 11, League Cup 27, Other 5.
*Goals:*             League 40, FA Cup 0, League Cup 6, Other 0.
*Debut:*            8 March 1995 v Queen's Park Rangers (a) lost 0–2.
*Also played for:*  Liverpool, Birmingham City, Wigan Athletic, Aston Villa, England
                   (62 Caps).

Built like a gladiator and with the strength of a bear, Emile Heskey has fulfilled all of his early potential to become one of the true footballing greats to emerge from the city of Leicester. Capped more than 50 times for his country, the striker helped the Foxes to become a Premiership force to be reckoned with.

As a youngster he played for the successful Ratby Groby Juniors side before being spotted and invited to begin his association with City by joining the club's school of excellence. His progress through the ranks was swift, and he was then given a timely boost thanks to a mystery virus which swept through the first-team ranks.

'I was still only 17,' recalls Emile. 'Just prior to a match at Queen's Park Rangers a lot of the guys were feeling unwell, and we had a few injuries within the squad as well. When we got in the dressing room Mark McGhee, the manager, read the side out, and he told me I was playing.'

Although this was not a fairytale introduction – the depleted visitors went down by a couple of goals – it put Emile's name in the City record books as their youngest-ever Premiership player.

The following season, with City now in the second tier, first-team appearances became more and more frequent, and his opening League goal is still etched clearly in the back of Emile's mind. 'It was away at Norwich City, and I'd come on as a late substitute. Simon Grayson put a cross in, and I just got there ahead of the defender to nick it in at the near post.'

## 'To play at Wembley whilst I was still only 18 was a terrific experience for me, and to win it in such dramatic circumstances made it even more special.'

That would be just one of a host of great memories to take away from a first full season that would end with an appearance in the Play-off Final. 'To play at Wembley whilst I was still only 18 was a terrific experience for me, and to win it in such dramatic circumstances made it even more special.'

Wembley was to become something of a second home to the Foxes and their supporters over the next few seasons, with the side, now under Martin O'Neill, reaching three League Cup Finals in four seasons. The first, against Middlesbrough in the 1996–97 season, holds special significance for Emile. Not only did the Foxes win it after a replay, but it was also his late equaliser that earned City their second chance. 'Middlesbrough were a good side then with some really great players, and they were leading right at the end of extra-time. Then we had a chance. The ball came down off the bar and in the scramble I just got there before Steve Claridge to toe-poke the equaliser.'

If that Cup Final strike was one of Emile's most important City goals, he remembers an effort from earlier that season as being his favourite. 'It was at home to Southampton. I got the ball from Neil Lennon, turned, took a couple of touches and hit it into the top corner past Dave Beasant from around 25 yards – a lovely feeling.'

During 1998–99 Leicester City again reached the League Cup Final, this time losing against Spurs. 'I sustained a back injury early on in that match,' reveals Emile. 'It was frustrating not being 100 per cent fit and even more so as we lost to a late goal.'

Emile's development was being closely monitored. Tall, muscular and with a rapid turn of pace, his physical attributes were impressive. Unimaginatively tagged 'Bruno' because of his size and raw strength (a handle that Emile himself did not care too much for), he was closing in on being the finished article as far as being a top-quality striker was concerned, and his inevitable chance at international level came with a first cap against Hungary in 1999.

His elevation to the full England side brought him new admirers, and City were frequently being asked about his availability. Shortly after another League Cup success, the 2–1 win over Tranmere Rovers in 2000, Liverpool broke their own transfer record by signing Emile for £11 million.

'I'd got a taste for winning trophies and was ambitious to go on and win more, and felt that at that time I would have a better chance of doing so at Liverpool. Also, it was probably the right time of my career to make a move, and it was a very good offer for Leicester as well.'

Emile has returned to play against the Foxes many times since leaving and has always received a great ovation. One of his proudest moments in the game came during another return visit. 'The only time I've worn the captain's armband for England was at the Walkers Stadium, when we played against Serbia and Montenegro in 2003. Michael Owen was substituted, and he gave me the armband to wear as he went off.'

While some members of the media would observe that Emile's goal tally could be improved upon, teammates and managers have always leapt to point out that his worth to any side has been immeasurable. His selfless running and constant hounding of defenders has created countless opportunities for those around him – qualities that the very best in the game have envied.

# ROGER HEYWOOD

*Born:* 4 May 1909, Chorley, Lancashire.

*Died:* 30 December 1985, Leicester.

## Leicester City record:

*Appearances:* League 228, FA Cup 12, Other (wartime) 40.

*Goals:* League 2, FA Cup, Other (wartime) 2.

*Debut:* 3 May 1930 v Birmingham City (a) lost 0–3.

*Also played for:* Chorley St James, Chorley, Corby Town.


Central-defender Roger Heywood was another Fox who topped the 200 mark in terms of League appearances for the club, yet he could have played many more times but for a succession of niggling injuries and then the onset of World War Two.

Tall and athletic, Roger had excelled at cricket as well as football as a youngster, and in later years he would return to Lancashire whenever he could to play the summer game at a decent League standard.

Career-wise, football won out though, and he picked up a couple of Lancashire Combination title successes with home-town club Chorley before attracting the attention of Leicester boss Willie Orr, who eventually agreed on a fee of £575 to bring the 20-year-old to Filbert Street. Almost immediately he was injured, however, and had to wait until the final day of the 1929–30 season to make his League bow, in an away defeat to Birmingham City.

During the following campaign the number-five jersey changed hands several times, with Roger making 21 League appearances, but Orr also continued to use both George Carr and Albert Harrison in that position as well; however, both players soon moved on, with their opportunities having been clearly limited by the younger man.

Roger played in all but one of the games in 1931–32; although, like his defensive colleagues, it became a tall order to prevent City from sliding out of the division. Twenty of the 42 games were lost and 92 goals were conceded, with two huge hammerings recorded – a 2–9 reversal at Everton and an 8–3 home thrashing against Aston Villa.

A year later Villa again provided the opposition when Roger managed to get himself on the score sheet for the first time. Although that was in a losing cause, his second and final League goal was rather more memorable, being the winner at Anfield Road against Liverpool on 18 February 1933.

Now with the club under the management of Peter Hodge, City's fortunes looked to be turning around a little, and much of that was due to the fact that Roger had succeeded Adam Black as club skipper.

## 'the Lancastrian was highly instrumental in the FA Cup run that took the side to within 90 minutes of their first Wembley Final in 1934, losing to Portsmouth at St Andrew's in a hugely anti-climactic semi-final.'

As such then, it provided the highlight of his career when the Lancastrian was highly instrumental in the FA Cup run that took the side to within 90 minutes of their first Wembley Final in 1934, losing to Portsmouth at St Andrew's in a hugely anti-climactic semi-final.

Manager and captain were forming a close bond – but the summer of 1934 brought the devastating news of Hodge's untimely death. Roger travelled to Scotland for the funeral and, along with five of his teammates, acted as pall-bearer.

It is probably understandable that the angst felt by all at Filbert Street could not be shaken off, and the side slid into Division Two for the first time in 10 seasons.

Though twice just missing one game, it was a constant frustration to Roger that he was so susceptible to a variety of knee and ankle problems that he was unable to complete one single ever-present season in his time at Leicester. Indeed, his frequent absences cost him dearly during what should have been the best time of his career, the 1936–37 Division Two title campaign, when he was restricted to just five outings, thus missing out on a Championship medal.

He was only able to play in seven League matches during the next term, but a minor milestone was notched up with the Final one of them. It is not known if Roger was aware that the trip to Wolves on 15 April 1938 marked the occasion of his 200th League match for City, but had he done so then there would have been no cause for celebration as the home side ran out winners 10–1, and even the consolation was a gift from the home side's England star Stan Cullis.

Relegation again followed, and Roger was in and out of the line up during the period immediately preceding the outbreak of the war – playing in only one of the three matches at the start of the 1939–40 season before League football was suspended.

During the first two years of wartime football Roger appeared in a further 40 matches for the club, playing in the Regional League Midland Division, the South Regional League and the Wartime Cup – in which City were narrowly defeated by Arsenal in a two-legged semi-final.

His final outing for City was in a 2–0 home win over Nottingham Forest on 2 June 1941, although for a brief period he continued to coach the club's youth team. He also 'guested' in a handful of matches for Northampton Town.

Having remained in Leicester into retirement, City's first FA Cup semi-final skipper passed away in 1985, aged 76.

# COLIN HILL

*Born:*  12 November 1963, Uxbridge, Middlesex.

## Leicester City record:

*Appearances:*  League 145, FA Cup 8, League Cup 12, Other 10.
*Goals:*  League 0, FA Cup 0, League Cup 1, Other 0.
*Debut:*  27 March 1992 v Tranmere Rovers (a) won 2–1.
*Also played for:*  Glebe Athletic, Park Lane, Hillingdon Borough, Arsenal, Brighton and Hove Albion, CS Maritimo (Portugal), Colchester United, Sheffield United, Northern Ireland (27 caps).

Colin Hill was one of the mainstays of the Foxes defence during 'the Play-off years' of the 1990s. The Uxbridge-born Northern Ireland international enjoyed a successful five-year stint at Filbert Street which saw him collect a Player of the Year award and become club captain.

He initially joined on loan from Sheffield United in March 1992: 'It was deadline day and Cambridge United were also after me, but Dave Bassett told me to speak to Brian Little and John Gregory at Leicester, and that made my mind up. John Beck and Gary Peters told me that I was doing the wrong thing in not joining them at Cambridge.'

As fate would have it, Colin soon had the opportunity to show that he had made the correct decision. 'We came up against Cambridge in the Play-off semi-final and battered them 5–0 at home. For some reason they refused to shake my hand afterwards!'

That victory put City through to a Wembley show-down against Blackburn Rovers. 'They were just beginning to assemble a decent side under Kenny Dalglish, but we had gone to Ewood Park and beaten them just a few weeks earlier. In fact, I played 10 League matches and we had won nine of them, so our confidence was sky-high.'

Wembley was not a totally new experience for Colin – he had appeared there in an international for Northern Ireland and his early football had been played very close to the Twin Towers at Hillingdon Borough.

A slender defeat to Blackburn condemned the Foxes to another season of second-tier football but it was touch-and-go for a while if Colin would be joining them. 'The transfer dragged on for a while, and in fact I went back to Sheffield United for pre-season training before Brian Little came up and signed me.'

Colin was an ever-present at the back for City throughout the 1992–93 season and lifted the Player of the Year award, but again there was the collective frustration of a Play-off Final setback, this time against Swindon Town. 'We were a grinding team that season. We would go to places like

Oxford just determined not to let them score against us. We had a really strong squad of around 24 or 25 players, and in training you could put any 11 against 11 and you wouldn't know who the first team were. The Final was a really topsy-turvy game and when we got them back to 3–1 we could see that Swindon were physically shattered, but then they got the penalty, and it was heart-breaking for The Cat [Kevin Poole, goalkeeper] as he was adamant that it shouldn't have been given.'

Promotion was eventually achieved 12 months later, but this time Colin had to sit out the Play-off victory over Derby County with a knee injury. The season was momentous for him for one reason, however, as it featured his only City goal, which came at Old Trafford of all places against Manchester United in the League Cup. Sadly City were 4–0 down at the time, though, and on their way to a 5–1 defeat.

*'I hit it into the wall and when it came back I hit it right-footed low past Peter Schmeichel from about 20 yards',*

'We had a free-kick and I think the ball should have been played to Steve Thompson, but the routine broke down and the ball just fell to me. I hit it into the wall and when it came back I hit it right-footed low past Peter Schmeichel from about 20 yards. Incredibly about a minute later I found myself having another shot from inside the area and wondered what was going on!'

Colin's spell as captain came during Mark McGhee's year in charge. Ironically he had just lost his place in the side. 'After a couple of games in the Premiership the manager decided he wanted to try some younger lads at the back then it all changed when Mark came in. His first game was against Aston Villa – ironically with Brian Little as their new manager – and I was put back in the team. As we were going out to warm up I was then told I was to be the skipper. From being out in the cold to being back in the Premiership as captain was quite a turn-around.'

Whether he was employed as a traditional central-defender or as the sweeper in a back three formation, Colin was good at organising those around him. 'Even if I wasn't playing particularly well myself, I was still one of those guys that liked to talk and to encourage those around me.'

For the Foxes' fourth Play-off Final in five years – the 1995–96 match against Crystal Palace – Colin began on the bench but recalls that he did not actually spend much time sitting there. 'From the first few minutes Steve Walsh came over and said that he was struggling – I was told to warm-up, and this went on all through the first half and well into the second until I eventually got on.'

Colin eventually left Filbert Street to join Northampton Town – via Sweden. 'Pontus Kaamark fixed me up with a summer playing with Trelleborgs, which I really enjoyed. When I came back Martin O'Neill said that I was welcome back at Leicester, but he couldn't guarantee that I'd play every week, so I opted for the chance to move where I'd get regular football.'

# ERNIE HINE

*Born:* 9 April 1901, Smithy Cross, Yorkshire.

*Died:* April 1974, Huddersfield, Yorkshire.

## Leicester City record:

*Appearances:* League 247, FA Cup 12.

*Goals:* League 148, FA Cup 8.

*Debut:* 16 January 1926 v Burnley (h) won 3–2.

*Also played for:* New Mills, Staincross Station, Barnsley, Huddersfield Town, Manchester United, England (6 caps).

Ernie Hine was a goal-machine who found the net over 300 times during a playing career which spanned more than 17 seasons. Six and a half of those campaigns were spent at Filbert Street, where he cemented his place in the Foxes record books by becoming a member of the elite group of just six City players who have scored a century of goals for the club. Indeed, his aggregate tally of 156 is bettered only by 1950s legend Arthur Rowley and by Arthur Chandler, with whom Ernie terrorised defences in the 1920s and 30s.

After beginning his working life down the coal mines, Ernie was given an opportunity in League football with Barnsley and made an instant impression by scoring on his first appearance in a 2–1 win away at Norwich in January 1922.

Ernie went on to become part of Barnsley's folklore with a record tally of goals spread over two lengthy periods at Oakwell, the first of which was interrupted in January 1926 when he signed for the Foxes for a fee of around £3,000.

Up to that point he had played all of his football in Division Two, but he quickly demonstrated that the step up to the top flight would not be an issue. As at his previous club he got off to the best possible start on his debut with a couple of goals in a 3–2 home win over Burnley. It could have been even better though, as he also missed a penalty-kick that day!

The following season – his first full one with Leicester – Ernie scored 17 times, including a hat-trick against Sheffield Wednesday. They were good times for the club and the League Championship trophy came tantalisingly close to being won. Third in 1927–28 was bettered the following year, as the Foxes achieved their highest-ever finishing position, just one point behind Sheffield Wednesday.

Representative honours came Ernie's way via the traditional route, selection for four trial matches, four further appearances for the Football League side and eventually a first England cap, which was awarded against Ireland at Goodison Park in October 1928. All six of Ernie's full caps were won while he was a serving Leicester player, and they yielded a return of four goals.

*For five consecutive seasons Ernie scored over 20 League goals, a staggering testimony to his consistency, yet it was only in the latter two that he had actually finished as top scorer. They were heady days for City fans!*

At whatever level he played and against any opposition, the nippy inside-right had the capacity to be in the right place to convert chances. It is often overlooked that he scored a hat-trick on the day of the club's record 10–0 victory over Portsmouth (overlooked because Chandler scored six that day!). He also netted another triple (against Bury on Boxing Day) on the way to a seasonal tally of 32, just two behind the great Arthur.

Ernie scored another Foxes hat-trick in an away win at Sunderland on Christmas Day 1930 and netted again when the two sides met at Filbert Street 24 hours later (to think that modern-day managers tend to complain about the fixture scheduling).

The former miner (and new club captain by this time) set a new club record for most goals scored in an FA Cup tie for City when he hit five in a 7–0 victory over non-League Crook Town in 1932. The north-easterners had actually drawn home advantage for the tie but happily agreed to a switch to play the game at Filbert Street.

For five consecutive seasons Ernie scored over 20 League goals, a staggering testimony to his consistency, yet it was only in the latter two that he had actually finished as top scorer. They were heady days for City fans!

There were grumbles of discontent when, in May 1932, City began a re-building programme and to generate the necessary funding Ernie was sold to Huddersfield Town for £4,000 – at the time that was a club record fee for the sale of one of their players.

He did not stay long at Leeds Road, however, nor at Old Trafford after a move there, but the goals began to flow once more after a return to his beloved Barnsley towards the end of 1934. To City's cost he showed his magical touch one more time, scoring all three goals for the South Yorkshire club in a 3–3 draw against the Foxes in December 1935.

His aggregate tally of 123 League goals for Barnsley has yet to be bettered, but the bulk of his goals were scored while playing for Leicester City.

In today's inflated market what price would a club pay to acquire the services of such a phenomenal goalscorer as the great Ernie Hine?

# DEREK HINES

*Born:*  8 February 1931, Woodville, Derbyshire.
*Died:*  2001.

## Leicester City record:
*Appearances:*  League 299, FA Cup 18.
*Goals:*  League 116, FA Cup 1.
*Debut:*  27 March 1948 v Tottenham Hotspur (a) drew 0–0.
*Also played for:*  Moira United, Shrewsbury Town.

In any other era Derek Hines would have been hailed as a goalscoring sensation. As it was, however, for a large bulk of his Leicester City career he played alongside the most prolific scorer in Football League history, Arthur Rowley. That said, Derek can still reflect on a decade of service to the Foxes which brought him two Second Division Championship medals, a place on City's elite list of scorers with more than 100 goals for the club and the honour of being the last Fox to score four goals – and five goals – in a single League match!

Derek was an outstanding schoolboy footballer, who went on to win England Youth caps before being given a trial in Southend United's reserve team while still only 15. He decided instead to accept an offer to join City, signing as an amateur in the summer of 1947.

Manager Johnny Duncan threw the youngster into the heat of Second Division conflict towards the latter end of the 1947–48 season and was rewarded with a healthy return of six goals from his nine starts, including two on his home debut against Doncaster Rovers.

While National Service may have hampered Derek's first-team prospects over the next couple of seasons, it did hone his fitness levels, as well as bring him Army representative hours.

Back at City, the young forward was given an extended run in the side from the 1950–51 season onwards, grabbing 13 goals in his first full campaign and 17 a year later. His best season in front of goal was during the 1953–54 Division Two Championship-winning campaign when he notched 19 goals (to Rowley's 30 in the League). Of those 19, 13 of them came at home, with the haul including a hat-trick against Leeds United in a 5–0 romp, and then even greater success followed in a fixture against Lincoln City.

On 21 November 1953 (four days before the Hungarians revolutionised the game with their 6–3 win over England at Wembley) Derek recorded his own piece of footballing magic. Within 10 seconds of the kick-off City's number nine had opened the floodgates to score one of the club's quickest-ever goals. Ninety minutes later, in front of a largely disbelieving but celebratory crowd of 30,343, the Imps 'keeper Jerry Lowery had been beaten eight more times – with Derek getting five in the 9–2 annihilation.

The goals continued to flow throughout that season for Norman Bullock's side – a record 97 in the League, which proved hugely significant as the title was only claimed on goal average from runners-up Everton, who had finished on the same points total of 56.

Derek's performances were obviously being scrutinised because he was selected to play in the traditional end-of-season trial fixture between Young England and England; although he scored – and played again in the same fixture a year later – further recognition did not arrive.

This was a typical period in City's history because no sooner had they gained promotion than they were back in the lower tier, but the yo-yo existence continued with yet another title charge in 1956–57 – though this time with plenty to spare!

Champions by a full seven points ahead of Nottingham Forest, City clocked up six new records: most wins, most away wins, fewest defeats, most points, most goals and highest individual scorer (Rowley 44). Derek had missed the first couple of months of the season through injury but still contributed a healthy 14 goals from his 29 games.

*'Derek was able to take some small measure of satisfaction from the defeat at Sunderland on 4 September 1957 because he recorded his 100th League goal for the club, becoming the fifth Fox to reach that milestone.'*

Back in Division One City began poorly, losing six of their first seven matches, but Derek was able to take some small measure of satisfaction from the defeat at Sunderland on 4 September 1957 because he recorded his 100th League goal for the club, becoming the fifth Fox to reach that milestone.

Despite their poor start, City recovered to move away from the drop zone and retain their place in Division One, but the club were thrust into turmoil when Rowley was allowed to join Shrewsbury and then in November manager Dave Halliday resigned.

New boss Matt Gillies presided in a temporary capacity at first, but Derek must have gone some way to sealing the job for him with another finishing masterclass, which remained in the record book for the rest of the 20th century. Against Aston Villa on 15 November 1958, Gillies' first home game in charge, Derek scored four times in a 6–3 win, in doing so becoming the last Fox to score as many in a single game.

Having achieved so much at Leicester, it is a shame that Derek Hines did not make just one more League appearance because his final outing for the club – a goalless draw away at Preston on 25 March 1961 – was his 299th and final League outing for the club.

He missed out on a place in the squad during the FA Cup run that year and then decided to hook up with his old strike partner, playing under Rowley for a brief spell at Gay Meadow, which brought eight goals from 20 League and Cup matches, before later returning to Filbert Street as the youth-team coach.

Four goals – and even five goals – in a match are individual targets that have been beyond a plethora of Leicester strikers for over 60 years. Who will be the next man to oust Derek's name from the record books?

# PETER HODGE

*Born:*         1871, Dunfermline, Scotland.

*Died:*         18 August 1934, Perth, Scotland.

## Leicester City record:

*Managed:*         September 1919–May 1926 and March 1932–August 1934.

*Also managed:*    Raith Rovers, Stoke City, Manchester City.

It is clear that much of Leicester City's early consolidation was due to the meticulous dedication that Peter Hodge brought to his position as joint manager and secretary.

Although not a gifted player himself, Peter fell in love with football at an early age and quickly identified that his talents could benefit the game as a whole in other directions.

Born and raised in Dunfermline, he became a knowledgeable and well-respected administrator in local league circles before becoming honorary secretary at Dunfermline Athletic. He managed to combine this role while advancing his own understanding of the game by becoming involved in refereeing, and he officiated in matches in the Scottish Second Division from 1897 to 1906.

In the summer of 1907 the prospect of a more hands-on role tempted him to apply and be accepted to the position of Raith Rovers' first full-time professional manager. Peter's organisational skills shone through immediately with the winning of the Second Division Championship. Automatic promotion was not a feature at this time and the club were not elected, nor were they the following year when they finished as runners-up. Eventually, after finishing joint-top in 1909–10, they were duly elected to the First Division of the Scottish League.

Despite a couple of 15th-place finishes, and a first historic win over Celtic, the ambitious but unrealistic Raith board relieved Peter of his post in November 1912, citing poor results as the sole reason.

His return to the game came south of the border when he took over at Stoke City in June 1914 and led them to the top of the Southern League's Second Division. As in Scotland, his future hopes rested on an off-the-field vote rather than success on the pitch, but the side from the Potteries were successful in their attempt to be re-elected to the Football League. Sadly, though, the outbreak of war meant that they had to wait until 1919 before taking their allotted place.

Peter returned to Kirkcaldy, where his attention was diverted from football for a while as he was employed as a local military recruiting officer. Soon, however, he was lured back into the fold at Starks Park, resuming his old role in the managerial seat at Raith.

Meanwhile, there had been much activity at Filbert Street. The Leicester Fosse club had run into considerable financial difficulties and been wound up, and a newly reconstructed club, Leicester City, formed in its place.

During early 1919 negotiations were completed with Peter for his resignation from Raith and his appointment as the new Leicester City manager – with the position coupled with a secretarial role. The squad he inherited were largely made up of an inadequate mix of pre-war veterans and youthful inexperience, but contacts – principally from his homeland – soon replenished the existing staff, with a total of 30 players being utilised during his first season.

Over the next five years his signings included the likes of Adam Black, John Duncan and Arthur Chandler, all of whom became Leicester heroes in their own right. The assembled jigsaw finally lifted the Second Division title in 1924–25, a success largely founded on the back of an 18-match unbeaten run from December to March.

Peter remained for one year of top-flight football, then in May 1926 he stunned everyone at Filbert Street by resigning to take over at Manchester City, themselves just relegated. Within two seasons he had emulated what he had achieved at Leicester by taking his new side back up as champions.

The Foxes, meanwhile, had continued to progress – the side that Peter had built finished third and then second in the top division – and it was with relish that he accepted the offer to re-join them in March 1932.

An FA Cup semi-final defeat to Portsmouth denied City the opportunity of a trip to Wembley towards the end of the 1933–34 campaign and hopes were high that Peter would be able to steer the club towards an era of dominance in the English game. Those hopes were dashed, however, when, while enjoying his close-season break back home in Scotland, Peter complained of feeling unwell with chest pains and was admitted to Perth Infirmary on 30 July. His condition failed to improve and on 18 August he passed away.

His death was a huge blow to all at Filbert Street, as the club prepared to embark on its Golden Jubilee season. Six of his players, Hughie Adcock, Adam Black, Arthur Chandler, Roger Heywood, Alex McLaren and Arthur Lochhead, acted as pall-bearers at his funeral. The latter, Lochhead, was later persuaded to turn his attention away from the playing side to become Peter's full-time replacement.

*'Over the next five years his signings included the likes of Adam Black, John Duncan and Arthur Chandler, all of whom became Leicester heroes in their own right. The assembled jigsaw finally lifted the Second Division title in 1924–25, a success largely founded on the back of an 18-match unbeaten run from December to March.'*

# DEREK HOGG

*Born:*        4 November 1930, Stockton Heath, Lancashire.

## Leicester City record:

*Appearances:*    League 161, FA Cup 4.
*Goals:*    League 26, FA Cup 0.
*Debut:*    14 February 1953 v Leeds United (h) drew 3–3.
*Also played for:*    Chorley, West Bromwich Albion, Cardiff City, Kettering Town.

Derek Hogg was a tricky winger whose primary role in the City side of the 1950s was to create opportunities for those two lethal front men, Rowley and Hines. His success in the role would have been particularly painful for both Preston North End and Blackburn Rovers, who both had chances to sign him.

'I was on Preston's books as an amateur prior to my doing National Service,' recalls Derek. 'Afterwards I went back but the club wouldn't offer me part-time terms so I went to Chorley as a part-time professional – by day I was working as an estimator in an office.'

'I was quite a prominent player in the Lancashire Combination – and was quite fit after my National Service – and both Blackburn and Bolton had both been interested in me. I thought I was on my way to Blackburn, who seemed more interested in signing me. Then a Leicester scout came and watched me on a Saturday and manager Norman Bullock came up on the Sunday and the signing was completed in a hotel in Chorley.'

'My debut was at home against Leeds United, and I seem to remember that I had quite a reasonable game. Certainly the fans took to me straight away – in fact they were always good towards me – they only gave me any stick when I went back in later years to play against Leicester!'

Derek played eight games between joining and the end of the season, and he had the satisfaction of scoring his first goal for the club in a home derby against local rivals Nottingham Forest.

Although he had always played on the right flank previously, Derek found his path to the number-seven jersey obstructed by the form and fitness of Mal Griffiths, who had been on City's books since before the war.

'I was pretty quick then and predominantly right footed, but I had two good feet really, so Mal stayed on the right and I began on the left as they were short of left-sided players.'

Apart from Griffiths (City's scorer at Wembley in 1949), Derek recalls some of the other outstanding talent at the club: 'Jack Froggatt was a really good footballer at that time, I thought Johnny Morris was brilliant – one of the best inside-forwards I ever played with – he would always pass at the right time and would never put you in any trouble.'

# 'Jack Froggatt was a really good footballer at that time, I thought Johnny Morris was brilliant – one of the best inside-forwards I ever played with – he would always pass at the right time and would never put you in any trouble.'

Derek saw his role as being the chief supply-line for two of the great centre-forwards. 'I generally used to try and beat the full-back and then pull it back for either Derek Hines or Arthur Rowley.'

This was a style of play that the Lancastrian had developed from watching his own heroes in action. 'It was a different game in those days – Tom Finney and Stan Matthews were the players I looked up to in my position. I watched them and their style of play – if you come in from the flank you have to go on and shoot at goal yourself, but if you stay on the outside you can beat them and cause havoc. I played against them both many times but I particularly enjoyed watching Tom play for Preston at the end of the war, when I was about 14 or 15.'

Although he did manage to get the occasional spectacular goal himself, Derek gets most fun out of remembering one he was credited with against Everton, which owed a little bit to some good fortune. 'It was straight from a corner, at the Spion Kop End at Filbert Street. I took it right footed, an in-swinger, and it caught a bit of wind and sailed straight over the head of the 'keeper Albert Dunlop.'

As Derek recalls, football was a very different game in the 1950s. 'The conditions were nowhere near as good then. In the time before floodlights you just had to play the matches – there was no chance of them being re-arranged, so in the depths of winter the snow was rolled flat and you got on with it.'

'Clearly we weren't as fit as the players of today, but they should be fit as they don't play nearly as many games as we had to. I played week in week out and that's far more taxing on your body – I've had three hips and there's no doubt that football was a contributory factor in that.'

After hanging up his boots, Derek went into the licensing trade, initially at Osgathorpe, near Loughborough, and then near to Market Rasen. At retirement age he moved to Cromer in Norfolk, to enjoy golf – and life; although he still readily accepts the opportunity to help out behind the bar of a local hotel 'just for weddings and other big functions.'

Derek's love for Leicester City has never diminished and he gets to the Walkers Stadium as often as he can – a ground that he would have enjoyed playing on. 'I wish we could have played on a surface like that – I remember Filbert Street when it had mud at one end and frost at the other!'

# IAIN HUME

*Born:*  31 October 1983, Edinburgh.

**Leicester City record:**

*Appearances:*  League 122, FA Cup 4, League Cup 6.
*Goals:*  League 33, FA Cup 0, League Cup 1.
*Debut:*  10 September 2005 v Sheffield Wednesday (h) won 2–0.
*Also played for:*  Tranmere Rovers, Barnsley, Canada (3 caps).

Striker Iain Hume became something of a cult figure during his three-year spell with Leicester City. His darting runs and powerful shots were idolised by the Walkers Stadium faithful, who developed their own way of showing their respect towards him.

Iain joined the Foxes from Tranmere Rovers in August 2005, for a fee of £500,000, and he admits the transfer came as a bit of a surprise to him: 'Craig Levein signed me out of the blue in the dying moments of the transfer window. I was surprised as they'd just come down from the Premiership and they still had big name players like Dion Dublin and Danny Tiatto, but once I knew of their interest I couldn't wait for the move to go through.'

Some of that enthusiasm disappeared a little, however, when Iain thought his new fans had not taken to him. 'I made my debut coming on as a substitute against Sheffield Wednesday. I came on and hit a post and the crowd started the H-O-O-O-O-O-M-E chant. My parents were there and they thought I was being booed. I couldn't understand why I was being jeered either, but afterwards I was collared by a couple of the fans who asked me what I thought of the way they shouted my name, and then I realised what was going on. I must have heard that H-O-O-O-O-O-M-E thing a thousand times since!'

Iain's first goal for the club soon followed, and it came in a match away at one of City's big local rivals. 'It was at Derby and it was a massive thing because I realised just how much that match meant

> **'I made my debut coming on as a substitute against Sheffield Wednesday. I came on and hit a post and the crowd started the H-O-O-O-O-O-M-E chant. My parents were there and they thought I was being booed.**

to the fans. Patrik Gerrbrand cleared the ball upfield and I've just run past the centre-half. Kevin Poole was in goal for them and as he's come out I've hit it over him with the outside of my right boot. It was important for me to score early in my City career and it's probably my favourite goal for them.'

Although he was born in Edinburgh, Iain has played international football for Canada. 'The family moved out there when I was only about a year and a half old. We came back when I was about 16 but under the residency regulations I qualified to play for them.'

A great striker of the ball and a good team player, Iain is modest in appraising his own value to a side. 'My main quality is that I like to give everything I've got. I know I'm not a world-beater but I wear my heart on my sleeve and give 110 per cent all of the time – and occasionally I'll pop in a decent long-ranger!'

Iain recalls that there was sadness, sportsmanship and a shock win during the early rounds of the 2007–08 League Cup campaign. During the half-time interval of City's tie at Nottingham Forest, Clive Clarke, on-loan from Sunderland, was taken ill. 'Clive was sat next to me when it happened – between me and Darren Kenton in fact – it was a frightening episode for all of us and there were a lot of tears at the time. We were told that it was being reported in the media that a Leicester City player had suffered a heart-attack so we were all trying to ring home as quickly as possible to reassure people – but our thoughts were mainly with Clive and his family.'

The match was abandoned at half-time, and thankfully Clive made a full recovery, but when the tie was re-staged three weeks later City made one of the most sporting gestures of all time – from the kick-off they allowed the Forest goalkeeper Paul Smith to walk from the halfway line and score, unopposed. Iain says the team agreed it was the right thing to do. 'Forest were leading 1–0 at the time of the abandonment and thoroughly deserved to be in front. The gaffer mentioned it just before the kick-off and we agreed with it. We probably didn't play as well as we could have done but still managed to go through 3–2, and in terms of comebacks it was perhaps one of the club's most famous results.'

There was drama of a different kind in the next round when the Foxes went to Aston Villa and defeated Martin O'Neill's Premiership side 1–0, with a goal from Iain's striker partner, Matty Fryatt. 'In fairness I think we played really well that evening,' he says.

Iain endured a fairly turbulent time with City in terms of managerial changes. He served under seven different bosses in just three years before moving on to join Barnsley. The 'Willo-the-Wisp' striker suffered a serious head injury while playing for the Tykes but returned to action in time to make an emotional playing return against City in August 2009. 'It was nice to go back. I just love playing at the Walkers – it's a great Stadium and a great pitch. I've tried to change shirts when I've played against former teammates in the past and I made sure I swapped with Matty. Apart from being a good friend I just know he'll go on to become a really great player. The crowd gave me a really great ovation, and only the Barnsley lads afterwards – and those close to me – will know how much that meant to me.'

# MUZZY IZZET

*Born:*          31 October 1974, Mile End, London.

## Leicester City record:

*Appearances:*    League 269, FA Cup 16, League Cup 27, Other 7.
*Goals:*          League 38, FA Cup 4, League Cup 4, Other 1.
*Debut:*          30 March 1996 v Sheffield United (h) lost 0–2.
*Also played for:* Chelsea (trainee), Birmingham City, Turkey (8 caps).

Regarded by many as being one of the finest midfielders to represent Leicester City, Muzzy Izzet gave the club yeoman service during the successful Martin O'Neill era and played in three League Cup Finals, a Play-off Final and another promotion-winning season.

Muzzy began as a trainee at Chelsea, but with opportunities for youngsters being at a premium there he was allowed to join City on loan in March 1996, helping them into the end-of-season Play-offs, where they defeated Crystal Palace 2–1 at Wembley.

Muzzy's impact and attitude had impressed Martin O'Neill, and the City boss made the move permanent during the close season, forking out £650,000 for his signature. Adapting instantly to life in the Premiership, his was a highly successful return to the big time with a ninth-placed finish in the League, plus further success in the knock-out form of the game.

City's return to the big time had been flourished with the capture of the League Cup – won for the first time since 1964 – and it provided Muzzy with the first major medal of his career.

Sharing duties with him in the centre of the park during that season had been Neil Lennon, and by the start of the following campaign the duo had become a triumvirate with the addition of Robbie Savage to the City roster. Together, they comprised probably the best central unit the club has ever had, and possibly one of the best in the history of the Premiership.

Complementing each other magnificently, sometimes seemingly by telepathy, they could hold, tackle, pass and shoot with the very best – and their style enabled Muzzy to be the player to 'bomb on' and support the attackers.

Muzzy's deadball expertise also became something of a speciality, and he provided countless number of assists as well as striking a few stunning free-kicks home himself. Usually clinical from the penalty spot, his conversion rate helped him tot up a healthy quota of goals each season.

It is usually possible to typecast a player by the manner in which he usually gets his goals. With Muzzy, this was impossible. Among his City collection were long-range strikes, diving headers, cool one-on-one finishes and even, towards the latter part of his Leicester days, an unbelievable overhead-kick away at Grimsby Town.

*Muzzy's deadball expertise also became something of a speciality, and he provided countless number of assists as well as striking a few stunning free-kicks home himself. Usually clinical from the penalty spot, his conversion rate helped him tot up a healthy quota of goals each season.*

Muzzy played in two more domestic Cup Finals for City as the setback of losing the 1999 League Cup Final to Tottenham Hotspur was tempered a year later when Tranmere Rovers were beaten 2–1.

In absolutely golden form, Muzzy was then able to step up and perform on an even higher platform. His father's background had qualified Muzzy for selection when the Turkish selectors enquired about his availability prior to the 2000 European Championships, and the midfielder made his international debut against Sweden in Eindhoven during that tournament. Although further appearances were infrequent, Muzzy was also selected for the 2002 World Cup, and his eighth and final appearance at that level came as a substitute against Brazil in the semi-final of that competition.

During the 2000–01 season Muzzy led the City scoring charts with a total of 11 – a haul that included a UEFA Cup goal in Belgrade against Red Star.

Following relegation at the end of the 2001–02 season there were enquiries made about Muzzy's availability, but he remained loyal to the Foxes, stating that he wanted to help them get back into the top flight. This he did, achieving automatic promotion with Leicester as runners-up behind Portsmouth.

City's number six had assumed the captaincy on a stand-in basis on many occasions, but he took over permanently during the latter stages of a Foxes career that eventually ended after yet another brief stay in the Premiership. In nine years of loyal service he had appeared in 319 first-team games and had netted on 47 occasions.

Out of contract, he was entitled to a Bosman free transfer and he joined Birmingham City, hoping to resurrect his international standing. Persistent knee injuries wrecked his two seasons at St Andrew's, however, and he was only available for League selection on 26 occasions.

Accepting the demands being putting on his body, Muzzy reluctantly brought a premature end to his playing career.

Whenever he is not supporting younger brother Kemal (the Colchester United midfielder), Muzzy is a frequent visitor to the Walkers Stadium, where he always receives a hero's welcome.

He pulled on the Leicester City 'blue' once again during the summer of 2009 when he helped his old club to the regional Masters title.

# JULIAN JOACHIM

*Born:*  20 September 1974, Peterborough, Cambridgeshire.

## Leicester City record:

*Appearances:*  League 99, FA Cup 5, League Cup 9, Other 6.

*Goals:*  League 25, FA Cup 1, League Cup 3, Other 2.

*Debut:*  3 October 1992 v Barnsley (h) won 2–1.

*Also played for:*  Aston Villa, Coventry City, Leeds United, Walsall (loan), Boston United, Darlington, Kings Lynn.

Jet-heeled striker Julian Joachim burst into the City first team during the 1992–93 season, aged just 18. Over the course of the next three and a half years his breathtaking sprints, youthful exuberance and keen eye for goal catapulted him into the hearts of all City fans. By the time of his sizeable transfer to Aston Villa he had appeared in two Play-off Finals and scored some memorable strikes for the Foxes.

Although he appeared to burst on to the first-team scene overnight, he admits it had been a long process to get to that stage. 'I lived in Boston as a youngster and was first spotted playing for the Lincolnshire county side as a schoolboy. Les Gray, one of the Leicester scouts, invited me to go down there from the age of 10 or 11.'

Graduating through the junior ranks, Julian was still a first-year YTS when he was called in by Brian Little to sign pro forms for the club, and he did not have to wait much longer for an unexpected early introduction into the League side, but he admits he had a slight tinge of frustration about one incident in his first match. 'I had a great chance to score but Simon Grayson took it off my toe to put it in,' he says.

That same season the FA Cup draw gave Julian the opportunity of doing something he had not achieved on debut, when he scored against Barnsley – and what a goal it was too! 'It was probably my best goal for the club', he reflects. 'It won the Goal of the Month award and was the overall runner-up for Goal of the Season. They had a corner, and it was cleared to the edge of our box to Steve Thompson. I'd been back defending as well so broke out and "Thommo" fed me, and I just took it on and on. I went right then cut back inside and hit it with the outside of my right foot into the top corner from about 25 yards – very pleasing!'

With Filbert Street undergoing development, City's home Play-off semi-final against Portsmouth at the end of that term was staged at Nottingham Forest's City Ground. Julian came on as a late substitute and made a telling impact with a stunning solo effort for the only goal of the evening. 'The ball was played up to me on the halfway line – I turned my marker and then set off – there were a couple of defenders between me and the goal – they had five yards on me, but I pushed it passed them and went. Luckily enough I got there and poked it between the 'keeper's legs to score.'

Turning his marker proved to be one of the strengths of Julian's play – that and his blistering pace. 'I was quick but wouldn't say I was an out-and-out goalscorer. I did manage to score a lot of good quality goals and had a decent first touch, plus a low centre of gravity which also helps.'

Being selected to start in the 1993 Play-off Final against Swindon Town was a totally new experience for the youngster. 'It was not only the first time I'd played at Wembley, but it was also the very first time I'd ever been there at all, and at 3–0 down it was all going horribly wrong then "Walshy" got his head onto a cross, the ball hit the upright and came out straight into my path in front of goal, and I was able to tuck it away. Once we'd got it back to three-all we had all the momentum, only for them to be awarded a debatable penalty right at the end.'

Nicknames have always played their part around football grounds, and Julian had his fair share – with JJ and Jocky the favourites amongst his teammates – and the slightly more imaginative 'Crown Jules' being popular among the supporters.

During the summer of 1993, JJ's qualities were displayed to a much wider audience as England's Under-18 side captured the European Championships in their home country. With the matches being televised live, the outstanding talents of players like Robbie Fowler, Sol Campbell, Paul Scholes, Gary Neville and Julian himself were put in the spotlight.

The 1994 Wembley match against Derby provided Julian with contrasting emotions as he began the contest on the bench, only to come on later. '"Walshy" really emerged as the hero that day, but I was pleased to come on and experience the atmosphere,' he says.

JJ scored City's very first Premiership goal (in a 3–1 reversal at home to Newcastle United) and then he suffered the first set-back of his pro career. 'I got a metatarsal injury, and it took a long time to heal properly. I was out for about four or five months altogether.'

In February 1996 JJ left Filbert Street to be reunited with his former manager.

'I did not ask for a move, but Martin O'Neill rang me and said he needed to raise some money and would I like to go and play for Brian again, as he was interested in taking me to Aston Villa, so I just decided it was time for a new challenge. I'd really enjoyed my time at Leicester – I learnt my trade there, and the fans were always different class towards me.'

*'I was quick but wouldn't say I was an out-and-out goalscorer. I did manage to score a lot of good quality goals and had a decent first touch, plus a low centre of gravity which also helps.'*

# BERT JOHNSON

*Born:*          4 June 1916, Stockton-on-Tees.
*Died:*          30 June 2009, Evington, Leicestershire.

## Leicester City record:

*Caretaker manager:* January–April 1968.
*Played for:*      Southbank, Stockton, Spennymoor United, Charlton Athletic,
                 Bexleyheath and Welling, Cambridge United, England (2 caps).
*Managed:*       Cambridge United (1955–59).

Although he did not play a single game for Leicester City – nor was he ever appointed full-time manager – Bert Johnson's influence on the club's success during the 1960s is immeasurable.

Fiercely loyal to manager and long-time friend Matt Gillies, the pair oversaw a period in the Foxes history when Cup Finals were commonplace and League dominance appeared achievable.

Bert's own playing career had begun in his native North East, where he had stepped up from local Youth football to play in the strong Northern League with Spennymoor United. Charlton Athletic's manager, Jimmy Seed, was scouting in the North East looking at other players when he first noticed Bert and took him to the Valley in March 1939 for a fee of £400.

The outbreak of World War Two prevented Bert from making his first-team debut, and he joined the RAF, graduating to the rank of Sergeant. He took every opportunity to continue playing football, however, and 'guested' for Bolton Wanderers, developing into an outstanding wing-half and playing in more than 100 consecutive matches for the club. It was while playing for the Trotters that he first met Gillies.

Although he also 'guested' for both Wolverhampton Wanderers and Middlesbrough during the years of the conflict, he returned to the Valley to resume his football career and made his Addicks debut in January 1946 in a winning FA Cup third-round tie against Fulham. That was the start of a run which took the south-east London side to their first Wembley Final; although in front of 98,000 fans Charlton lost 1–4 to Derby County after extra-time. Shortly afterwards Bert was called up to play in two Victory Internationals for the full England side, appearing against Switzerland at Stamford Bridge and against France in Paris.

The 1946–47 season saw Charlton return for their second successive FA Cup Final, and this time Bert and his teammates collected winners' medals after a 1–0 triumph over Burnley, again after extra-time.

He carried on playing for Charlton until 1953, totting up 162 League and Cup appearances in the process, before taking a player-manager role at nearby Bexleyheath and Welling. Two years later, he accepted a similar position at Cambridge United.

In the summer of 1959 Bert was reunited with his wartime friend when Matt Gillies invited him to become Leicester City's chief scout – and early players to benefit and move to Filbert Street were Davie Gibson, Mike Stringfellow and Bobby Roberts.

Bert would do much more than recommend signings, however, as he became a sounding board for the manager; the pair would spend hours talking about tactics and innovations that would take the club forward. They also encouraged the players to be frank, honest and open and to have weekly discussions as to what had gone right and what had gone wrong in the previous game – regular occurrences nowadays but revolutionary at the time.

*That was the first of four domestic Cup Finals that the Foxes would reach in the early 1960s, and it hurt Bert as much as any man that only one of them – the 1964 League Cup – was won.*

Bert's position at the club 'metamorphosised' into one of much more importance – he took over the coaching duties and became Matt's 'number two'. His thoughts on the game were considered and practical – he believed that players should be able to adapt to different strategies and formations; the successful interchanging of positions between Frank McLintock and Graham Cross was always credited to the canny Teessider.

The official match programme for the 1961 FA Cup Final paid appropriate credit to Bert for the part he had played in helping City to get there, describing him as, 'genial and quiet' before adding, 'Bert Johnson is a devout churchgoer who winces at the cuss as much as the misguided pass.'

That was the first of four domestic Cup Finals that the Foxes would reach in the early 1960s, and it hurt Bert as much as any man that only one of them – the 1964 League Cup – was won.

The League and Cup double was even a possibility in 1963 – on 8 April City topped the First Division table – but by the end of the season they had slipped to fourth and lost their second Cup Final in three years. Having taken City to such heights, it was equally frustrating that the period of success was not maintained.

Matt Gillies' stress-related problems necessitated a period of absence from the club in January 1968, and Bert was put in temporary charge until the end of the season.

Despite the club breaking the British transfer record in signing Allan Clarke from Fulham for £150,000 at the start of the next season, results were poor after the manager's return and there was general talk of dressing room unrest. At a special board meeting on 28 November 1968 the directors decided to relieve Bert of his position. It was no surprise to anyone that Gillies – who was strongly against this decision – tendered his own resignation the next day.

The pair were soon back working together at Nottingham Forest, however, but they were unable to transform the City Ground side in the way they had been able to do it at Leicester.

Later Bert went to coach in Zambia – he made such a success of looking after the youth set up that he was invited to take over the national side, but he refused as they played on Sundays. Returning to the UK, he worked as a scout for Southampton and then as general manager at Walsall before retiring to his Wigston home.

Bert was 93 years of age when he died in a nursing home in Evington in June 2009.

# PONTUS KAAMARK

*Born:*  5 April 1969, Vasteras, Sweden.

**Leicester City record:**
*Appearances:*  League 65, FA Cup 4, League Cup 6, Other 2.
*Debut:*  5 November 1995 v West Bromwich Albion (a) won 3–2.
*Also played for:*  Vasteras SK, IFK Gothenburg, AIK (all Sweden), Sweden (57 caps).

Already a seasoned international defender when he arrived at Leicester City, Pontus Kaamark enhanced his reputation during a four-year stint at Filbert Street, which was crowned by a starring performance in the 1997 League Cup Final win.

The opportunity to challenge himself abroad was a major factor in his decision to move from his homeland. 'The Bosman ruling had just come into force,' recalls the Swede. 'Before then my club, IFK Gothenburg, did not want to sell their best players, but they were then unable to stop any player who wanted to move to another country. Leicester City made me a very serious offer. I liked the club, and all the staff were very nice. I was made to feel welcome, and it was very easy to settle in there.'

With Simon Grayson inked in to the right-back spot Pontus had just one outing in his first part-season in England – a 3–2 win at West Brom – but the club's Play-off promotion at the end of that season enabled him the opportunity of pitting himself against some of the best in the game.

It will be as a man marker that Pontus is best remembered by City fans, but he enjoys the freedom of the right-back position above all else. 'I prefer to play there, in a 4–4–2, when I'm allowed to push forward. If I was to assess my own qualities I think they would have to be strength and speed.'

Manager Martin O'Neill displayed a little cunning, though, whenever his side faced one of the so-called top-flight 'flair players' by getting Pontus to keep very close proximity to them for 90 minutes. 'I was given the job of man-marking guys like McManaman, Bergkamp, Overmars, Yorke and, of course, Juninho,' he says.

## 'Leicester City made me a very serious offer. I liked the club, and all the staff were very nice. I was made to feel welcome, and it was very easy to settle in there.'

Leicester's biggest obstacle as they prepared to face Middlesbrough in the 1997 League Cup Final was the form of Juninho – their brilliant Brazilian midfield maestro. Pontus admits his own preparations in the weeks leading up to the game were jeopardised by injury – but a teammate helped with his recovery. 'Myself and Mike Whitlow played hours and hours of badminton, which helped me recover my fitness and strength – and just for the record I beat him every game!'

Having proved his fitness to the manager, Pontus's role was clear and one that he relished. 'I've been given the man-marking role many times, perhaps most famously in the 1994 World Cup for Sweden against Brazil when I managed to keep Romario fairly quiet – at the time he was the best player in the world.'

'I used to play Ice hockey when I was younger, so that helped me to have strong legs and I've got a low centre of gravity which helps to follow quick players.'

If Juninho was frustrated by Pontus stifling his involvement in the Final, he did not show it to the Swede. 'He didn't say anything to me at all, but even if he had, my Portuguese isn't very good.'

It was certainly a full-time occupation keeping the Brazilian number 10 out of the contest, but Pontus did have time to take in a little of the atmosphere. 'I remember it was an amazing day at Wembley, seeing half of the arena just totally "blue" with the Leicester fans. It was a proud day for me because my parents had flown in from Sweden to watch the match – the highlight of the replay was obviously Steve's goal – everything just went mad!'

Apart from the League Cup triumph, Pontus was part of City sides that won a lot of big matches, stand-out games being at Liverpool and Manchester United. 'Usually when we won big games it was because Emile Heskey had one of his fantastic days. I rate him as one of the best players in the world. All of my defensive friends who have played against him say he is one of the toughest to play against. Olof Mellberg, when he was playing for Aston Villa, made that statement to a Swedish newspaper.'

With an understandable priority being given to either his defensive duties or his man-marking roles, it is not surprising that Pontus did not manage a goal in City's colours, although he remembers a couple of close calls. 'In my first match I hit a post and then against Manchester United at Filbert Street I was inches away – I got an "ooooooooooo" from the crowd at least.'

Having done such a good job in the Middlesbrough match, Pontus admits his omission from the 1999 League Cup Final defeat against Spurs was a defining moment for him. 'I felt that Martin made a mistake in not picking me for that game to mark David Ginola. I was very disappointed, and that was also one of the reasons why I decided to move on in my career. I remember making my decision on the bus after that game and went to Martin and told him. The main reason was my five-year-old daughter who was living in Sweden – but that day made my decision definite!'

Since retiring from the game Pontus has worked as a football expert for TV4 in his home country. 'I'm one of those guys you see on telly in a suit – either in a studio or at the matches – and I just love to talk football all day!'

# KEN KEYWORTH

| *Born:* | 24 February 1934, Rotherham, South Yorkshire. |
| *Died:* | 7 January 2000, Rotherham, South Yorkshire. |

## Leicester City record:

| *Appearances:* | League 177, FA Cup 23, League Cup 11, Other 4. |
| *Goals:* | League 63, FA Cup 7, League Cup 4, Other 3. |
| *Debut:* | 23 August 1958 v Everton (h) won 2–0. |
| *Also played for:* | Rotherham United, Coventry City, Swindon Town. |

Only two players managed to score for Leicester City during the four Wembley FA Cup Finals they reached during the 20th century. In 1949, as the Foxes went down to Wolves it was Welshman Mal Griffiths who registered the club's first goal beneath the Twin Towers. Fourteen years later, in City's loss to Manchester United, their consolation came from their centre-forward, Ken Keyworth.

Ken had begun his League career at his home-town club Rotherham United; although he had had trials for Wolves as a junior. National Service completed, he made his League debut for the Millers in the 1955–56 season, playing at left-half. Over the next couple of years he cemented his place in the side, missing just one match in 1957–58, when he also chipped in with four goals.

His form had been monitored by several clubs, but it was City boss David Halliday who stepped in to offer Ken the chance of First Division football. During his first season at Filbert Street the Yorkshireman made 32 appearances in the League and bolstered his contribution with a couple of important goals, in away wins at West Ham United and Nottingham Forest.

That season Matt Gillies replaced Halliday and the new manager, along with coach Bert Johnson, felt that Ken's game was ideally suited to a more advanced role. He was switched initially to an inside-forward position and wore the number-10 shirt when City progressed to the 1961 Cup Final, but he then became the fulcrum of the attack and for three consecutive seasons he was the club's top-scorer.

In 1961–62 his tally of 19 included three in Europe; two against Glenavon and one against Atletico Madrid (City taking the English spot in the Cup-Winners' Cup as Spurs had won the double the previous year and were playing in the European Cup).

The following year was Ken's most prolific, scoring 21 League goals, plus six more in the domestic Cup competitions. His haul included a hat-trick in a 4–3 home win over Manchester United, who then advanced to face the Foxes in the FA Cup Final.

En-route to their second Final in three years City had defeated Grimsby Town, Ipswich Town, Leyton Orient, Norwich City and then Liverpool but, although they were strongly fancied to end their Wembley hoo-doo, Ken and his teammates had a collective off-day and the Cup went back to Old Trafford.

The only highspot for the disappointed Leicester following was their goal, which came nine minutes from time. Frank McLintock tried a speculative effort which was flashing wide at around knee-height – Ken threw himself forward from a distance of around eight yards out to flash a diving header beyond the reach of United's 'keeper David Gaskell.

Sixteen goals in 1963–64 included three in the League Cup competition, which provided Ken – and City – with winners' medals at last, after they defeated Stoke City in the two-legged Final.

Injuries sustained in a car accident then restricted his appearances, and in December 1964 he was granted a free transfer to join Coventry City, the move going through on the day that the Foxes triumphed 8–1 over the Sky Blues in a League Cup tie!

He did not stay at Highfield Road for long and had a season with Swindon Town before bidding the game farewell and returning to his Rotherham roots. Later Ken worked as a quantity surveyor for a while and then later as an office manager for a building contractor.

Although sometimes viewed as being rather a blunt, straight-talking man, it is clear he had a great sense of humour and was highly respected within the game by teammates and opponents alike. The pen portraits from the two official FA Cup Final programmes in which he played give an insight into his standing at the time. From 1961, when he played inside-left: 'City's third first-team player from Yorkshire and quite a comedian in a droll way. Says of Banks, Appleton and himself "Yorkshire only export the best".' It goes on to add, 'Tremendous worker who does a lot of the carrying and fetching for his colleagues.'

# A vastly underrated centre-forward and clever ball player. A typical example of the supreme versatility running through the team.'

Two years later, they had this to say, 'A vastly underrated centre-forward and clever ball player. A typical example of the supreme versatility running through the team.'

Ken enjoyed his days at Leicester, but he would have hoped that he does not remain in the record books as their last FA Cup Final goalscorer for too much longer.

# IAN KING

*Born:*          27 May 1937, Loanhead, Midlothian.

## Leicester City record:
*Appearances:*   League 244, FA Cup 27, League Cup 22, Other 4.
*Goals:*         League 6, FA Cup 0, League Cup 1, Other 0.
*Debut:*         11 September 1957 v Sheffield Wednesday (a) lost 1–2.
*Also played for:* Broughton Star, Arniston Rangers, Charlton Athletic, Burton Albion.

Ian King was a defensive lynchpin who played in all four of City's domestic Cup Finals in the early 1960s and completed almost 300 appearances for the club during his nine-year stay at Filbert Street.

Born John Aitken King, he knows the first question he will always be asked: 'Everyone wants to know why it's "Ian", but when you were named John and went to school, they all called you Ian – it's a Scottish tradition, and it has stuck with me ever since. It's a similar thing with Matt Gillies – he was always "Jimmy" for the same reasons!'

'Jimmy' Gillies played a significant part in bringing the young centre-half to Leicester. 'I'd had a few trials with Hearts as a schoolboy, but the manager decided I wasn't going to make it, but I was playing in some Junior Cup Final or other and he turned up to watch. He must have given a good report to Dave Halliday, the City manager at the time, because he came up and I signed for the club in the old North British Hotel in Edinburgh.'

The new acquisition was not a complete novice, however, and already had an impressive footballing pedigree. 'I'd played for Scotland Schoolboys three or four times and was captain against England at Wembley. My opposite number as England captain was Duncan Edwards – he was built like a man and played like a man – he was much too good for us, and regrettably it was my only meeting with him.'

It did not take too long for Ian to break into the first-team ranks; although he did not have long to prepare: 'My debut was a night match at Sheffield Wednesday. I'd only had about three games in the A Team, but I was told on the morning that I'd be travelling, and when I got there I was picked to play. Our side had a lot of experience at that time – people like Arthur Rowley and Johnny Morris, who were all good to listen to and to play alongside.'

Ian's profile, both within the club and within the game as a whole, was raised over the next couple of seasons, although he did have a lengthy lay-off after a match against Blackburn Rovers. 'I went for a challenge with Roy Vernon and was caught on the left ankle, and there was cartilage damage and further injury to the ankle which troubled me for quite a while afterwards.'

Restored to full fitness, Ian took over as the club's penalty-taker, but a successful sequence was halted in another match against Blackburn. 'I thought I'd try something different and just chip one straight down the middle – they do it a lot nowadays – most 'keepers move one way or another, but Fred Else just stood there and caught it!'

There was another high-profile miss, during an epic FA Cup semi-final second replay against Sheffield United. 'They weren't a bad side, and it became a protracted affair and went to a third game. I remember the pitch being bone-hard, but I was a little unlucky with the penalty – he dived and it hit his heel, but in the end we won easily.'

That put City through to the Cup Final, and Ian admits the pre-match drama was a little unsettling. 'Ken Leek was left out, and no-one would ever say why. He was a bit of a character, but he had scored twice against Spurs in a League meeting, but it hit us to discover he'd been left out, and then Lennie got injured and Frank was put at right-back.'

The Scot admits he did not really take in too much of the Wembley experience. 'It was my first time in a Cup Final, and everything just passed me by – the occasion was so big.'

More disappointment came two years later. 'In the 1963 Cup Final we were strong favourites to win but, in truth, we hadn't played well in the month leading up to the game. United hadn't had a great season, but they turned up and played on the day, whereas we didn't.'

Five of the six League goals that Ian scored for City came from the penalty-spot, with the exception coming in a 4–0 away romp against Cardiff City. 'The ball was played out to Howard Riley on the right – I kept on running straight down the middle. Howard continued, then fired in a shot which the 'keeper could only parry out for me to tap home the loose ball.'

Domestic Cup success was finally achieved with the League Cup win over Stoke City in 1964, and although the trophy was not retained after defeat in the Final the following year (Ian missed the second leg versus Chelsea), he feels that this was the most outstanding period in Leicester City's history. 'After "Jimmy" [Gillies] took over he created the most successful side the club has ever had, in my opinion. He was always able to call on the country's best goalkeeper, Gordon Banks, and had a side with really outstanding players in it like McLintock, Gibson, Stringfellow and Appleton.'

It was with the latter that Ian enjoyed such a fine working relationship. 'Colin was an accurate passer and good at hitting long diagonal balls, but I didn't just stand there and head it – I'd like to think I could play a little bit as well!'

*'In the 1963 Cup Final we were strong favourites to win but, in truth, we hadn't played well in the month leading up to the game. United hadn't had a great season, but they turned up and played on the day, whereas we didn't.'*

# TEDDY KING

Born:                  1884, Leicester.
Died:                  7 July 1952, Braunstone, Leicestershire.

## Leicester City record:

Appearances:      League 227, FA Cup 9, Other (wartime) 121.
Goals:                 League 26, FA Cup 0, Other (wartime) 24.
Debut:                6 April 1907 v West Bromwich Albion (a) won 1–0.
Also played for:   Aylestone Swifts, St Andrews, Leicester Imperial.

Edwin 'Teddy' King was one of the truly outstanding servants to the Leicester club. Over the course of an 18-year period – both before and after the transition from Fosse to City – he made over 350 appearances for the first team, before going on to become a valued member of the backroom staff. He was also a very capable wicket-keeper, who made a couple of first-class appearances for Leicestershire CCC.

Leicester born and bred, he had played for local sides Aylestone Swifts, St Andrews and Leicester Imperial before joining the League side in 1906, directly after helping the 'Imps' to success in the County Cup Final.

While many other youngsters were given decent opportunities to prove their worth, Teddy remained a fringe player until the 1910–11 season, whereupon he began to nail down a regular place in the first team.

He had scored his first League goal a year earlier against Birmingham during a rare promotion to the side, but his chance to establish himself came in particularly tragic circumstances. Andy Aitken, the former Scottish international, had been appointed as player-manager, and although centre-half was his own preferred position he had signed Ted Pheasant – the former Wolves and West Brom star – to wear the number-five jersey instead; however, Pheasant had only been at the club for a fortnight when he was admitted to Leicester

*Preferring to remain on the sidelines, Aitken made the bold decision to switch Teddy from his favoured wing-half berth to the central role, and he responded with a series of hugely consistent performances.*

infirmary, where he died from peritonitis. Preferring to remain on the sidelines, Aitken made the bold decision to switch Teddy from his favoured wing-half berth to the central role, and he responded with a series of hugely consistent performances.

Over the next five seasons he enjoyed lengthy runs in the side, playing right across the half-back line. It was a hugely significant period in the club's history. In the summer of 1913 they made their first overseas trip – to Sweden, winning all five of the matches played during a 10-day stay.

Teddy's versatility was implemented yet again when he was deployed as a makeshift striker during the 1914–15 season. He responded by finishing as second top scorer with 10 goals – including the final one of a 5–1 win over Leeds City that would be the club's last before the League programme was cancelled due to the hostilities.

Financial restraints were seriously bedevilling the club, and the outbreak of World War One marked the end of the Fosse era.

At 31 years of age at the time the conflict began, Teddy was able to remain in the Leicester area during the next four years, and he provided an element of permanency during the club's wartime fixtures, playing in 121 of the matches. Only Sam Currie, with 123, played in more of these games.

The reconstruction of the club from Fosse to City went through in time for the resumption of the League programme at the start of the 1919–20 season. This opened up the prospect of lots of new 'firsts' to be accomplished, and Teddy unfortunately entered the record books in two categories that he would rather not have!

Playing away against Fulham on 20 September 1919 he was sent off (along with the Cottagers' Johnny McIntyre) to become the first City player to be dismissed, and then against Burnley in the FA Cup on 8 January 1921 he was 'credited' with scoring an own-goal in the 3–7 defeat; again, the first time that had happened since the reconstruction.

The League match against Stockport County in February 1920 was designated as a well-deserved Benefit game for Teddy; although he carried on playing for another couple of seasons. He scored twice against Stoke on 11 February 1922, in what turned out to be his final home match for the club, although he played once more away at Leeds a week later.

He was then appointed as coach of City's reserves, a position he held for two years before stepping up to assist Willie Orr with the first team, most notably helping the side to the Division One runners'-up spot at the end of the 1928–29 campaign.

Teddy's summers had been spent performing behind the stumps for Leicestershire's second XI for a number of seasons, and he fulfilled all of his cricketing ambitions when he was called-up to play a couple of matches for the full county side in 1925 at the grand old age of 41.

After leaving City, Teddy coached the Leicester Nomads side for a number of seasons; although he remained a keen supporter and follower of the professional side right up until his death in 1952.

# KEN LEEK

*Born:*          26 July 1935, Ynysybwl, South Wales.

*Died:*           19 November 2007, Daventry, Northamptonshire.

## Leicester City record:

*Appearances:*     League 93, FA Cup 17, League Cup 1.

*Goals:*            League 34, FA Cup 9, League Cup 0.

*Debut:*           23 August 1958 v Everton (h) won 2–0.

*Also played for:*   Pontypridd YC, Northampton Town, Newcastle United, Montreal Concordia (Canada, loan), Birmingham City, Bradford City, Wales (13 caps).

Ken Leek is a name that perhaps became as well known with the general sporting public for a game he did not participate in, rather than for all of those in which he did. Missing the 1961 FA Cup Final for City was a devastating blow to a man who had contributed so much towards ensuring that his club had a big day out at Wembley to enjoy.

During the run to the Twin Towers, which ultimately ended in a 2–0 defeat to Tottenham Hotspur, Ken had scored goals in every round of the competition, yet he was controversially left out of the starting XI on the big day. The disappointment was so hard to take that the Welsh international left Filbert Street shortly afterwards to resurrect his career and ultimately gain iconic status with Birmingham City.

He had already won Welsh Under-23 honours while at Fourth Division Northampton Town and was invited to guest for a City XI in a friendly against touring Brazilian side Canto do Rio in April 1958. Such was the impression made by Ken he was signed a few days later, for £5,750. That summer he went with Wales to the World Cup Finals in Sweden but did not make an appearance; although he would later earn 13 full caps for his country – six of them while he was at City.

Ken made his mark on the opening day of the new season, scoring his side's first goal of the campaign and helping to christen his debut with a 2–0 victory over Everton. (It would be another 12 years before the Foxes tasted a win on the opening afternoon!)

*Ken made his mark on the opening day of the new season, scoring his side's first goal of the campaign and helping to christen his debut with a 2–0 victory over Everton.*

The striker bagged eight goals in his first season as the club successfully fought off relegation and 10 the year after as they climbed to 12th. Neither team nor individual exploits would have indicated that Leicester City, their fans and their number nine would be about to embark on such an exciting campaign the next time around, especially after having not made the brightest of starts.

Both Leicester City and Ken himself would experience happier times in later League Cup competitions, but it was a brand new venture when City entered for the first time in 1960, and the striker was part of the side that completed a routine 4–0 home victory over Mansfield Town. A rather less acceptable loss to Rotherham United (eventual finalists) followed in the next round.

That Cup exit was soon erased from memory as the Foxes embarked on the FA Cup trail. In routine home victories, 3–1 versus Oxford United and 5–1 versus Bristol City (after an original half-time abandonment for a waterlogged pitch), Ken was among the goals as City eased into the fifth round.

At that stage they were drawn away for the first time but earned a home replay after a 1–1 draw at Birmingham City. Ken's double saw his side through, and he kept his scoring spree going with an extra-time headed winner at Oakwell in a sixth-round replay win over Barnsley. This goal was always fondly referred to as the striker's favourite for the club.

City had already played six (and a half) matches to reach the last four, and Second Division Sheffield United were in no mood to make things any easier. In the pre sudden-death days, Cup-ties could go on forever and this 1961 semi threatened to. Goalless games at Elland Road and then the City Ground took the teams to a tension-filled third encounter at St Andrew's, where Leicester skipper Jimmy Walsh, and then our hero Ken, scored the goals that finally saw off the Blades' stubborn resistance.

Spurs, runaway First Division champions, had also made their way to Wembley and lay in wait, hoping to claim the Holy Grail of the League and Cup double. Three months earlier Leicester had gone to White Hart Lane and triumphed 3–2, with Ken among the scorers.

While Bill Nicholson was anxiously wondering how his defence would be able to cope with Leek, his opposite number was about to drop a huge bombshell. City's League form had not been great in the run-up to the Final, and, so the story goes, Gillies felt that Leicester's chances would be improved with young Hugh McIlmoyle (with four goals from only seven League appearances) leading the line inside of his more recognised and established centre-forward. No other explanation has ever been forthcoming but the hunch, if that is what it was, did not pay off, as the London side triumphed by two goals to nil.

Ken's immediate desire to move on was understandable, and he had a brief spell at Newcastle United and a few loan games in Canada before getting his career back on track with Birmingham City.

The highlight of his time at St Andrew's was scoring two of the goals in the aggregate 3–1 win over arch-rivals Aston Villa in the 1963 League Cup Final. He later returned to Northampton Town and helped the Cobblers achieve top-flight status for the first time ever before being sold to Bradford City for a then-club record fee of £10,000.

Ken managed several non-League sides in Wales after ending his playing days before taking a job with Ford Motors, in Daventry, until his retirement in 1995.

# NEIL LENNON

*Born:*                 25 June 1971, Lurgan, Northern Ireland.

## Leicester City record:

*Appearances:*   League 170, FA Cup 8, League Cup 23, Other 7.
*Goals:*            League 6, FA Cup 0, League Cup 3, Other 0.
*Debut:*            24 February 1996 v Reading (a) drew 1–1.
*Also played for:* Manchester City, Crewe Alexandra, Glasgow Celtic, Nottingham
                Forest, Wycombe Wanderers, Northern Ireland (39 caps).
*Managed:*        Glasgow Celtic.

It says much for the esteem in which Neil Lennon was held within the game that when Martin O'Neill left Leicester City to take over as manager of Glasgow Celtic, he returned to his former club to persuade Neil to join him at Parkhead.

The transfer meant that Neil's Leicester career had gone full circle because he had been Martin's first Filbert Street signing four years earlier. During a wonderfully consistent spell with the Foxes he played in a winning Play-off Final side, plus three League Cup Finals – two of which were won. No wonder he became a true City cult hero!

Neil had played junior football at home in Lurgan before being taken on as a trainee at Manchester City. Boyhood pal Gerry Taggart followed a similar route and both eventually ended up at Leicester City together. The young midfielder only made one senior appearance for the Maine Road club before being allowed to move to Crewe Alexandra on a free transfer.

Over the next five and a half years he learned his craft, benefiting from the sage guidance and wisdom of manager Dario Gradi. Regular visitors to Gresty Road could not help but be impressed by the rapidly-improving 'Lenny', and his status received a boost with his initial call-up to the full Northern Ireland side in 1994.

Neil helped Crewe to two promotions, but his career was put in doubt for a while after a serious back injury. Fully recovered, it was not long before he was ready to move up to the next level.

A fee of £750,000 was paid to the Railwaymen for Neil's services in February 1996 and within three months it looked a bargain as the new recruit helped his side to progress successfully through the end-of-season Play-offs, defeating Crystal Palace at Wembley to take their place in the Premiership.

Along with Muzzy Izzet and former Crewe teammate Robbie Savage, Neil became one third of the most talked about central midfield unit in the country. Each had their own carefully defined responsibilities but also enough all-round talent to cover each other when needed. 'Lenny' was

*'Lenny' was principally a defensive-minded player, always in the right place to extinguish an opposition threat and always capable of picking out the correct pass to release a colleague.*

principally a defensive-minded player, always in the right place to extinguish an opposition threat and always capable of picking out the correct pass to release a colleague.

In 1997, the League Cup Final win over Middlesbrough brought Neil the first major medal of his career, and he played in two more Finals in the same competition – losing to Spurs in 1999 and being on the winning team 12 months later against Tranmere Rovers.

Between these two Finals Neil had found himself to be the unwitting victim in a highly-publicised incident against Newcastle United. A challenge on Alan Shearer, close to the touchline, saw both men fall clumsily. The striker's boot caught 'Lenny' in the face but the former England player was cleared by the FA of any wrong-doing.

The softly-spoken Ulsterman was a firm favourite with the City supporters for his whole-hearted commitment and never-say-die attitude. Normally nugget-haired, he became even more of a noticeable figure after dying his locks bleach-blonde.

His relationship with his manager was close and it was no surprise when O'Neill identified the need to take him to Glasgow soon after he had swapped life in the East Midlands to take over at Celtic. Leicester's tears were soothed a little by the £5 million profit they had accrued on Neil.

Over the next six and a half years, 'Lenny' set about cementing his place as an all-time Hoops legend. He played in five SPL-winning seasons, won three Scottish Cups and two League Cups – as well as playing in the 2003 UEFA Cup Final defeat to Porto.

In January 2006, following the dismissal of Craig Levein, there were reports linking Neil with a return to Leicester City as player-manager, but although he went on record as saying he was flattered by the speculation, he declared himself happy at Celtic.

Neil's final act for the Glasgow club was to skipper them to the 2007 Cup Final victory over Dunfermline Athletic which clinched the double that season.

A return to the English game did materialise, with a short spell at Nottingham Forest and then an equally brief period at Wycombe Wanderers, before he got the opportunity to return to his beloved Celtic as a member of the coaching staff, and he began the 2009–10 season as the club's reserve-team manager. By the season's end he had succeeded Tony Mowbray as caretaker manager of the first team, and the position was officially handed to Neil on 9 June 2010.

# DANNY LIDDLE

*Born:*          17 February 1912, Borrowstouness (Bo'ness), West Midlothian.

*Died:*          9 June 1982, Wigston, Leicestershire.

## Leicester City record:

*Appearances:*     League 255, FA Cup 19, Other (wartime) 115.

*Goals:*          League 64, FA Cup 7, Other (wartime) 21.

*Debut:*         27 August 1932 v Sheffield United (h) drew 1–1.

*Also played for:*   Bo'ness, Wallyford Bluebell, East Fife, Mansfield Town, Scotland (3 caps).

During the summer of 1932 Leicester City manager Peter Hodge – so knowledgeable about the Scottish football scene – raided East Fife to snap up both of their wide players for a combined sum of £1,320. The proportion of that fee that went on right-winger Ted Lowery was not such good business, as he only played 14 times for the Foxes before heading south-west, initially on loan to Yeovil Town and then permanently to Torquay United. The other signing proved to be rather better value for money, however, because Danny Liddle's association with City lasted for 14 years; although the last six campaigns were during the restructured programmes put in place during World War Two.

He had arrived in the East Midlands as a Scottish international, having featured in recent matches against Austria, Italy and Switzerland (though he was unluckily never chosen again), and thus in doing he had become the first player from East Fife to gain such recognition.

Danny scored eight times in his first season, no mean feat considering that City remained in the nether regions of the First Division throughout, but he banged in half that tally in one game at the start of the new term.

*The Scot was becoming no stranger to the scoring charts himself, leading the pack again in 1934–35, but his 14 goals needed better support from his colleagues because the relegation noose hung around City's neck all season and ultimately could not be shaken off.*

On 28 August 1933, in front of a delighted Bank Holiday crowd at Filbert Street, Danny scored all four of City's goals in a 4–0 rout of Sheffield United – the side he had made his debut against 12 months earlier.

That season the short, nippy, left-footer was a permanent fixture in the side and top-scored with 14 goals, all but one of which came in the League. His other goal came at Millwall in an FA Cup run which was eventually halted at the semi-final stage, Portsmouth being just too strong on the day as they ran out 4–1 winners at St Andrew's. Of minor consolation to Danny was the part he played in setting up City's goal, converted by Arthur Lochhead.

The Scot was becoming no stranger to the scoring charts himself, leading the pack again in 1934–35, but his 14 goals needed better support from his colleagues because the relegation noose hung around City's neck all season and ultimately could not be shaken off.

Thankfully, it only took two years for the Second Division Championship trophy to be returned to the City boardroom (it had been won 12 years earlier) as Frank Womack's side lifted the title by just one point from runners-up Blackpool.

The arrival at the club of another natural left-winger, Eric Stubbs from Nottingham Forest, had resulted in Danny moving inside, and his link-up play, vision and keen eye for goal were utilised to good effect in a more centralised role.

His 250th League game for the club came away at Brentford on 1 April 1939, and not only was the 2–0 defeat a personal disappointment for Danny, but it also virtually condemned bottom-placed City to their second relegation of the decade.

The loss of their First Division status, although unwelcome, was but a side issue, as the world prepared for hostilities. At the start of the scheduled 1939–40 campaign Danny played in all three of City's opening League fixtures, but it was on the way home from the third – at West Ham United – that a black-out was enforced and war was declared the following day. The entire Football League programme was abandoned and the three fixtures that had been played were expunged from the record books.

For most of the conflict Danny remained in the Leicester area and was able to 'guest' for City in more than a century of matches, the highlight of which was success in the Midlands Cup Final, with victory over Walsall in May 1941.

Apart from his matches for City, Danny was very much in demand as a 'guest' player, and he appeared from time to time for the likes of Northampton Town, Notts County, Leicester City Police and Mansfield Town, and it was with the latter that Danny made one sole League appearance after the war before finally hanging up his boots for good and settling in the Leicester area.

In all competitions Danny played in a total of 389 matches for Leicester City – scoring 92 times – a very decent return on the investment shelled out to East Fife for his services!

# GARY LINEKER

*Born:*            30 November 1960, Leicester.

## Leicester City record:

*Appearances:*     League 194, FA Cup 13, League Cup 9.
*Goals:*           League 95, FA Cup 6, League Cup 2.
*Debut:*           1 January 1979 v Oldham Athletic (h) won 2–0.
*Also played for:* Everton, Barcelona (Spain), Tottenham Hotspur, Nagoya Grampus
                   Eight (Japan), England (80 caps).

If you were to ask almost anyone living in Britain to suggest a sports star who came from the city of Leicester then it is pretty much odds-on that they would respond with the name of Gary Lineker.

To a whole new generation Gary has become one of the most familiar faces on BBC Television. For many years he has been the host of the station's flagship football programme *Match of the Day*, although his boyish charm and easy-on-the-eye presenting style has enriched 'Auntie's' coverage of the Masters and The Open Golf Championships, as well as the Sports Personality of the Year Award.

Leicester City fans, however, particularly of a certain age, will view Gary differently from the articulate and likeable sports presenter he has become, because the home-town boy achieved iconic status as the definitive 'Fox-in-the-box'.

Having amassed a record-breaking 112 goals in just 32 matches for the Aylestone Park juniors side, Gary was on City's radar from an early age and graduated through their youth ranks before making his League debut on New Year's Day 1979.

With extreme pace as his closest friend, Gary was initially blooded wide on the right before his predatory instincts and goal-poaching qualities came to the fore in a more central striking position.

His first goal for the club came during his fourth outing, with a 1–0 winner away at Notts County in April 1979, and he experienced both promotion and relegation during the next two campaigns as he began to find his feet in the professional game.

Between 1981–82 and 1984–85 he was the club's leading marksman for four consecutive seasons – netting an incredible 96 goals during the period. He had appeared in City's FA Cup semi-final side

*Frequently he would be 'ribbed' for the amount of one-yard tap-ins he accumulated, but those doing so were ignoring his wonderful reading of the game and the anticipation that had got him into a scoring position in the first place.*

in the first of those campaigns and then helped plunder the goals that would guarantee a return to the top division.

Frequently he would be 'ribbed' for the amount of one-yard tap-ins he accumulated, but those doing so were ignoring his wonderful reading of the game and the anticipation that had got him into a scoring position in the first place.

Four League hat-tricks for City – against Carlisle United, Derby County, Notts County and Aston Villa – would ensure that his progress was being monitored at the highest of levels. A further one came against Burton Albion in the FA Cup, although the tie was ordered to be replayed after crowd trouble.

The striker was first capped against Scotland in May 1984 and the first seven of his overall total of 80 England appearances came as a City player. Having become only the sixth Fox to score a century of League goals for the club, Gary, who was out of contract, then joined Everton during the summer of 1985 for a fee set by tribunal at £800,000 plus a share of any future sale.

While his club career brought deserved success, both at home and abroad (he played and scored in an FA Cup Final for Everton, won the Spanish Cup and the European Cup-Winners' Cup while at Barcelona and then won an FA Cup-winners' medal with Spurs), his performances at international level both united and excited a nation at successive World Cup Finals.

His hat-trick against Poland at Mexico in 1986 revived England's hopes in that tournament and, although his clinical finish in the 'Hand of God' match against Argentina was not enough to take his side through, his six-goal haul earned him the Golden Boot as the leading marksman.

Four years later in Italy, Gary had coolly converted two late penalties to defeat Cameroon in the quarter-finals before playing a central role in one of the most vivid matches of all-time, the semi-final showdown against West Germany. The image of Gary drawing the manager's attention to the teary and distressed Paul Gascoigne (who had realised that his booking would keep him out of the Final should England get there) was replayed millions of times around the globe.

England's late equaliser in that match had been scored by Gary, but although the former Leicester man converted his own spot-kick England eventually lost out on penalties.

Following that tournament Gary took over as captain of the national team for the next two years but ended his own international goal tally on 48 – just one behind record-holder Sir Bobby Charlton. His playing days ended in Japan after a succession of toe injuries had marred his time there, but he returned to the UK to embark on a successful media career.

A former recipient of the FIFA Fair Play Award, in recognition for his never having been cautioned during his playing career, Gary was awarded the OBE in 1992 and given the 'Freedom of the City of Leicester' three years later. He was later inducted into football's Hall of Fame.

A wonderful servant and ambassador for his club, Gary Lineker is as much a part of Leicester as the River Soar, De Montfort University or Walkers Crisps!

# BRIAN LITTLE

*Born:*　　　　　25 November 1953, Newcastle-upon-Tyne.

## Leicester City record:
*Manager:*　　　　May 1991–November 1994.
*Played for:*　　　Aston Villa, England (1 cap).
*Also Managed:*　Wolverhampton Wanderers, Darlington, Aston Villa, Stoke City, West Bromwich Albion, Hull City, Tranmere Rovers, Wrexham, Gainsborough Trinity.

The old adage 'if at first you don't succeed, then try, try and try again' was never more apt than in Brian Little's quest to take Leicester City into the top flight.

Shrugging off the disappointment of failing to win automatic promotion with the Foxes, he twice had to endure the cruellest of hammer blows with defeat in Play-off Finals before eventually leading his gallant troops to glory.

Brian's own playing career had been spent solely at Aston Villa, where he had progressed through the youth ranks, winning an FA Youth Cup-winners' medal before advancing into the senior side, where he won League Cups in 1975 and 1977.

At the height of his career, and aged only 26, a persistent knee injury brought a highly promising career to a disappointingly early end. The inside-forward had made 247 appearances for Villa, scoring 60 times, and he had made one substitute appearance for the full England side.

He joined Villa's backroom staff as youth-team coach before joining Wolves, initially as first-team coach and then in overall charge after the dismissal of Sammy Chapman. With the club in financial strife Brian left to become coach at Middlesbrough, serving under Bruce Rioch.

In 1989 he was persuaded to become manager of Darlington, who were bottom of the Football League at the time. Although they were already in a downward spiral and were relegated into the Conference, they bounced back at the first time of asking under Brian's stewardship. There was more success with the capturing of the Fourth Division title, and understandably their manager was being fêted for his achievements.

One of his admirers was Leicester City chairman Martin George, and in May 1991 he not only identified Brian as the man to lead the Foxes out of their second tier misery, but he was also able to prise him away from Feethams.

Brian almost succeeded in leading City into the top division at the first time of asking. In the first half of the season they led the table and looked good value for one of the automatic promotion slots, but they fell away after Christmas and had to be content with a final finishing position of fourth and a place in the end-of-season Play-offs. They overcame Cambridge United in the two-legged semi-final to advance through to Wembley Stadium, where Kenny Dalglish's Blackburn Rovers lay in wait. A desperately poor affair went the way of the Lancashire side thanks to a hotly-contested penalty, converted against his old club by former Fox Mike Newell.

Having come so close, it was bitterly cruel on City, but Brian ensured they regrouped and acquitted themselves equally well, and they found themselves back in a similar situation at the end of the following season.

This time it was Portsmouth who were defeated in the semi-finals and then Swindon Town who were the opponents in the Final. In the cruellest twist of fate, another controversial spot-kick turned the day out at Wembley into another huge anti-climax, especially after City had come back from a three-goal deficit to draw level, only to eventually lose 4—3.

Fortunately the City board backed their manager – after all, only severe misfortune had stood in the way of Brian leading his team to promotion in two successive seasons.

The softy-spoken Geordie, ably assisted by his two lieutenants, John Gregory and Allan Evans, galvanised City into a third Herculean effort to get out of the division in 1993–94, but again they finished fourth, which meant that familiar well-trodden route had to be faced once again.

Brian showed a touch of compassion before the Wembley Final, inviting injured skipper Gary Mills to lead out the side on their big day – and it really did become third time lucky as City shrugged off the hammer blow of going one down to Midland rivals Derby County before bouncing back to win thanks to two goals from Steve Walsh.

Having brought the new shiny Premiership to Leicester for the first time, it seemed that Brian could do no wrong in the eyes of the Blue Army; however, that theory was quickly disproved when he resigned from his post, only to take over immediately at Aston Villa, the club he had served with such distinction as a player.

There was an acute sense of dejection at City; although the lure provided by Brian's affiliation with Villa was partially understandable. Although he led his new charges to League Cup glory in 1996, he could not recapture their former glories and left two years later.

Always in demand, Brian has since managed (with varying degrees of success) Stoke City, West Bromwich Albion, Hull City, Tranmere Rovers and Wrexham.

In September 2009 he was appointed as boss at Blue Square North side Gainsborough Trinity, who were hoping that – if nothing else – their new manager still retained the same determination to get the job done – however many attempts were needed!

*The softy-spoken Geordie, ably assisted by his two lieutenants, John Gregory and Allan Evans, galvanised City into a third Herculean effort to get out of the division in 1993–94, but again they finished fourth, which meant that familiar well-trodden route had to be faced once again.*

# ARTHUR LOCHHEAD

*Born:* 8 December 1897, Busby, East Renfrewshire.

*Died:* 30 December 1966, Edinburgh.

## Leicester City record:

*Appearances:* League 303, FA Cup 17.

*Goals:* League 106, FA Cup 8.

*Debut:* 17 October 1925 v West Bromwich Albion (h) won 3–0.

*Managed:* October 1934–October 1936.

*Also played for:* Heart of Midlothian, Clyde (loan), Manchester United.

Arthur William Lochhead is a member of two very small and select bands connected with Leicester City. His tally of 114 goals for the club puts him alongside Chandler, Rowley, Hine, Hines and Lineker as those who have scored more than a century of goals, and he is also one of just a handful who have both played for and been full-time manager – joining the likes of Frank Gardner, Johnny Duncan, Matt Gillies and Frank McLintock.

He became 'boss' in tragic circumstances, though, with the club still reeling from the sudden death of their influential manager Peter Hodge, the man who had signed Arthur nine years earlier. As a senior pro, approaching the end of his playing days, the Scot was considered the most suitable successor.

Hodge had parted with City's highest-ever transfer fee to sign the inside-forward from Manchester United but considered that the £3,300 asking price was good value, a judgement based on first-hand experience as Arthur had netted twice in a 3–2 win over the Foxes less than a month earlier. There was to be no 'first night nerves' either as Arthur was blooded straight into City's side and triumphantly added another couple of goals in a 3–0 pounding of West Bromwich Albion.

A clever link-up player, with a keen eye for goal himself, Arthur had joined a club that were clearly in the ascendancy and it seemed to be only a matter of time before silverware would be brought to Leicester. Those thoughts were temporarily stalled when Hodge resigned to take over at Manchester City, but early in the new campaign, under his successor Willie Orr, the Filberts briefly took over at the summit of Division One.

Alas, the momentum could not be maintained and the season petered out a little with a final placing of seventh, but hopes remained high that success might be just around the corner.

Arthur had begun his career with Hearts and had displayed such early promise that he had warranted selection for one of the Scottish trial fixtures, playing for the Home Scots against the Anglo-Scots in March 1920. It says much of Scotland's strength in depth and also their small programme of fixtures that he was not called-up again; although many years later, during his peak years at Leicester, he was invited to participate in another trial.

During his time with Hearts – and for a long time afterwards – he was fêted for scoring the winner at Parkhead in a Scottish Cup quarter-final triumph over Celtic. The euphoria of victory was soon deflated with a semi-final defeat against Partick Thistle.

His popularity at Tynecastle ensured there would be something of an outcry when the Hearts board decided to use him as bait in a swap-deal to sign Tom Miller from Manchester United. Although he was a Scottish international, Miller was considered to be past his prime by many and his value of £2,850 – and Arthur's of £2,300 – meant that United were felt to have got the better end of the bargain, and so it proved as Arthur netted 50 goals in 153 appearances for the Old Trafford club.

His arrival at Leicester coincided with the club's best-ever League positioning – third in 1927–28 and then one place better at the end of the next campaign. For a predominantly left-sided inside-forward, Arthur had a phenomenal goal output, reaching double figures in each of his first eight seasons at City.

During the ninth (1933–34 ) there was more heartbreak for the Leicester faithful as they fell just short of a first-ever trip to Wembley. Arthur had scored in earlier rounds against Lincoln City and Millwall, and by 17 March only Portsmouth stood in the way of a place in the FA Cup Final.

Six years earlier Arthur had been part of the City side that had routed Pompey 10–0 to create a new record League victory – now the south coast side relished their moment of revenge, subjecting a dispirited Leicester side to a 4–1 defeat. Even Arthur's cool finish, after a sweeping move involving Archie Gardiner and Danny Liddle which brought the scoreline back to 2–1, was scant consolation.

Peter Hodge had returned to the Filbert Street hot seat in 1932, but despite the Cup run he was aware that his aging side were on the wane and needed bolstering. He took those thoughts on his summer sojourn back to Scotland but sadly did not return, falling ill and then passing away.

Arthur was one of the City contingency that attended the funeral, and, indeed, he acted as a pall-bearer. He played four more times for the club then was approached by the board to take over the managerial reins.

His new charges were under-prepared and ill-equipped for the battle that lay ahead and relegation ended City's 10-year stay in the highest division. A respectable sixth-place finish in 1935–36 was not enough to prevent Arthur from handing in his resignation in October 1936.

He returned to Edinburgh – and turned his back on football – but his achievements had cemented his name in the Leicester City record books forever.

*His arrival at Leicester coincided with the club's best-ever League positioning – third in 1927–28 and then one place better at the end of the next campaign. For a predominantly left-sided inside-forward, Arthur had a phenomenal goal output, reaching double figures in each of his first eight seasons at City.*

# STEVE LYNEX

*Born:*          23 January 1958, West Bromwich, West Midlands.

## Leicester City record:
*Appearances:*   League 213, FA Cup 12, League Cup 15.
*Goals:*         League 57, FA Cup 1, League Cup 2.
*Debut:*         14 February 1981 v Sunderland (a) lost 0–1.
*Also played for:* Sandwell Rangers, West Bromwich Albion, Sligo Rovers, Shamrock Rovers, Birmingham City, Cardiff City, Telford United, Mitchells & Butlers.

Steve Lynex was a uniquely thrilling wide player in the City side of the early 1980s. Quick, tricky and a difficult proposition for any opposing defender, he had spent time playing in Ireland before Jock Wallace pounced to bring him to Filbert Street.

'I had just started to break into the Birmingham City side and had scored a few important goals, but I was being used mainly just as a "super-sub". One day I was told that Leicester were interested in signing me, and straight away Jock sold me on the club.'

Following a defeat at Sunderland and a win at Spurs, where Steve scored his first goal for the club, there came a home debut which he will never forget: 'It was against Nottingham Forest – there was a terrific atmosphere, and I managed to score. The ball was knocked over the top of the defender, I just ran on to it and slid it past Peter Shilton. It was a great start for me at a new club, and it obviously helped my relationship with the fans.'

The following season, with City back in the second tier after relegation, Steve played in every game bar one and scored 10 goals in the League. It was a campaign, however, that is best remembered for the club's exploits in the FA Cup, where they reached the last four after eventually overcoming the spirited resistance posed by Shrewsbury in the sixth round. Although the tie was finally won 5–2, nerves were jangling when City lost their 'keeper through injury.

'I'd often go in goal during training and have a bit of a go, but when Mark Wallington went off they decided to put Alan Young between the sticks – mainly because of his size. Then he got a knock on the head so Jock told me to get the gloves off him and go in goal. I played there for about 15 minutes while Alan cleared his head and thankfully kept a clean sheet in that time and made one decent save where I tipped it over. I told everyone to look out for that save on *Match of the Day*, but they edited it out!'

The highs of that afternoon were soon forgotten as Spurs ended the dream at the semi-final stage. 'It was a disappointing day for everybody – we just didn't perform and, of course, Tommy Williams broke his leg. It was a shame because we'd done well to get there, and the fans were really up for it.'

The same Tommy Williams is allegedly responsible for Steve's Leicester nickname. 'They all reckoned I looked to be squinting on team photos and I had a little handlebar moustache at the time, so Tommy started calling me "Charlie Chang" because of it – they all cottoned on, and it was "Charlie" from then on.'

A third-place finish in 1983 was enough to seal promotion back into the top division, and for Steve came an afternoon that he will never forget – a 6–0 home win against Carlisle United. 'I scored a hat-trick of penalties that day. At 5–0 we were awarded another one, but as Gary Lineker had scored the other two goals he took the final spot-kick to get his hat-trick as well. I was told later, though, that nobody has ever scored four penalties in the same League match.'

Although Steve did not mind missing out on the chance to be a record-breaker, he would have liked the match-ball. 'Gary got it – and they gave me the spare ball. I've still got it, though – a memento of my only League hat-trick!'

*Although Steve did not mind missing out on the chance to be a record-breaker, he would have liked the match-ball. 'Gary got it – and they gave me the spare ball. I've still got it, though – a memento of my only League hat-trick!'*

Scoring penalties was almost second-nature for Steve; 23 of his 57 League goals came via that route. 'I scored 21 in succession, then slid one wide against Luton. I always hit it low and hard, to the 'keeper's left if I could.'

Penalties aside, there is one strike from open play that he fondly recalls. 'It was against Liverpool in a thrilling 3–3 match. I hit it right-footed past Bruce Grobbelaar from just outside the box – that is probably my favourite City goal.'

The 1983–84 season was perhaps Steve's finest in a City shirt, and it culminated in him winning the Player of the Year award, although he remembers the shock at finding out the news: 'It was a terrific honour because we all thought Gary Lineker was going to win it. I chose to pop to the toilet at the exact moment they announced that I'd won, and when I came out – believing that Gary had got it – I just blurted out, "The best man won it." It was very embarrassing when I realised what had happened.'

There is one less happy memory of that season, however, the home draw against Manchester United. 'They thought for some reason I should stand in front of one of their defenders at corners, and as the ball came across there was the inevitable contact and my tooth disappeared onto the Filbert Street turf – gone forever!'

Steve admits that being blessed with great pace helped his rapport with the fans. 'I was a speed merchant – that was clearly my best asset – I played inside a few times but really did prefer playing wide on the flank, and I consider myself to be lucky because the supporters always seemed to appreciate what I was doing and were fantastic towards me.'

# KEVIN MACDONALD

*Born:*          22 November 1960, Inverness, Scotland.

## Leicester City record:
*Appearances:*     League 141, FA Cup 4, League Cup 10.
*Goals:*          League 8, FA Cup 0, League Cup 0.
*Debut:*          29 November 1980 v Norwich City (h) lost 1–2.
*Caretaker manager:* 22 November 1994 – 14 December 1994.
*Also played for:*  Inverness Caledonian, Liverpool, Glasgow Rangers (loan), Coventry City, Cardiff City (loan), Walsall.

Kevin MacDonald proved that there are real nuggets to be found within the non-League game. From the honest endeavour of the Highland League to the lofty branches of the English domestic tree he took it all in his stride and developed into one of the most sought-after midfielders in the game.

'I was playing part-time in Inverness and working for the Civil Service', says Kevin. 'There were a few rumours that clubs were looking at me, but then Leicester came in with a decent bid, and I signed straight away.'

It says much of Kevin's maturity, as well as his undoubted ability, that he was able to handle the step up almost immediately. 'I'd had a brief substitute's appearance and then played at Birmingham City. The next match was my full home debut against Middlesbrough, and after about seven or eight minutes we were awarded a penalty.'

With regular taker Alan Young out injured Kevin stepped forward to show he was prepared to accept whatever responsibility was thrown his way. 'I used to take penalties at Inverness and wanted to try my luck. I was a confident lad and wanted to repay Jock Wallace for having sufficient faith to sign me – and fortunately I scored!'

The club suffered the disappointment of relegation at the end of Kevin's first season, but a march to the FA Cup semi-finals the following year brought some cheer to the beleagured Foxes; although it did not work out too well for the young Scot. 'At the start of the Cup run Jock decided to play Andy Peake, Eddie Kelly and Ian Wilson in the middle of the park. I was coming back in for all the League matches and playing some decent stuff, but as with most managers once they try something

*'I used to take penalties at Inverness and wanted to try my luck. I was a confident lad and wanted to repay Jock Wallace for having sufficient faith to sign me – and fortunately I scored!'*

and it works they tend to stick to the tried and tested.'

Sitting on the outside as City advanced to within 90 minutes of Wembley could not have been easy for any ambitious player desperate to make his own mark in the game. 'I was disappointed for myself, but it was the manager's prerogative and there was no animosity from me about the selection. We were a tight group and all pulled together.'

Kevin's combative style was winning him lots of admirers – both within the game and on the terraces. 'I was a competitive player – I suppose that comes from my Scottish genes. I always wanted to win, whether it was in training or in a match.'

Asked to assess his worth to a side, Kevin is slightly reticent. 'I had good energy and liked to get from box to box. If anything I lacked a little bit of pace, but it is hard to say what my qualities were – I've always said self-praise is no praise!'

Once Gordon Milne had succeeded Jock Wallace as Leicester boss he installed Kevin as the club captain. 'I was always a very vociferous player – whether I was captain or not – but it was a great honour for me to be made Leicester captain. It filled me with a lot of pride.'

Although 'Mac' was clearly at his best in the middle of the park he was asked to adapt to a new role in the run-in towards the end of the 1982–83 season. 'When Larry May got injured I filled in at centre-half for the last nine or 10 games of the season – I enjoyed it and we had a great run which helped to clinch promotion.'

It was during his stint at the back that Kevin scored his favourite City goal. 'It was against Sheffield Wednesday at Hillsborough in a match that finished 2–2. I got the ball on the edge of our own box and played a couple of one-twos and made my way right down the pitch and into their box then "mis-hit it" into the top corner. Perhaps the biggest criticism of my game was that I did not score enough goals, but I enjoyed that one!'

A £400,000 move to Liverpool brought in some much-needed revenue for City and gave Kevin the chance to test himself with one of the top sides in the country. 'I heard a year or so later that Gordon had been told that he had to sell either me or Gary Lineker and his thinking was that Gary might get enough goals to keep us up. If I'd known I'd have wanted to go anyway – it was always a dream to challenge myself at the very highest level, although I was a little disappointed to leave behind a good group of players who I thought were on the verge of going on to do good things.'

Kevin briefly returned to City on loan in 1987–88 as he looked to recover his sharpness after a broken leg. 'I didn't play particularly well and think it was too early in my rehabilitation, but that is what happened.'

He later returned to the club as a coach under Brian Little and even took over the reins as caretaker boss for a brief period between managerial appointments.

'I'll always have a great affinity for Leicester City – I started my playing career there, and I started my coaching career there, so it's a club that are close to my heart, and I always like to see them doing well.'

# GARY McALLISTER

Born:                25 December 1964, Motherwell, Lanarkshire.

**Leicester City record:**

Appearances:    League 201, FA Cup 5, League Cup 15, Other 4.

Goals:              League 47, FA Cup 2, League Cup 3, Other 0.

Debut:              28 September 1985 v Ipswich Town (h) won 1–0.

Also played for:  Fir Park Boys' Club, Motherwell, Leeds United, Liverpool, Coventry City, Scotland (57 caps).

Managed:         Coventry City, Leeds United.


Very few midfielders have brought the Blue Army to their feet in the way that Gary McAllister did. A true 'Rolls Royce' of a footballer, the Scot possessed elegance and sophistication in abundance and could drop a pass on a sixpence.

He began in the professional game with his home-town club Motherwell, and he scored eight times in 70 first-team appearances for them before joining Leicester City as part of the £250,000 deal that also brought the more experienced Ali Mauchlen to Filbert Street.

Quickly settling into the rarefied air of the First Division, Gary showed himself equally adaptable in both a central midfield berth or wide on either flank. His temperament was matched only by his acute vision. The ability to spot a pass created openings aplenty – particularly for Alan Smith, whose goal output increased significantly with 'Macca' in the side.

Gary also became the club's deadball expert, and after demonstrating his worth with corners and free-kicks, he succeeded Steve Lynex as the first choice penalty-taker.

To the fans he was 'Super-Mac', but to those in the game he was known as 'the Enforcer', a moniker that remained with him throughout his career.

Late in his second season with the Foxes (1986–87), Gary's first Scottish call-up became something of a mixed blessing. A scoring debut for

*Quickly settling into the rarefied air of the First Division, Gary showed himself equally adaptable in both a central midfield berth or wide on either flank. His temperament was matched only by his acute vision. The ability to spot a pass created openings aplenty – particularly for Alan Smith, whose goal output increased significantly with 'Macca' in the side.*

the B team against France B ended early due to injury – a blow that would ultimately see him miss the final three games of his club season. Hindsight is a wonderful thing, but had the playmaker been available perhaps City would not have gone down. (Charlton Athletic survived by a margin of just two points.)

Inspirational to those around him, 'Macca' was good for the development of City's younger pros, but nearing the peak of his own career it was clear that he needed to be playing at the highest level to fulfil his own potential.

In a wonderfully consistent three-year stretch he scored 31 goals in 131 League matches – no wonder the top-flight scouts and the Scottish selectors were regularly in attendance at Filbert Street.

His first three Scottish caps came while he was still a Fox – and he was selected for the 1990 World Cup Finals squad (although he did not play).

After five years at City – and having rejected various overtures from other clubs – Gary signed for Leeds United for a fee of £1 million. The Elland Road club finished fourth in his first season with them before being crowned champions of England in 1991–92.

The midfield maestro enhanced his reputation with several seasons of consistent form and took over the captain's armband, leading his side to the 1996 League Cup Final, as well as skippering Scotland during that summer's European Championships.

Six years at Leeds ended with a £3 million transfer to Coventry City, where Gary played under Ron Atkinson and then his old Leeds teammate Gordon Strachan.

At the age of 35 – when many players are looking to wind down their careers – 'Macca' was surprisingly snapped up by Liverpool, who then proceeded to enjoy one of their most successful campaigns of knock-out football ever. With Gary to the fore, they defeated Birmingham City in the League Cup Final, Arsenal in the FA Cup Final and then beat Alaves of Spain to seal a memorable UEFA Cup triumph. In the Reds' 5–4 win, the Scot collected the Man of the Match award for a five star performance.

He also scored a goal in the Charity Shield win, played his part in the European Super Cup victory over Bayern Munich and achieved hero status on the red half of Merseyside for a memorable 40-yard free-kick winner in the derby against Everton. Rather than accepting a golden clock on retirement, Gary had lifted a sack full of medals in the final two years of his career and earned lifetime status as an Anfield legend.

He was awarded the MBE in the New Year's Honours List in 2001 in recognition for his services to the sport and then moved into management, serving at two of the clubs where he had performed so admirably as a player – Coventry City and Leeds United.

Gary McAllister was a shining diamond of a footballer, and his ability to spray the ball around with pinpoint accuracy over any distance, short or long, made many a fan stand open-mouthed in admiration. Selected 57 times for his country, he deservedly has been inducted into the Scotland Hall of Fame.

# FRANK McLINTOCK

*Born:*            28 December 1939, Glasgow.

## Leicester City record:
*Appearances:*     League 168, FA Cup 20, League Cup 11, Other 1.
*Goals:*           League 25, FA Cup 0, League Cup 3, Other 0.
*Debut:*           14 September 1959 v Blackpool (a) drew 3–3.
*Manager:*         July 1977–April 1978.
*Also played for:* Shawfield Juniors, Arsenal, Queen's Park Rangers, Scotland (9 caps).
*Also managed:*    Brentford.


One of the truly outstanding players of his generation was Frank McLintock, an athletic Scot brought down to Filbert Street at an early age and who went on to appear in two FA Cup Finals for City before going on to achieve phenomenal success at Arsenal.

'I was just 16 when I was invited down to Leicester for a trial', recalls Frank. 'I'd been playing as a wing-half in Scotland and had been spotted by the club's scout there, Walter McLean. I thought I'd played terribly – everyone was just shouting all the time, "Man On" and that sort of stuff. But I must have done OK because they wanted me, and I signed on my 17th birthday. My mother thought I'd be back straight away, but I was given digs at Broadgate Park and just loved Leicester. It wasn't like being in Glasgow or one of the other big cities where there are several teams.'

According to Frank, acclimatisation was made much easier by the people he had to work for. 'As a young player you couldn't wish to meet two nicer people than Matt Gillies or Bert Johnson. They didn't try and over-complicate things but just let you go out and express yourself. I also formed a friendship with Davie Gibson, a fellow Scot, that has remained true to this day.'

Frank's debut match was fairly extraordinary in itself – a 3–3 draw away at Blackpool. 'There were one or two who thought I wasn't quite ready for the first team, and I thought, "I'll show you" and went out, and everyone said I was Man of the Match. It was before substitutes were introduced and Blackpool lost a player through injury. It was the guy I was supposed to be marking, and after he went off I was a little unsure of where I should be, but overall I was pleased with that and the first few games in general.'

Athletically-built and with a solid all-round game, Frank became a permanent fixture in the Foxes ranks and provided some versatility with his ability and awareness. 'I was basically a midfield player but capable of making forward runs or coming back to cover defensively, and almost by accident they hit upon the idea of myself and Graham Cross switching positions during games. It was quite innovative then, and we were a good foil for each other. It fooled many of the teams we came up against.'

City established themselves as redoubtable Cup opponents during Frank's time at the club, reaching two Wembley FA Cup Finals. 'In 1961 against Spurs we were a little unlucky, having to play with 10 men for much of the match. I thought we played really well before collapsing in the final few minutes. In 1963 we just didn't perform and deserved to be beaten.'

Aside from his two FA Cup runners'-up medals Frank should also have picked up some League Cup silverware. Having scored in both legs of the semi-final victory over West Ham in 1964 he missed the Final against Stoke City due to injury.

Frank was always likely to pop up with a vital

> *"I'll step over it and you dummy it etc" – but I told him to stop over-elaborating. "Just pass it to the side of me," I said. He did, and I smashed it into the net!'*

score, but he recalls a fairly simple free-kick routine as being one of his most memorable Foxes goals. 'It was against Wolves and we'd been awarded an indirect free-kick inside the box, just seven or eight yards out. Davie Gibson was always full of tricks, and he was planning all sorts – "I'll step over it and you dummy it etc" – but I told him to stop over-elaborating. "Just pass it to the side of me," I said. He did, and I smashed it into the net!'

The clamour to sign Frank intensified and, although they were not keen to let him go, the Foxes board realised that they could not stand in his way when the chance came for him to join Arsenal.

'I have every respect for the chairman Mr Needham and his family, for the way they ran that football club. They let me go reluctantly because they knew I was ambitious, and it wasn't about the money.'

Frank went on to enjoy great success at Highbury, having been totally converted into a central-defender. He skippered the Gunners to the League and FA Cup double in 1971, as well as to an Inter-Cities Fairs Cup success earlier and took his total of full Scottish international appearances to nine – the first three of which had been won during his time at Leicester. The former Fox won the Footballer of the Year award in 1971 and was awarded the MBE a year later.

Once Frank's playing days were over he turned his hand to management and returned to Filbert Street for a short, unsuccessful stint. 'It was the most disappointing time of my sporting life,' Frank admits. 'I'd had great success there as a player, but it was the wrong job at the wrong time.'

A popular media pundit and after-dinner speaker, Frank remains hugely involved in the game and was inducted into Football's Hall of Fame in 2009.

# IAN MARSHALL

**Born:**              20 March 1966, Liverpool, Merseyside.

## Leicester City record:
*Appearances:*    League 83, FA Cup 8, League Cup 6, Other 2.
*Goals:*              League 18, FA Cup 3, League Cup 4, Other 1.
*Debut:*              22 September 1996 v Tottenham Hotspur (a) won 2–1.
*Also played for:*  Everton, Oldham Athletic, Ipswich Town, Bolton Wanderers, Blackpool.

Instantly recognisable with his flowing locks and stylish sideburns, Ian Marshall became one of the real characters of the game during the 1990s, but City fans, quite rightly, recall him as being an integral part of the Martin O'Neill squad that so successfully mixed it with the Premiership big boys.

A fee of £800,000 was needed to prise him away from his third professional club, Ipswich Town, but Ian admits to having some doubts about the transfer. 'To be honest, at first I didn't really want to leave Ipswich, but I was starting to get pushed out because they needed the money and I was considered an "asset", but when I met up with Martin he sold me on the idea – but at the time it was still a big decision for me to make the move.'

Any reservations soon evaporated when Ian got off to the best possible start, making an immediate impact for his new club. 'I came on as sub for the injured Steve Claridge in a match against Spurs at White Hart Lane. The score was 1–1 when I got my head on a late corner to grab the winner.'

One of the most memorable matches of Ian's career came on 22 February 1997 at home to Derby County. City trailed early on – yet by the break they led 3–1 on the way to a 4–2 victory, and Ian had bagged all three of those first-half goals. 'I only scored two hat-tricks in my whole career, so that was a very special occasion. I can remember feeling under the weather before the game, and we had a few players missing – but what a tonic.'

Shortly afterwards came an even more significant moment in City's history and Ian had to sit it out, unfortunately. 'I'd played for Ipswich in the first round of the League Cup back in early August, so I was Cup-tied for Leicester's run to the Final. I remember that Matty Elliott was also Cup-tied, but Martin used to take us to the away games as part of the squad and we would have a great night out afterwards.'

One spin-off of the Cup win was a place in the UEFA Cup, City's first foray into major European competition since 1961–62. Incredibly, the same opposition that ended their participation back then, Atletico Madrid, were paired with the Foxes. Ian's 11th-minute strike in the Spanish capital opened the scoring in the tie, but the more experienced European competitors rallied to knock City out 4–1 on aggregate.

*'I always liked playing up front. It was the main reason I left Oldham Athletic, earlier in my career, because Joe Royle preferred me in defence and said that I would have played for England if I'd stayed as a centre-back. If you've ever scored a goal, though, there's no better feeling!'*

Closer to home, Ian's earlier hat-trick would still have been fresh in the minds of the Derby defenders when Leicester travelled there on 26 April 1998 – but by the time he had scored City's fourth the Rams had other worries! 'It was an unbelievable game – and I know our fans absolutely loved it. It was pretty much all over after 15 minutes with us leading 4–0. For some reason I had a pretty good scoring record against them throughout my career.'

Although Ian began his career as an apprentice at Everton, he had grown up as a Liverpool fan – he therefore has no hesitation in nominating his favourite Leicester goal – a last-minute winner at Anfield. 'It was probably my career highlight – scoring against my boyhood heroes, and it was a great strike as well. I'd always dreamed of scoring a goal at the Kop End. I didn't ever realise that I would go on to do it for a different team though!'

Ian's versatility – and prowess in the air – meant that he was equally adaptable in defence or in attack, but given the choice it is clear which position he favoured. 'I always liked playing up front. It was the main reason I left Oldham Athletic, earlier in my career, because Joe Royle preferred me in defence and said that I would have played for England if I'd stayed as a centre-back. If you've ever scored a goal, though, there's no better feeling!'

Having scored twice in an epic League Cup quarter-final tie against Fulham, which eventually was won on penalty-kicks, Ian sustained an injury in the next game which ruled him out for six weeks. His return came in the closing stages of the Final, against Tranmere Rovers at Wembley. 'It was such a shame to get injured when I did, but I still have good memories of the part I played – it was a great occasion.'

Nicknamed 'Marsh' or 'Marshy' by his teammates ('they are the ones you can print!'), the charismatic and likeable Scouser says with hindsight he could have stayed at Leicester a little longer. 'Martin O'Neill let me go, but sadly only a few days later he left to go to Glasgow Celtic, so in hindsight he could have given me another year.'

Ian moved to Canada after his playing days had come to a natural conclusion and began running Soccer Camps. For a while he ran a restaurant: 'It was easier marking Tony Adams or Jaap Stam!'

Marshy looks back on his time at Filbert Street with great affection. 'Martin built a team with great spirit and determination, and there was a great camaraderie in the dressing room that I don't think you find in the game these days.'

# ALI MAUCHLEN

*Born:*              29 June 1960, Kilwinning, Scotland.

## Leicester City record:

*Appearances:*    League 239, FA Cup 7, League Cup 18, Other 9.
*Goals:*          League 11, FA Cup 0, League Cup 1, Other 0.
*Debut:*          24 August 1985 v Oxford United (a) lost 0–5.
*Also played for:*  Irvine Meadow, Kilmarnock, Motherwell, Leeds United, Heart of
                    Midlothian, Glenavon, Ballymena United (both Northern Ireland).

When Ali Mauchlen ventured south to join Leicester City in 1985 he can have had little thought that a quarter of a century later he would be as much a part of the club as the *Post Horn Gallop*. Like so many who have worn the blue jersey, he simply fell in love with the Foxes and their supporters, and he has complemented his years of sterling play with a driven passion to uphold their heritage.

Without complaint, on his arrival he reverted to a less-favourable full-back position – and skippered the side through some of their darkest times – but throughout his career he was the very embodiment of 100 per cent commitment, and displaying such passion to the cause it was no wonder the fans adored him.

Alister Henry Mauchlen began his professional career with Kilmarnock but first began to make his mark in the game after moving to join former City boss Jock Wallace at Motherwell.

The fiery midfield ball-winner was instrumental in helping the Fir Park club to the First Division title in 1984–85, as well as extending Celtic to a replay in the Scottish Cup semi-final.

In October of that year he was the experienced half of the joint deal which also brought Gary McAllister to Filbert Street – and he made his debut in far from idyllic circumstances, coming on as a late substitute in a trouncing away at Oxford United. Ironically, it was against the same opposition that he played in one of his most important games for City in May 1991. The 1–0 win over the U's that day prevented a first-ever drop into the third tier of the English domestic game (although that fate did eventually arrive at the end of the 2007–08 season).

A week after his debut, Ali made his first start for the Foxes – playing out of position, at left-back, away at Arsenal. For the remainder of that initial term he was back in a more familiar area of the pitch – wearing number 10 and occupying the centre of the park, where his snappy, tidying up duties, just in front of the back four, blunted many an opposition attack.

His role, and associated defensive responsibilities, dictated that Ali was never going to be a regular goalscorer, but his two strikes that season were vital. He helped secure a point away at Chelsea and on the final day he hit the first in the 2–0 win over Newcastle United that effectively kept City up.

The drop was only postponed for 12 months, however, and in the second tier boss David Pleat chose to utilise Ali's pace and intuition as an emergency right-back. His willingness to get forward added a new dimension to his play, and his overlaps helped create a significant number of opportunities for the front men.

Ali became a senior figure within the side and assumed not only the captaincy for a while but also the responsibility of a player-coach role during Gordon Lee's tenure.

His 'tache bristling with pride every time he stepped onto the field of play, it was evident how much representing City meant to him. Some footballers are often quoted as saying 'they'd play for nothing' – with Ali you felt he meant it!

After seven fully driven campaigns, Brian Little allowed him to join Leeds United on loan towards the end of the 1991–92 season; although he did not feature in any first-team action for the Elland Road club (who were on their way to clinching the League title), and a free transfer to Hearts was completed during the summer months.

In October 1993 Ali joined Glenavon, helping the Northern Ireland side to their most successful season in 34 years – but for two late goals conceded in the final game they would have been crowned champions. Ali briefly took over as caretaker manager during the following term before embarking on a short stint at Ballymena United.

Back in the East Midlands, Ali remains very much involved with his beloved Foxes. He became chairman of the ex-Leicester City Players' Association, after helping form it in 2004, and has sacrificed much of his own time to bring together past teammates to attend social functions, play in charity fixtures or publicise good causes. He has successfully skippered the City Masters side for many years and twice they have claimed national titles, as well as winning their fifth straight regional crown in 2009.

His forthright and incisive opinions on City's fortunes and the game in general, whether as a matchday summariser or as a 'phone-in' panellist, has helped him become a popular and much-valued member of BBC Radio Leicester's sports coverage.

Always keen to promote football in the region, Ali has also thrown his weight behind the move to bring the World Cup to the Walkers Stadium, should England's bid to host the 2018 games prove successful.

# GARY MILLS

*Born:*           11 November 1961, Northampton.

## Leicester City record:

*Appearances:*   League 200, FA Cup 7, League Cup 10, Other 15.

*Goals:*           League 16, FA Cup 0, League Cup 1, Other 0.

*Debut:*           4 March 1989 v Walsall (h) won 1–0.

*Also played for:*   Nottingham Forest, Seattle Sounders (USA), Derby County (loan), Notts County, Grantham Town, Gresley Rovers, Boston United, Tamworth, Glapwell.

*Managed:*      Grantham Town, Kings Lynn, Notts County, Tamworth, Alfreton Town.

Gary Mills became an iconic figure during his five-year term at Filbert Street – the former European Cup winner twice won City's Player of the Year award as well as amassing a club record number of appearances for a single season!

Apart from a brief stint in the North American Soccer League and a short loan spell at Derby County, Gary had played all of his professional football in Nottingham – initially with Forest and then at Notts County – and he admits that the prospect of staying fairly local was a decisive factor in his move to Leicester 'I'd spoken to a couple of other clubs, but they were further afield, and I didn't want to be driving an hour and a half each way into training each day – it just felt right to go to Leicester, and I've never regretted it.'

Capable of playing in a variety of roles, either across the back or in midfield, Gary enjoyed the role he was given by his new manager. 'Brian Little liked to play with wing-backs, and that suited me as I liked to defend and I liked to get forward.'

The Play-off trilogy between 1992–94 would seem from the outside to be a work of fiction but, one way or another, Millsy was involved in all three of City's back-to-back Finals. 'In 1992 against Blackburn I thought it was a fairly equal game, although we didn't create too much. The penalty was disappointing – some would have given it, some wouldn't.'

Defeat is never easy to take at Wembley, especially when the stakes are so high. 'We were probably more disappointed that we hadn't gone up automatically,' he says.

If the previous Final had been nervy, there is not really enough words in the dictionary to sum up the roller-coaster, edge-of-the-seat nail-biter that took place beneath the Twin Towers on 31 May 1993 when the Foxes faced Swindon Town. It was the 61st match of the season for City – and Gary had played in every one!

'I suppose neutrals would say it was one of the better Play-off Finals', he laughs. 'At 3–0 down the game was over but we just kept going and got back level only to lose to another penalty. It was heartbreaking for it to happen two years running. The decision certainly wasn't clear cut.'

The result again left a sour taste – and ruined what should have been the proudest day of Gary's career. 'I was captain, and it's just everybody's dream to lead the team out at Wembley – sadly it wasn't our day again.'

In 1994 Gary played a full part in the day; although that seemed unlikely when injury ruled him out of Brian Little's selection plans. 'I'd got injured before the Play-offs and was absolutely devastated not to be playing. On the morning of the game the gaffer called me aside and asked if I'd like to lead the team out – what a gesture. It showed what respect he had for me.'

*'I'd got injured before the Play-offs and was absolutely devastated not to be playing. On the morning of the game the gaffer called me aside and asked if I'd like to lead the team out – what a gesture. It showed what respect he had for me.'*

That was only part of Gary's duties on the day, as he had agreed to commentate on the match for BBC Radio Leicester. Recalling the occasion is the former sports editor of the station, Geoff Peters: 'I was commentating on Walshie's winner when Gary Mills jumped up, screamed [audible to all listeners] and grabbed Neville Foulger, the co-commentator, around the neck in joyous celebration, and I had to keep talking until he regained his composure to get his thoughts on the goal. We did a tape of the game and, to this day, Millsy tells me he still gets people mentioning it to him who remember his screams and listen to the tape on the way to City games. It was utter brilliance from Millsy to be fair. Real, raw emotion!'

Gary briefly figured in the next Premiership campaign, enough to take his City total to exactly 200 League appearances. 'It was nice to reach that milestone and to do it in just under five years shows pretty decent consistency,' he says.

Despite his Wembley appearances, Gary is clear about the most significant match he played in for the club – 11 May 1991 at home to Oxford United. It was a match that City went into knowing they faced the real possibility of life in the third tier had they lost, but thanks to a solitary strike from Tony James and a starring performance from Gary, near-disaster was averted.

'It had been a poor season for the club, although a good one for me personally, but that day we had to win. If we'd drawn or lost we'd have gone down, and who knows where the club would have ended up? Fortunately we won and I was voted Man of the Match. As far as I'm concerned that was the most important game of them all.'

Reflecting on his days as a Fox, Gary is fulsome in his praise for the club and their fans. 'I had a fantastic five years there – I played without doubt the best football of my career. I've always thought the Leicester City supporters were second to none – they were always absolutely brilliant with me and I enjoy going back whenever I can.'

# JOHNNY MORRIS

*Born:*                27 September 1923, Radcliffe, Lancashire.

## Leicester City record:

*Appearances:*    League 206, FA Cup 14.
*Goals:*           League 33, FA Cup 1.
*Debut:*           4 October 1952 v Plymouth Argyle (h) won 2–0.
*Also played for:* Manchester United, Derby County, Corby Town, Kettering Town,
                   England (3 caps).
*Managed:*         Corby Town, Kettering Town.


Former England international Johnny Morris had been considered something of a handful at his previous clubs – and his playing career at Filbert Street was not without incident – but he helped the club to two Second Division titles and was wonderfully consistent in notching up more than 200 appearances in less than six full seasons.

Like so many talented players of his generation, football was a welcome distraction during the years of World War Two. Johnny had been on Manchester United's books as a junior but his first appearances for the club were in wartime fixtures.

In between service with the Royal Armoured Corps he had also 'guested' in matches for Bolton Wanderers, Wrexham and Charlton Athletic, but it was to United he returned – winning an FA Cup-winners' medal in 1948 after Blackpool had been defeated 4–2 in the Wembley Final.

An inside-forward who liked to get his head down and attempt mazy runs, sometimes successfully, sometimes not, Johnny was also an astute passer and a fearsome striker of the ball.

He was popular with his teammates and the fans, but his clashes with authority came when he disagreed with Matt Busby about tactics and was put on the transfer list and omitted from United's semi-final clash against Wolves in 1949 (some blame the flare-up for the defeat which allowed the men from Molyneux to go on and face Leicester City in the Cup Final!).

Derby County then signed Johnny for a British record transfer fee of £24,500, and the midfield schemer recaptured his best form almost immediately and won three caps for England (and scored three times as well). He also played in a further four matches for the Football League representative side (to add to one he had won at this level while at Manchester).

It was regarded as a great surprise when Johnny was allowed to join Second Division City three years later for a club record fee of £21,500, but it was an astute capture by Norman Bullock. He took over the number-eight jersey and made an immediate impact, scoring two tremendous goals against Everton in just his third game for his new club.

*It was regarded as a great surprise when Johnny was allowed to join Second Division City three years later for a club record fee of £21,500, but it was an astute capture by Norman Bullock. He took over the number-eight jersey and made an immediate impact, scoring two tremendous goals against Everton in just his third game for his new club.*

Away form let City down badly, however, and they could only muster a final position of fifth in the table, but at least the City supporters had begun to experience hope that they would again see top flight football at Filbert Street.

That wait was for only another 12 months as Johnny's guile and experience came to the fore to inspire City to promotion – as well as the title. Although Arthur Rowley, with 30, and Derek Hines, 19, led the way with League goals, Johnny chipped in with 13 goals himself from the inside-right position, including one in the 9–2 demolition of Lincoln City, the club's biggest win since the 10–0 trouncing of Portsmouth in 1929.

Despite the euphoria of going up, Johnny was not seeing eye-to-eye with the manager and asked to go on the transfer list through the summer months. The lack of any firm offers persuaded him to remain at City, but it was only a short while before another brush with authority surfaced – and this time it soured relations irreparably.

Following an away defeat at Newcastle United in February 1955, the team had stayed overnight at a hotel in Whitley Bay. An incident ensued which resulted in the board of directors asking manager Bullock to resign immediately. For his involvement Johnny was suspended for 14 days.

Managerless for the last three months of the season, it was not surprising that City's stay in the top flight – where they had not been for 16 years – was all too brief. They had been cut adrift early on after failing to strengthen the squad and became dispirited as their fate became clear.

Johnny switched roles at the start of the 1956–57 campaign, moving slightly deeper to take over the right-half position. There, his resolute tackling and ball-winning skills came into their own, while his accurate distribution and inciteful probing remained to the fore. He enjoyed one of the best seasons of his career and remaining injury-free, he was an ever-present and collected his second Championship medal in four years.

If there was any thought that his competitive edge was softening, they were dispelled when Johnny got himself sent off in a public practice match ahead of the next campaign. Allegedly, it was for 'insulting the referee', but it was costly for both the player and his club, as he was handed a 14-day suspension!

City consolidated their status in the highest division at the end of the 1957–58 campaign – at which point Johnny wound down his League career and accepted an appointment as player-manager at non-League Corby Town. Three years later he succeeded former City great Jack Froggatt when accepting a similar role at Kettering Town.

# DAVID NISH

*Born:*        26 September 1947, Burton upon Trent.

## Leicester City record:

*Appearances:*    League 228, FA Cup 28, League Cup 16.

*Goals:*          League 25, FA Cup 4, League Cup 2.

*Debut:*          3 December 1966 v Stoke City (h) won 4–2.

*Also played for:*  Measham, Derby County, Tulsa Roughnecks (USA), Seattle Sounders (USA), Shepshed Charterhouse, Gresley Rovers, England (5 caps).

In 1969 Leicester City's David Nish became the youngest FA Cup Final captain of all time. The record books will tell that the day ended in huge disappointment for the youngster, but it heralded the start of an outstanding career that ultimately saw him move across the East Midlands for a British record transfer fee before going on to win a League Championship and five full England caps.

Having been on City's books as a youngster, David was eventually rewarded with his first start in December 1966, but it almost came earlier that year in rather unusual circumstances. 'I'd stayed on at Grammar School and we had to attend lessons on a Saturday morning. I remember the school got a phone call one Friday asking if I could be excused the next day as I was needed to be substitute for Leicester City. It was away at Leeds United, and I was scared stiff that nobody got injured – every time one of our players went down I was praying that they'd be alright!'

Although he did not get into the action at Elland Road he was soon handed his full debut and commemorated the day with a goal in the 4–2 home win over Stoke City. 'I think it was our third, and I just took it off a defender and put it in at the Spion Kop End,' he says. He was an ever-present the following season as City finished 13th in the top division.

Although he was later to spend most of his career playing at left-back, David spent all of this campaign in midfield and says it was by accident really that he ended up in the number-three position. 'The truth is, I ended up playing at left-back because nobody else could – it was the same after I'd gone to Derby. Left-backs were very few and far between in those days, and I always said that I was out of position because I was right-footed, but I must have done OK there, I suppose!'

The 1968–69 season was a turbulent one for the Foxes. Matt Gillies had resigned after a 10-year stint as manager, new boss Frank O'Farrell had taken over the reins, David had been appointed club captain and then there was the fight against relegation, not to mention reaching their fourth FA Cup Final.

On 26 April 1969 City lined up at Wembley against Manchester City with David, at the age of 21 years 212 days, becoming the youngest-ever Cup Final skipper. 'It was a great honour to lead the team out', he recalls. 'But in truth I was overawed on the day and didn't play well enough. All week I'd been doing interviews for the media – so much was being made about my age, and I couldn't concentrate properly in the build-up to the game.'

Protocol dictated that the Foxes captain would introduce his team to the Royal Guest. 'It was Princess Anne, and I remember her asking me if I'd been here before. "No, I'm too young" was my answer!'

After the dejection of defeat in the Final the side had the little matter of a relegation scrap to contend with and still had five matches to play. 'It had been a bad winter with lots of matches called off, and we went into our final game at Old Trafford knowing we had to beat Manchester United to have any chance of staying up. I managed to score in the first minute – side-footing in a corner – but after 10 minutes we were 2–1 down and eventually lost 3–2. I tell people that I led City to the double – a Cup Final defeat and relegation!'

By this stage of his career David had been handed even more responsibility by taking over penalty-taking duties, and he boasted a pretty impressive conversion rate: 'I scored my first 12 out of 12 until Norwich's Kevin Keelan saved one at Carrow Road.'

It took two seasons for City to regain their top-flight status, with David being able to lift the Championship trophy at Portsmouth's Fratton Park after a last day win there in May 1971.

There was more silverware for him to raise in August 1971 when City beat Liverpool to win the Charity Shield, beginning an ever-present season that confirmed that David had matured into an outstandingly gifted player. 'I was comfortable on the ball and could make time for myself', he reflects. 'I could see passes and hopefully could read the game pretty well.'

A then British record fee of £225,000 was paid out by Derby County in the summer of 1972 to secure his services – a deal that David believes suited all parties involved. 'The move was good for me as I'd been a pro for six years and had the chance of playing in Europe for the first time with Derby, and the money was good for Leicester.'

Later, during the Brian Little regime at Filbert Street, David returned to join the Foxes backroom staff – working as chief scout, youth development officer and also youth-team coach.

> 'It was a great honour to lead the team out', he recalls. 'But in truth I was overawed on the day and didn't play well enough. All week I'd been doing interviews for the media – so much was being made about my age, and I couldn't concentrate properly in the build-up to the game.'

# RICHIE NORMAN

*Born:*          5 September 1935, Newcastle-upon-Tyne.

## Leicester City record:

*Appearances:*   League 303, FA Cup 30, League Cup 28, Other 4.

*Goals:*           League 2, FA Cup 0, League Cup 3, Other 0.

*Debut:*           23 January 1960 v Newcastle United (a) won 2–0.

*Also played for:*  Ferryhill Athletic, Horden Colliery Welfare, Peterborough United, Burton Albion.

One of the most solid and dependable full-backs ever to wear the Leicester blue was the likeable Geordie, Richie Norman. In the top 12 on the club's all-time appearance list, Richie played in two FA Cup Finals and two League Cup Finals for City, as well as compiling a record run for consecutive first-team outings.

Having starred for top non-League outfit Ferryhill Athletic, the defender had just moved to join the Horden Colliery Welfare side when he was signed by City. 'I was only there for about six matches', says Richie, 'Then I was signed by Leicester City. I travelled down on the train, met Dave Halliday the manager, and as he shook my hand he told me that he was leaving the club.'

New boss Matt Gillies made Richie wait for his League introduction, but when it arrived it came at a ground he knew extremely well. 'I made my debut away at Newcastle, which was quite unbelievable really as I'd been brought up there and had supported them as a lad. There were so many of many family, friends and even old school mates there that Ken Leek, one of my new teammates, complained that he was unable to get a spare ticket!'

Richie settled quickly into the demands of a professional footballer and embarked on a run of consecutive appearances that stretched from 20 August 1960 to 29 February 1964 – 194 games in all. 'I knew it was approaching the 200 game mark, but against Nottingham Forest I turned, sprinted and pulled my hamstring and that put me out for a month.'

Modern-day managers may well have offered him a break, no matter how consistently he was playing, but squad rotation was not considered in the 1960s.

'There were times when I may have been left out, particularly when I sustained a bad cut on my eye that required stitches, after I'd been caught by a stray elbow. I told the manager that I may have to sit one out as I was concerned about the wound re-opening, but he told me that I'd be fine and put me in the team anyway.'

Richie's unbroken stretch not only meant that he had been an ever-present through three full League campaigns, but it also lasted through a couple of FA Cup runs which both culminated in Final defeats.

'In 1961 I thought we played really well against a great side. It was unfortunate that Len Chalmers got injured, and we had to re-shuffle as I thought we were getting on top of them and that knocked us out of our rhythm a bit. You see all of the substitutes sat on benches nowadays, and it's crazy to think that you weren't allowed to replace an injured player back then. To reach Wembley in my first full season though was a great feeling.'

'In 1961 I thought we played really well against a great side. It was unfortunate that Len Chalmers got injured, and we had to re-shuffle as I thought we were getting on top of them and that knocked us out of our rhythm a bit. You see all of the substitutes sat on benches nowadays, and it's crazy to think that you weren't allowed to replace an injured player back then. To reach Wembley in my first full season though was a great feeling.'

Defeat was a little harder to take two years later, however. 'In 1963 we were the favourites to win, but Manchester United did the business on the day and we just didn't perform.'

City went into that game justifiably full of confidence as they had managed a win and a draw against United over the Easter period. The 2–2 match at Old Trafford still provides Richie with one of his favourite anecdotes. 'We were attacking the Stretford End, and I received the ball from a throw in around the halfway line. I took it on 10 or 15 yards, beat someone and heard a cry of "Go on, have a shot", so I let fly and it screamed into the top corner past Harry Gregg. I remember seeing the likes of Best, Law and Charlton all looking at me absolutely flabbergasted!'

That was one of just five goals that Richie contributed to the City cause, so it is fairly remarkable that he once found himself on a hat-trick! 'It was at Coventry City in the League Cup', reflects the former left-back. 'Jimmy Hill was their manager at the time, and I remember we stopped off at the Leofric Hotel in the city prior to the game. A few of us saw their local evening paper in which Hill had written that his side were going to give us a thrashing. That really spurred us on and we paralysed them 8–1, and I scored twice from long-range.'

Asked to sum up his overall worth to the team, Richie reflects on a description once given to him in the *Leicester Mercury*, 'It said I was a left-back who was very fast, was consistent, reliable but an unorthodox tackler. It went on to say that I had a confidence based on speed.'

After retiring as a player Richie remained in the game as a physiotherapist and had given Nuneaton Borough 15 years of loyal service by the end of the 2009–10 season.

# MATT OAKLEY

*Born:*          17 August 1977, Peterborough, Cambridgeshire.

**Leicester City record:** (to the end of season 2009–10).
*Appearances:*   League 103 FA Cup 4 League Cup 2 Other 1.
*Goals:*         League 8 FA Cup 0 League Cup 0 Other 0.
*Debut:*         12 January 2008 v Coventry City (h) won 2–0.
*Also played for:*  Southampton, Derby County.

There is a little more to captaincy than choosing ends after the coin toss and running around with a distinctive armband on. It requires a variety of skills, which all come under the 'leadership' banner – there's knowledge, experience, character, guidance, sensitivity and many more traits, all of which were displayed in abundance by Matt Oakley as he led Leicester City to the Football League Division One Championship in 2008–09.

Given that Matt was officially only the club's vice-captain adds even more punch to the manner in which he helped ensure that City's first visit to the third tier of the English domestic game would be an extremely brief one.

The inspirational midfielder had joined City from local rivals Derby County, signing on 11 January 2008 for a fee of £500,000. He made his debut the following day, starring in a 2–0 home victory over Coventry City, but too many of the closing games were lost and relegation was confirmed, alongside Colchester United and Scunthorpe United.

A serious Achilles injury to club captain Stephen Clemence became a long-term issue and ruled him out of the final weeks of the season, plus all of the 2008–09 campaign, and Matt, who had worn the armband at his previous club, took over.

The immediate aim from everybody at the Walkers Stadium was to win promotion at the first time of asking, and with new manager Nigel Pearson at the helm – and Matt in charge on the park – they set about their mission with gusto.

*The immediate aim from everybody at the Walkers Stadium was to win promotion at the first time of asking, and with new manager Nigel Pearson at the helm – and Matt in charge on the park – they set about their mission with gusto.*

An unbeaten run of 23 matches stretching from 1 November 2008 to 7 March 2009 (before they were eventually defeated 2–0 at Tranmere Rovers) not only smashed a 38-year-old club record but also sent the Foxes sailing 10 points clear at the top of the table.

Matt's own form was spectacular throughout this run – prompting, cajoling and inspiring those around, he deservedly won the League One Player of the Month Award for January 2009. His predilection for a 'pot-shot' enabled him to contribute some vital goals from the centre of the park – or from a wide-right position where his manager often utilised him – and his overall tally of eight goals in the League signified the best return of his entire career. His wonderful finish – after some fine approach work – at home to Cheltenham won him another trophy, after being voted the club's Goal of the Season.

Having secured the title away at Southend United with a couple of games to go, the presentation took place after the final home game against Scunthorpe United. It was an immensely proud Matt who collected the Division One silverware in front of a packed Walkers Stadium to initiate jubilant scenes, complete with the obligatory fireworks and chorus of *We are the Champions* from the Blue Army.

Coming off the back of a career that had seemed destined to be spent entirely on the south coast, Matt could have been forgiven for pinching himself a little. He had made his debut for Southampton at Everton on 6 May 1995, while still a trainee. Over the course of the next 11 years he played in over 300 first-team games for the Saints, playing both before and after their move from The Dell to St Mary's. The highlight of his time there was the FA Cup run of 2003, where he appeared in the losing Final against Arsenal.

During the early stages of Matt's career his promise and potential had been identified and rewarded with four selections for the England Under-21 side; although many observers' predictions that he would go on to earn senior recognition were not fulfilled.

Severing his long-standing connection with Southampton, Matt joined Derby County in August 2006 and in his first season there he captained them to their Play-off Final win over West Bromwich Albion at Wembley Stadium, thus securing them a return to the Premiership.

Having been a major contributor in putting the 'pride' back into Pride Park, Matt was somewhat surprised that the Rams agreed to Leicester City's bid for him halfway through their top flight return, but for the midfielder it signified a marvellous opportunity to revive another fallen East Midlands giant. No one at the Walkers Stadium was short-changed by his acquisition.

Away from the game Matt is something of a wine connoisseur, and together with his great friend, the sommelier Barry Skarin, they formed their own company, Nebuchadnezzar Wines.

The 2008–09 campaign was truly a great vintage for Leicester City, and for once the Foxes fans were able to crack open the champagne and celebrate a truly magnificent season.

Matt played his 100th competitive match for the club during February 2010 and a month later, against Reading, he reached a century of League appearances for City.

# DAVID OLDFIELD

*Born:*  30 May 1968, Perth, Australia.

## Leicester City record:

*Appearances:*  League 188, FA Cup 7, League Cup12, Other 14.

*Goals:*  League 26, FA Cup 3, League Cup 1, Other 2.

*Debut:*  13 January 1990 v Newcastle United (a) lost 4–5.

*Also played for:*  Luton Town, Manchester City, Millwall (loan), Stoke City, Peterborough United, Oxford United, Stafford Rangers.


Occupying the Leicester City right flank during the early part of the 1990s was former England Under-21 cap David Oldfield.

He had been blooded into the professional game with Luton Town and was then transferred to Manchester City, where his finest hour was scoring twice in a 5–1 mauling of fierce rivals United in 1989. After arriving at Filbert Street, David began life as a Fox in pretty unusual circumstances. 'I made my debut in a real roller-coaster of a game away at Newcastle. I remember we had got Kevin Campbell on loan from Arsenal at the time and he was excellent. We were leading 4–2 and then in the final few minutes they came back to win 5–4. The final goal was a penalty – I think from Mark McGhee. I remember trying to follow in hoping to be first to clear a rebound and receiving an elbow in the face from one of the defenders for my trouble.'

The feature of David's time at Leicester were the back-to-back-to-back attempts to get out of the second tier via the Russian roulette route – the Play-offs. 'I was there throughout the years of the three consecutive Play-off Finals, although I only played in one of them. I was really frustrated to miss out on the Blackburn Rovers match in 1992. I sustained a medial ligament injury in my knee and had to miss the final month of the season but got myself back into contention in time for the game. I was given a boost beforehand when one of the supporters' groups named me their Player of the Year, but I was left on the bench. It was a blazing hot day and felt that I might have had a run when some of the guys starting showing signs of fatigue, but it wasn't to be.'

Back again 12 months later and David was involved this time. 'I played the following year – the 4–3 match against Swindon Town – and again it was heartbreaking for the club and the supporters not just to lose, but to lose by conceding a late penalty as had happened the previous year.'

Having come so close on two occasions, it did not surprise David that City got it right at the third attempt. 'We felt really hard done by to lose both times, but the squad was so bubbly that I knew we'd come back again. Lots of clubs that experience Wembley heartbreak struggle the following season, but it showed our character that we bounced back yet again to contest the 1994 Play-off Final.'

David arrived at Leicester as an out-and-out striker but was switched on a hunch. 'One of the lads got injured, and I remember Brian Little tried me out in midfield in the reserves, and I did pretty well so he played me there in the next match and I stayed right side for the rest of my time at the club.'

Blessed with a pretty decent cardiovascular system, running up and down the flank was not a problem for David. 'I didn't have blistering pace but had lots of energy and could pretty much run all day – the football term is "a good engine", I think!'

Despite his own modest assessment, David's pace was what you would expect from a former school sprint champion, but he had to learn the rudiments of wing-play, and his manager was able to elevate his game with a simple tip. 'Brian always coached me not to run in straight lines but to cut inside when I could – it's very in-vogue now and I try to teach young players to do similar.'

Apart from his tricky dribbling skills and sheer hard graft, David also contributed with some important goals. 'I think the best I scored for City was in a losing cause, at Manchester City in the FA Cup. I hit it right-footed over 'keeper Tony Coton from about 25–30 yards. The only disappointment was that it must have flown in so quickly because the cameraman missed it and it wasn't caught on film at all.'

David was tagged with a couple of far-from original nicknames, due to being born on the far side of the globe. 'They first started calling me "Skippy" or "Ozzy" at Luton earlier in my career. I'd scored a couple of goals against Everton, and all the media boys knew about me was that I'd been born in Perth, Western Australia, so they put in all the match reports that I was an Aussie.'

Although in recent times David has been serving Peterborough United with distinction, as their reserve and youth-team manager, his association with the Foxes has been maintained thanks to the enthusiastic running of the Former Players' Association. 'I really enjoy catching up with the Leicester boys. I've been fortunate to keep my fitness levels up over the past few years and have been able to turn out for the "old side" in charity games that people like Ally Mauchlen and Paul Ramsey run.'

In addition, he played a starring role in helping the City side win the Masters indoor tournament in 2007 – collecting the Man of the Tournament award upon its completion.

*Blessed with a pretty decent cardiovascular system, running up and down the flank was not a problem for David. 'I didn't have blistering pace but had lots of energy and could pretty much run all day – the football term is "a good engine", I think!'*

# JOHN O'NEILL

*Born:* 11 March 1958, Derry, Northern Ireland.

## Leicester City record:

*Appearances:* League 313, FA Cup 19, League Cup 13.
*Goals:* League 10, FA Cup 1, League Cup 1.
*Debut:* 19 August 1978 v Burnley (a) drew 2–2.
*Also played for:* Derry Boys' Club, Queen's Park Rangers, Norwich City, Northern Ireland (39 caps).
*Managed:* Finn Harps (Republic of Ireland).

No-one has represented their country on more occasions as a Leicester City player than John O'Neill, who won 39 caps for Northern Ireland while on the Filbert Street books.

John was still studying at Loughborough University for his BSc in Economics and Accountancy when Jock Wallace handed him his City debut, as a non-contract player, at the start of the 1978–79 season, but he was soon offering the player professional terms.

'I had to train on my own for most of the time', recalls John. 'Perhaps I'd spend just one session a week at Leicester until I'd finished my studies.'

The tall, elegant central-defender made an immediate impression and showed from the start that he was a dominant force in the air and had a good understanding of what the position demanded. 'I could read the game alright, but critics always said that I lacked a little bit of pace – I had just enough to make a decent career out of it though!'

In his second full season at the club John helped the Foxes to the Second Division title, and there was an added bonus awaiting him. 'I went to the Player of the Year award and never thought in my wildest dreams that I'd be in with a shout. It came as a bolt out of the blue, but it was brilliant to win that, on top of the promotion.'

There had been one major set-back that season, however, the embarrassing third-round replay FA Cup exit at the hands of non-League Harlow Town, and it affected John more than most as he missed out on the chance of a short break. 'I didn't get back to Northern Ireland very often, and Jock had promised me that I could go home for a few days after the match –

*'I remember playing in the 1986 World Cup Finals against Brazil when they beat us 3–0 and we didn't get a kick. I watched the match back in 2009 and we actually played much better than I remember.'*

providing there wasn't a replay. They equalised with about 10 minutes to go and then beat us down there, where we were awful. I didn't get home for about another six weeks!'

John feels that defeat was typical of City's fortunes. 'Anyone who just liked to hump the ball forward had a chance against us, but we always did well against sides who liked to get the ball down and play football. That's because it was our strength as well. I think I played against Liverpool at Anfield four or five times and only remember losing once.'

The prospects of a Wembley Cup Final in 1982 seemed bright when City drew Spurs in the semi-final, but it did not turn out that way. 'We just didn't compete in that match. I remember thinking we might have a chance but they played us off the park, to be honest.'

John scored a dozen goals for City in all competitions but says there were not too many spectacular ones among the collection. 'They were mostly all either tap-ins or close-range headers. My first came against Leeds United from a free-kick outside of the box. Andy Peake had a shot that hit the wall, and it landed at my feet six yards out. I just stuck it in. The other I like to remember was against Watford on the Cup run – it was an easy header from a corner but it was very important at the time.'

A number of different managers came and went during the nine seasons that John played for City. He is clear about who is his favourite gaffer, though. 'I loved playing under Gordon Milne. I was captain when he arrived, and from a tactical and playing point of view it was the happiest time of my career.'

John admits that sometimes his memory distorts how a game had actually been played out. 'I remember playing in the 1986 World Cup Finals against Brazil when they beat us 3–0 and we didn't get a kick. I watched the match back in 2009 and we actually played much better than I remember.'

Memories of that game resurfaced at a recent get-together. 'Afterwards I swapped shirts with their number 19 Elzo, and I still have his shirt. I went to a function in Northern Ireland and a supporter came up with my shirt from that game. How it had got from Mexico – presumably back to Brazil – and then turned up in Northern Ireland 20 years later is anyone's guess, but the fan had bought it on-line, so I suppose Elzo had hit on hard times and decided to sell off his souvenirs!'

On leaving Leicester, John played briefly at Queen's Park Rangers then moved to Norwich City, where he sustained a career-ending knee injury in just his first game. 'I snapped knee ligaments and severed a nerve and knew straight away that it was serious.'

The Canaries granted John a testimonial, and a familiar face returned to take part in it. 'Gary Lineker came back from Barcelona and scored four in that match – one of them would surely be the best goal he ever scored in his career.'

City's all-time record cap-holder now lives in Lurgan but regards his days as a Fox with great affection. 'Leicester City is a club that will always stay dear to my heart. Had things turned out differently I would have loved to have stayed there a little longer, but I'll always be grateful for the time I had there.'

# MARTIN O'NEILL

Born:          1 March 1952 Kilrea, County Londonderry, Northern Ireland.

## Leicester City record:
*Manager:*       December 1995–June 2000.
*Played for:*     Distillery, Nottingham Forest, Norwich City, Manchester City, Notts County, Northern Ireland (64 caps).
*Also Managed:*  Grantham Town, Shepshed Charterhouse, Wycombe Wanderers, Norwich City, Glasgow Celtic, Aston Villa.

Older Leicester City supporters may reminisce fondly about the Matt Gillies era, which yielded four domestic Cup Finals in five years, or the Jimmy Bloomfield side of the 70s who were dubbed 'the great entertainers', but in terms of bringing major silverware to the trophy cabinet then the stewardship of Martin O'Neill would be statistically the most successful in the club's history.

After taking over with the Foxes in the second tier, Martin's side won a Play-off Final then went to on to secure two League Cup Final victories, as well as reaching a third. He also brought European football back to Filbert Street for the first time since 1961.

Martin's own playing career had peaked during a magnificent decade of service at Nottingham Forest – most of which was spent playing under legendary boss Brian Clough. Among his own medal haul was a League title win, two League Cup triumphs, success in the 1980 European Cup Final and a Charity Shield victory over Ipswich Town, in which he scored a couple of times at Wembley Stadium.

His international career stretched from 1971–1984 and brought him 64 full caps. He skippered his country to the 1982 World Cup Finals, where one of his proudest moments was leading his side to a memorable victory over the host country in Valencia.

After hanging up his boots, Martin gained invaluable managerial experience in the lower leagues, before pioneering Wycombe Wanderers' journey into the Football League.

A brief spell at Norwich City ended in December 1995 and almost immediately he was appointed as manager of Leicester City. At the end of that first season he took his new charges to the Play-off Final, where Crystal Palace were defeated in dramatic fashion.

With the game entering the final minute of extra-time – and the scores level at one-all – Martin, preparing for a penalty shoot-out, substituted his goalkeeper Kevin Poole in favour of the much taller deputy Zeljko 'Spider' Kalac.

Whether this bold gamble had backfired on Martin – or had proved to be one of the most inspirational pieces of management ever – did not have to be dissected, because Steve Claridge fired a dramatic winner for Leicester with the last kick of the match.

A watching television audience had been able to witness with close scrutiny how emotionally involved Martin had been on the sidelines. Reactions which became commonplace over the following years endeared O'Neill to his supporters, as he enthusiastically appeared to 'kick every ball' with his players and rejoice in their success. City supporters could see that their manager cared as much as they did – and they loved him all the more for it.

Erudite and bespectacled, Martin could be mistaken for a school-master or perhaps even a lawyer; although he had opted not to complete his own law degree at the Queen's University of Belfast when signing for Forest.

His interests include criminology, and it is clear an inquisitive mind is no handicap when it comes to football management. Martin enjoyed pitting his wits against the best in the Premiership following City's promotion – and his decision to shackle the Brazilian playmaker Juninho by deploying Pontus Kaamark as a man-marker was pivotal in the League Cup Final win over Middlesbrough in 1997.

Ably assisted by loyal backroom staff (and good friends) John Robertson and Steve Walford, Martin turned Leicester City into a force to be reckoned with. Four consecutive seasons each brought top-10 finishing positions, plus two further League Cup Finals – one lost versus Spurs in 1999 and one won versus Tranmere Rovers the following year.

The good times were certainly back at Filbert Street; though, sadly, all good things come to an end, and the challenge of managing a club with the huge profile of Glasgow Celtic proved too much to resist for Martin and he joined them in the summer of 2000.

In his first season with the Hoops he led them to a domestic treble, and in his seven years at Parkhead he guided them to seven major honours – plus the 2003 UEFA Cup Final. There's no wonder the Celtic supporters dubbed him 'Martin the Magnificent'.

Awarded the OBE in 2004 for his services to sport, the softy spoken Irishman then took 15 months out of the game for personal reasons, but just prior to the 2006–07 season he returned to top-flight management once more by assuming the mantle at Aston Villa.

Like all other football fans, those of Leicester City love to dream – and love to hope – and under Martin O'Neill their club became one of most feared and respected in the land. They were certainly good times to be a Fox – maybe even the very best.

## 'City supporters could see that their manager cared as much as they did – and they loved him all the more for it.'

# IAN ORMONDROYD

*Born:*           22 September 1964, Bradford, Yorkshire.

## Leicester City record:

*Appearances:*    League 77, FA Cup 2, League Cup 6, Other 11.

*Goals:*            League 7, FA Cup 0, League Cup 2, Other 3.

*Debut:*            11 March 1992 v Portsmouth (h) drew 2–2.

*Also played for:*  Bradford City, Oldham Athletic, Aston Villa, Derby County, Hull City (loan), Scunthorpe United.

As Leicester City discovered in the early 1990s, if you needed a goal to help you through a nervy Play-off semi-final you could do worse than select Ian Ormondroyd in your line up. Although Ian's role in the side was never as an out-an-out striker, he completed the remarkable feat of managing to score at that stage in three consecutive seasons.

In 1992 he netted against Cambridge United, Portsmouth suffered the following year and his timely goal against Tranmere Rovers in 1994 helped the Foxes to a third Wembley trip in as many years.

'I was extremely fortunate to play a part in that period of the club's history', says Ian. 'I'd joined from Derby County, who ironically had thrown a lot of money at trying to achieve promotion but missed out, and we had to overcome Cambridge United to get through. I don't remember too much about my goal that day, but it was a fairly routine tap-in as we won 5–0.'

A couple of weeks later the trip to the national stadium ended in huge disappointment but retrospectively gave the Leicester boys something to chuckle about in later years.

'Before the Final, Brian Little had told us that it was to be George Courtenay's last match as a referee and I remember him saying, "Don't be surprised if he gives a penalty today". Through the match there had been a bit of a feud developing between Steve Walsh and their player David Speedie. Anyway, he went down under a challenge from Walshy, and the ref gave the penalty – Walshy was adamant that he hadn't touched him. Later, of course, Speedie signed for us and Walshy still held that

# 'I had probably the best time of my career at Leicester – there was always a great camaraderie between the lads'

grudge and wouldn't have anything to do with him for a couple of weeks – it was really funny at the time, but eventually they became mates!'

The defeat condemned Leicester to another season in the second tier, but again they reached the Play-offs. 'Filbert Street was undergoing development towards the end of that season and we had to play our "home" leg at The City Ground, Nottingham, and managed a 1–0 victory, courtesy of a goal by Julian Joachim.'

In the return at Fratton Park Ian's goal settled any City nerves. 'It was another tap-in from close range, and their fans were convinced I was offside but I wasn't, and we were well worth our draw to reach Wembley yet again.'

Swindon Town provided the opposition for City on 31 May 1993, and there were more reasons for Ian to feel despondent. 'Against Swindon I was a sub and didn't get on. We were gutted to lose – and again it was to a late penalty, which we felt shouldn't have been given.'

At 6ft 4in tall, it is not difficult to envisage how Ian came to have the nickname 'Sticks'. 'Adie Thorpe – a mate back in Bradford – started calling me it years ago, and it just stuck! I think I suffered a little bit from the tall-player syndrome. It seemed that at some stages of my career teammates were conscious of my height and would just bang it up there, but I wasn't an old-fashioned centre-forward. I did play up front a lot, of course, but I actually preferred to be wide on the left of midfield or on the left of a three-pronged attack.'

In 1994, at the third time of asking, City won a Wembley Play-off Final. Again they were indebted to one of Ian's goals to get them there. 'The semi-final against Tranmere Rovers was quite a heated affair, but I managed to score after Mark Blake had hit a post, and I got a side-foot tap-in from around six yards from the rebound.'

Ian clearly recalls the part he also played in City's winner against Derby County in the Final. 'Simon Grayson crossed from the right. I'd made a near post run and headed it. Goalkeeper Martin Taylor could only parry it away at full-stretch and Walshy was there to tap in the rebound.'

Promotion to the Premiership, a change of manager and a desire to play every week then prompted Ian's decision to move on. 'It all changed when Mark McGhee took over. There was clearly a difference of opinion, and he didn't get on with me and bombed me out to Hull City on loan. Then he called me back to play against Wimbledon and didn't use me again. I was 30 then and needed to play regular first-team football, so I decided it was the right time to leave.'

It is clear that Ian enjoyed his time with City, however: 'I had probably the best time of my career at Leicester – there was always a great camaraderie between the lads, and the club did a lot to organise a lot of social activities for us. Brian Little was excellent, and I really enjoyed some of the individual sessions he would hold with the forwards. I got on well with the Leicester fans but just wished I'd been able to play even more during my time there.'

Ian is now back at Bradford City, working as the club's community officer and also covers all of their matches for local radio as an articulate and knowledgeable match summariser.

# GARRY PARKER

*Born:*          7 September 1965, Oxford.

## Leicester City record:

*Appearances:*    League 114, FA Cup 11, League Cup 17, Other 6.

*Goals:*          League 10, FA Cup 2, League Cup 2, Other 3.

*Debut:*         18 February 1995 v Wolverhampton Wanderers (a) lost 0–1.

*Caretaker manager:*      30 September 2001–10 October 2001.

*Also played for:*  Luton Town, Hull City, Nottingham Forest, Aston Villa.

Nearly every successful side will spend hours on the training ground practising their dead-ball routines, but no matter how much time and energy is applied, unless there is someone who can be relied upon to execute perfect delivery each time, then the practise is pointless.

Garry Parker was much more than just an accomplished taker of corners, free-kicks and penalties. He had proven himself at the highest level, and his versatility meant that he could be used in a number of midfield roles. He was no stranger to the big stage either, having appeared in two League Cup Finals and one FA Cup Final while with Nottingham Forest, and he had also scored one of the greatest-ever Wembley goals for them when he ran the length of the field to net in a Simod Cup Final against Everton.

After a further four years at Aston Villa he joined the Foxes; although he knew full well that they were about to lose their elevated status in the Premiership. 'I knew Leicester were a top side,' says Garry, 'but when I joined it was already virtually certain that we were going down.'

Despite him scoring a wonderful solo effort on the last day of the season, away at Southampton, Garry's fears were realised and the relegation was confirmed. It was then all about bouncing straight back as quickly as possible, and automatic promotion looked to be on the cards until a late-season loss of form. 'Crucially, we'd hit the top early in the season and had a few points in the bag, so when we had a poor run and lost a few we were still in contention for the Play-offs. It came down to the last game, though. We went to Watford and won 1–0 on a day when everything went right for us.'

Garry's stunning left-footed volley was the deciding moment – and only goal – of the two-legged semi-final against Stoke City, and it took the Foxes through to their fourth Play-off Final of the 1990s – with Crystal Palace standing in their way of going up – and it was the Eagles who scored first. 'Even when we were trailing at Wembley we didn't panic and were still very confident. Then we won the penalty. My immediate joy was diluted when I realised I'd have to take it. I knew I just had to score. As I put the ball down their player, Ray Houghton, who was an old teammate of mine, came up and said loudly, "You're gonna miss." Nigel Martyn was in goal and I'd taken a couple of penalties against him before and scored, so I was pretty confident – and fortunately I scored. That put us level with about 20 minutes to go. Who knows what would have happened if I'd missed it. Martin [O'Neill] always said that was the turning point.'

There was a further twist in City's favour with the game almost over. 'Of course, the game couldn't have finished any better. Martin had put Spider [Kalac] on for the penalties. We won a free-kick and I went to take it – I asked the ref how long was left and he said, "that's time". I just said, "let it go" and I hit the free-kick and it broke for Steve Claridge to mishit the winner.'

The final whistle sounded almost immediately and the realisation of what they had achieved hit the players. 'It was massive – they say the FA Cup Final is big but the Play-off Final is as big as it gets. There is a place in the Premiership at stake and that's where everybody wants to be. We had a whole season to look forward to of playing against the very best teams in the land.'

City not only consolidated their place in the top flight but also maintained their form in knock-out football by reaching the League Cup Final against Middlesbrough. A late Emile Heskey goal at Wembley earned his side a second bite of the cherry 10 days later at Hillsborough. 'We didn't play particularly well in the first game, but once we'd got the equaliser we were very confident of beating them and it was a different story in the replay – I thought we played pretty well.'

Even so, it was not until the extra-time period before Steve Claridge scored the only goal of the match after yet another well-directed free-kick from Garry had been headed into the striker's path.

'Parks' played for City until 1999, whereupon he joined the club's coaching staff. An unexpected challenge was handed to him in September 2001 when he was asked to take over as caretaker manager when the club relieved Peter Taylor from his post; although it won't be for his brief tenure as the 'gaffer' that Garry is remembered by City fans but for his ice-cool Wembley penalty, and those pinpoint free-kicks that resulted in Play-off Final and League Cup Final-winning goals.

'I loved every minute of my time at Leicester. I had a great rapport with the fans and really it was the best time of my life. We had no big timers there – everybody got on well together and Martin was a great manager, up there with the very best I've ever worked with.'

*'It was massive – they say the FA Cup Final is big but the Play-off Final is as big as it gets. There is a place in the Premiership at stake and that's where everybody wants to be. We had a whole season to look forward to of playing against the very best teams in the land.'*

# ANDY PEAKE

*Born:*          1 November 1961, Market Harborough, Leicestershire.

## Leicester City record:

*Appearances:*    League 147, FA Cup 9, League Cup 6.
*Goals:*          League 13, FA Cup 0, League Cup 0.
*Debut:*          6 January 1979 v Norwich City (h) won 3–0.
*Also played for:*  Grimsby Town, Charlton Athletic, Middlesbrough.

Very few footballers take it as a compliment when they are mainly remembered by supporters for just a handful of goals – particularly anyone as versatile and talented as Andy Peake – but when those strikes were long-range 'get you out of your seat' pile-drivers then it is not surprising that the midfielder had his reputation based on them.

Andy's debut for the City first team came in semi-fortunate circumstances and is widely remembered for a stunning goal by a teammate in tights!

A previous investment in a hot-air pitch cover enabled the FA Cup tie to go ahead when most of the other games were called off in near-Siberian temperatures. Television cameras were switched to Filbert Street and Jock Wallace plunged Andy in for an afternoon to look back on with immense pride as a mature display helped embarrass First Division Norwich City to the tune of three goals to nil – the most spectacular of which was converted by Keith Weller in his shiny white hose.

The fact that Leicester remained in the competition for another seven weeks was due entirely to the weather. Several times their fourth-round tie at Oldham Athletic was called off, and when it did go ahead (on 26 February) it was an occasion to instantly forget for the travelling faithful. Alan Young – who moved to Filbert Street just three months later – hit a hat-trick as the Boundary Park club progressed.

Andy's Cup dreams had evaporated as soon as they had begun; although the 17-year-old did not play against the Lancashire side as he was away adding to a burgeoning collection of England Youth caps.

His TV appearance (and more importantly his quality on the training ground) had convinced the manager that he was worth a run in the League side, however, and he played in 18 of the closing 20 Second Division fixtures and opened his scoring tally by registering against Newcastle United at home and Sheffield United away.

The 1979–80 campaign was memorable for City fans as they celebrated a return to the top tier by clinching promotion and the League title. Frustratingly for Andy – but sensibly in the long run – manager Wallace used Andy sparingly, particularly in the second half of the season, but his 25 appearances were still enough to earn him a Championship medal. He would not have been too disappointed at sitting out the 'egg-on-face humiliation' of the Cup exit at the hands of minnows Harlow Town.

The summer of 1980 was the last occasion in which his age group could play at international level, and he was a member of the England side that defeated Poland 2–1 to win the UEFA Youth tournament.

Buoyed by this success, the rapidly-maturing midfielder embarked on his first season playing at the highest level of the domestic game, and after defeats against Ipswich Town and Everton a win was desperately needed when reigning champions Liverpool came to town in August 1980.

City had enjoyed the better of the opening exchanges but needed something tangible on the score sheet. Receiving a square pass from left-back Willie Gibson 35 yards out, Andy took a touch then exploded a bomb of a shot past England 'keeper Ray Clemence into the top-left corner.

Commentator Hugh Johns screamed, 'What a Peake performance – his first goal in the First Division and he'll never score a better one.'

In terms of its impact it probably is Andy's most memorable score, although he did hit a couple of belters against Watford at home in March 1984. For the first he picked the ball up inside his own half and ran and ran before unleashing an unstoppable howitzer of a shot beyond Steve Sherwood and into the 'postage stamp' corner. His second was slightly closer but from a much narrower angle, and the bemused 'keeper barely saw it as it whistled past him into the other corner.

Andy had picked up one Under-21 cap while at City but his expected development into the higher echelons of the game failed to materialise, and after seven years with City he signed for Grimsby Town, with the Mariners breaking their own transfer record in paying £125,000 for him.

Within a year he had signed for Charlton Athletic, where he spent five seasons racking up 177 League outings. A move to Middlesbrough coincided with another successful promotion campaign, but at the age of 32 he decided to hang up his boots for good to join the Leicestershire Constabulary.

Imagine the joy of an errant City fan having his 'collar felt' by PC Peake – 'Hey, didn't you score that goal against Liverpool?'

'*Commentator Hugh Johns screamed, 'What a Peake performance – his first goal in the First Division and he'll never score a better one*'

# NIGEL PEARSON

*Born:*              21 August 1963, Nottingham.

## Leicester City record:
*Manager:*           20 June 2008–29 June 2010.
*Played for:*        Heanor Town, Shrewsbury Town, Sheffield Wednesday, Middlesbrough.
*Also managed:*      Carlisle United, Southampton, Hull City.

Leicester City's recent history has featured many twists and turns, but there has been one common denominator linking three of the most significant events – Nigel Pearson.

The former Middlesbrough central-defender was on the opposing team as Martin O'Neill's side lifted the 1997 League Cup after a replay at Hillsborough. Eleven years later – and having swapped his playing role for a managerial position – Nigel inspired his Southampton side to a dramatic last day of the season success which ensured their Championship survival at the expense of…Leicester City! Then, having taken over at the club he had just inadvertently helped to relegate, he oversaw a record-breaking campaign which brought the First Division Championship trophy back to the Walkers Stadium.

Nigel had begun his career with Heanor Town before being offered a professional contract with Shrewsbury Town. He made his League debut on the opening day of the 1982–83 season and went on to make over 180 first-team appearances before joining Sheffield Wednesday in 1987 for a fee of £250,000.

In a success-filled seven-year stretch with the Owls, Nigel assumed the club captaincy and scooped the Man of the Match award at Wembley in the 1991 League Cup win over Manchester United. Two years later he helped the club to both domestic Cup Finals but was unable to play in either after breaking his leg a few weeks earlier.

After making more than 200 appearances for Wednesday, the tall defender joined Middlesbrough where he spent a further four years, playing in three Cup Finals – including the 1997 defeat to the Foxes.

Nigel's first managerial appointment could hardly have been more dramatic – Carlisle United avoided being relegated from the Football League on the last day of the season thanks to an injury-time score from their goalkeeper Jimmy Glass.

Over the course of the next few seasons he was part of the backroom staff at Stoke City, West Bromwich Albion and Newcastle United – standing in as caretaker manager at both of his last two employers. During 2007 he also became assistant coach to the England Under-21 side and actually took charge for the 3–3 draw against Italy, the first game at the new Wembley Stadium.

Nigel's next mission was to keep Southampton in the Championship – this he did at Leicester's expense – but the south coast side's new owners did not display much gratitude by electing to opt for an overseas coach and not extend the short rolling contract they had given their manager.

Milan Mandaric leapt quickly to recruit him, making him City's sixth manager in just 16 months. The club's executive chairman said he hoped the appointment would be the beginning of a new era. He told BBC Sport: 'Nigel is the right man to take this club forward. He has a great mix of experience, integrity and enthusiasm. I interviewed a number of good candidates but Nigel's drive, passion and overall knowledge of the game was impossible to ignore.'

Pearson responded by saying, 'I am privileged to have been given the chance to turn around the fortunes of a club with so much history and such a strong fan base, and I am confident my style of management can help bring the good times back to Leicester City.'

*Despite some outstanding individual achievements from his players, Nigel deserved immense credit for the way he had galvanised his side and re-invigorated all at the Walkers Stadium.*

Over the course of the next nine months, Nigel's managerial style certainly proved itself. With some acute purchases, tactical nouse and able support from his handpicked assistants Craig Shakespeare and Steve Walsh, the reign began in typically promising fashion – three wins and a draw from the opening four matches secured the Manager of the Month Award for August 2008.

A 23-match unbeaten run broke a club record which had stood since 1971 – and enabled City to pull away from the chasing pack. Nigel picked up another Manager of the Month Award and a 2–0 victory away at Southend United on 18 April 2009 confirmed that the Blues would be promoted back to the Championship as title winners.

Dropping into the third tier for the first time had been one of the darkest moments in Leicester's history, but displaying something of a 'Dunkirk Spirit' they had reversed their recent trend and had begun the journey back towards the game's elite.

Despite some outstanding individual achievements from his players, Nigel deserved immense credit for the way he had galvanised his side and re-invigorated all at the Walkers Stadium.

This momentum was carried over into the 2009–10 season, in which City finished fifth, before losing to Cardiff City in the Play-off semi-finals.

On 29 June 2010, after almost exactly two years with the Foxes, Nigel moved on again to become the new manager of Hull City.

# KEVIN POOLE

*Born:*        21 July 1963, Bromsgrove, Worcestershire.

## Leicester City record:

*Appearances:*    League 163, FA Cup 8, League Cup 10, Other 13.

*Debut:*         17 August 1991 v Swindon Town (a) drew 0–0.

*Also played for:*    Aston Villa, Northampton, Middlesbrough, Hartlepool United (loan), Birmingham City, Bolton Wanderers, Derby County, Burton Albion.

Leicester City's reputation for fielding outstanding goalkeepers stretched right throughout the 20th century, and during the final decade City could always be relied upon to have strength in depth for its most crucial position.

Competing with the likes of Carl Muggleton, Russell Hoult, Gavin Ward and Kasey Keller was always likely to provide the sternest of tests for any aspirant to the City number-one jersey, yet Kevin Poole notched up almost 200 appearances during a near six-year stay, among which were a couple of Wembley Play-off Finals.

Kevin moved to Filbert Street from Middlesbrough for a fee of around £40,000, but his first season had a prematurely disappointing ending: 'I'd been a virtual ever-present but then got injured towards the end of the season and had to have a hernia operation which ruled me out of the last two or three games and meant that I had to miss out on the Play-off Final. I had to sit there, on the back of the bench at Wembley, as the lads played against Blackburn Rovers.'

Although there was more anguish 12 months later, at least Kevin did play in the 1993 Play-off Final. 'The Swindon game was memorable for so many reasons. From 3–0 down we came back to make it all-square and then a player – I think it was Steve White – tried to go around me and went down. I didn't touch him, but the referee was conned a little bit and gave the penalty. I remember being angry afterwards as it was never a penalty, but there's nothing you can do, you just have to get on with it.'

Kevin is usually listed in player profiles as being around the 5ft 10in mark, certainly not short but not the skyscraper height that some coaches would prefer. 'It's something of a pet hate to hear managers and coaches go on about 'keepers being not big enough. You only need to look at someone like Fabien Barthez who won a World Cup and a host of other medals despite his perceived lack of inches.'

If Kevin could not claim to be the tallest 'keeper around, his other qualities marked him out as one of the best of his generation. 'I always tried to maintain my fitness to aid my agility – I always felt I was a good decision maker and would always take ownership of the crosses and corners that would come into the box.'

Nicknamed either 'Pooley' or 'The Cat', the goalkeeper admits to being a great fan of another former City hero in his formative days. 'Peter Shilton was the goalkeeper I most admired when I was first getting into the game; he set the standard for others to aspire to. Again, he wasn't the tallest either!'

Kevin was out injured for much of the 1993–94 campaign, so he missed the third of the Foxes' trio of back-to-back Play-offs, but he regained fitness to have a hectic season in the Premiership.

'I won the Player of the Year Award then – mainly, I think, because of how busy I was! It was certainly a test as there were so many top strikers around.'

After a one-year stay at the highest level, City were back in familiar territory – and again they reached the Play-off Final. This time against Crystal Palace. Kevin recalls that one of his favourite saves as a City 'keeper came in that match: 'It was from a shot by Bruce Dyer, and I dived full-length towards the top corner to get a touch to tip it over. Apart from the personal satisfaction, it came at a crucial time with the game still goalless.'

Managers are paid to make tough decisions at key moments, and Martin O'Neill made one at Wembley that day, substituting his goalkeeper in the dying seconds of the match.

'I didn't know I was going to be taken off', reveals Kevin. 'We were moments away from a penalty shoot-out, and Martin obviously felt that Zeljko Kalac, at 6ft 7in, would be more of a physical presence in goal. I must admit I felt very dejected as I made my way off the field and sat down on the bench, but then within seconds Steve Claridge scored to win it for us, and I went from one extreme to the other. It was really emotional for everybody.'

The following season, although it was Kasey Keller who played in both the Final and the replay against Middlesbrough, Kevin picked up a League Cup-winners' medal.

'It doesn't really mean too much, to be honest', he reveals. 'I was on the bench and didn't play in any of the rounds. It was great to be part of the team spirit, and it is nice to know you're there to do a job if needed.'

Kevin admits there was always healthy competition for places at Leicester but has nothing but affection for the club and the supporters. Twelve years after leaving City 'The Cat' was still frustrating opposition strikers as he helped Burton Albion to the Blue Square title and a place in the Football League.

*'Peter Shilton was the goalkeeper I most admired when I was first getting into the game; he set the standard for others to aspire to. Again, he wasn't the tallest either!'*

# SPENCER PRIOR

*Born:*        22 April 1974, Southend, Essex.

## Leicester City record:
*Appearances:*    League 64, FA Cup 5, League Cup 7, Other 2.
*Debut:*        17 August 1996 v Sunderland (a) drew 0–0.
*Also played for:*  Southend United, Norwich City, Derby County, Manchester City,
            Cardiff City.


When the Foxes regained their Premiership status in time for the start of the 1996–97 campaign, manager Martin O'Neill strengthened his defence by signing a solid, dependable, win-at-all-costs defender who had previously played under him at Norwich City.

Spencer Prior joined from Norwich in August 1996 but admits he did not take much persuading to move to the Walkers Stadium. 'I didn't need to be sold on the club as I wanted to work under Martin again and I would have walked to Leicester if necessary! Seriously though, the club had just won promotion to the Premier League, they had one of the best managers in the country and everything about the direction the club was moving in sold itself to me.'

During Spencer's time with the Foxes the club were often thought to punch above their weight in the top flight, being particularly impressive on their travels. 'I'm not sure why that was really but we were a very tight group who loved the underdog status. The management team made sure we all knew our roles and responsibilities and it might also have been because if we didn't win then we always had to travel back on the bus – no matter what plans we had made that evening!'

Among those 'surprise' wins were some trips which were particularly memorable for the man called 'Spenner' by his teammates. 'We always seemed to do really well against Aston Villa, although winning at Tottenham was awesome, as there was nothing like coming down to London and winning. I've still got a photo of me and David Ginola wrestling for a ball and him finishing up on his backside!'

Perhaps even more stunning were a 2–1 victory at Liverpool and a 1–0 win at Old Trafford. 'The Manchester United game is one game I will never forget, just because Teddy Sheringham missed an absolute sitter right at the end! We never went anywhere and felt intimidated, even at places like those – or at St James' Park, where we should have won – 3–1 up but lost 4–3 to a late Alan Shearer hat-trick!'

Reaching the 1997 League Cup Final was a never-to-be-forgotten occasion for the City supporters, but Spencer recalls that all the players approached the match at Wembley in a thoroughly professional manner. 'Honestly, I really do not remember that much about the day as I was so focused on the game. It was a special occasion for the club admittedly – but we had a job to do, and if we

# 'Hopefully one day I will be able to return to Leicester as a coach – who knows, having worked under the great Martin O'Neill some of it must have rubbed off.'

had got caught up in the occasion then we might not have got our rewards. I can honestly say we all treated it as if it was just another game.'

After a drawn contest beneath the Twin Towers both sides had to head north to decide the outcome. 'The replay, however, felt really different, and the atmosphere at Hillsborough was electric. We went into the game believing we could win as always, and when KC [Keller] made a great save from Emerson we knew the Cup was ours. It was a fantastic achievement and something I feel proud to have been a part of – not just the Cup campaign, but the whole season. We were tipped to be relegation fodder, and we proved a lot of people wrong.'

In a total of 78 first-team games for City the big defender did not manage a single goal for the club, and on the occasion when he did come close he got a whack and a telling off! 'I should have scored in a game against Southampton but missed an absolute sitter. Five minutes later I got smashed in the back by Paul Jones, who was in goal for them, and finished up coming off with three broken ribs. "The Gaffer" turned round and said it served me right for missing that chance. He was right mind you!'

After a couple of years at City the fans were more than a little shocked when Spencer was transferred to East Midland rivals Derby County. 'I missed the opening day of the season with a damaged neck and the club had just signed Frank Sinclair, who went on to do great things for them. I did not want to leave but when the gaffer pulled me in and said the club had accepted an offer for me and that it might be better in my long-term football interests to move on, sometimes you need to take the hint!'

'I loved playing for Leicester, and the supporters were always awesome towards me when I came back, even as a Derby player. But for me the most memorable time was coming on at the Walkers Stadium for Southend United. It was quite emotional as I knew it was the final time I would get to see the supporters before I moved to Sydney.'

Spencer now lives in Australia with his wife Clare and three children Charlotte, Natasha and Millie. He works for Fox Sports covering the Premier League games and has recently completed his A Licence coaching badge. 'Hopefully one day I will be able to return to Leicester as a coach – who knows, having worked under the great Martin O'Neill some of it must have rubbed off.'

# PAUL RAMSEY

*Born:*            3 September 1962, Derry, Northern Ireland.

**Leicester City record:**

*Appearances:*    League 290, FA Cup 10, League Cup 19, Other 3.
*Goals:*          League 13, FA Cup 1, League Cup 1, Other 0.
*Debut:*          7 March 1981 v Arsenal (h) won 1–0.
*Also played for:* Derry City (Northern Ireland), Cardiff City, St Johnstone (Scotland), Telford United, Torquay United, Merthyr Tydfil, KPV (Finland), Rothwell Town, Grantham Town, Kings Lynn, Northern Ireland (14 caps).

Paul Ramsey was a hugely combative and immensely popular player who appeared in over 300 first-team matches for City during the 1980s and was rewarded with a well-deserved testimonial for his efforts.

After gaining schoolboy recognition for Northern Ireland his potential was clear, and it enabled him to follow a similar path to one of his countrymen. 'I was playing for Derry Athletic's youth team and my manager, Jim O'Hea, was also a scout for Leicester City – he'd sent John O'Neill over a few years earlier and arranged for me to go over for a trial. I played a few games and was then invited back and offered an apprenticeship at 16. Jock Wallace had taken over as the first-team manager and he took to me, which was a big turning point in my life.'

The young right-back settled in to life at Leicester and was handed an early opportunity. 'My debut came when I was just 18, and I went on as a sub in a 1–0 home win over Arsenal. It was a great day and a wonderful experience to be lining up against the likes of Pat Jennings, Liam Brady and Graham Rix, players I'd usually only seen on *Match of the Day*.'

It took until the 1982–83 season before Paul cemented his place in the team, and he played his part in a highly successful campaign, crowning it with his first goal for the club. 'It was a wonderful feeling to get promoted and good for me to get my first League goal – away at Oldham. It was a muddy day, and I remember

> **When David Pleat took over as manager Paul was handed the club captaincy: 'It was a great honour for me, and it inspired me to become a little more responsible.'**

we had got Gerry Daly playing for us on loan from Coventry. He was inspirational and really calmed us down. It was a decent goal – I think I played a couple of one-twos from the right-back position, first with Kevin McDonald then with Gerry, and then Alan Smith put me through and I stuck it in at the near post.'

Confirmation of Paul's advancement within the game came in the form of a first senior call-up for his country – with the first of his 14 caps coming against Austria.

As with many other predominantly defensive players his goals tended to be infrequent, and he scored one that very few people saw – against Burton Albion in an FA Cup tie that was played behind closed doors after trouble in the first match.

'It was played at Coventry City and was quite a surreal situation – it was a freezing cold day, and there was nobody there. I scored the only goal, and it got just a few handclaps from the direction of the directors' box.'

A rather more spectacular effort came against Queen's Park Rangers in March 1987 which won the Supporters' Goal of the Season award. 'There was a long ball downfield – their 'keeper came for it, but Ali Mauchlen kept chasing and got to it first, he passed it to me wide on the right edge of the box and I managed to hit it right-footed with the outside of the foot over the 'keeper and in from a widish position.'

By that stage of his career Paul had been more or less permanently advanced into a midfield role. I'd always been a right-back but moved forward to do the donkey work for the likes of Garry McAllister and the other more creative players. I didn't mind where I was really so long as I was involved – I loved getting into scrapes!'

When David Pleat took over as manager Paul was handed the club captaincy: 'It was a great honour for me, and it inspired me to become a little more responsible.'

Although the fans knew him as 'Rambo' there was another less well-known nickname which was kept within the confines of his close friends and family. 'It goes back to being with the Derry lads when I was just 16 or so – since then I've been known as "Penya" but there's only a couple of people who know the real reason why!'

Injuries finally began to catch up with Paul. He had initially damaged his left knee in a reserve-team fixture in 1984. But there was another golden performance to recall as the decade came to an end – at home to Leeds United in November 1989. 'I came on at half-time for the injured Alan Evans when we were 2–0 down and managed to score a couple of decent goals as we came back to win 4–3 – one was a run from the halfway line and the other a left-footed volley from the edge of the box!'

That same season Spurs provided the opposition for his testimonial match. 'Gary Lineker, Frank Worthington and Paul Gascoigne came and played – there were eight or nine thousand people there and my family came over from Ireland. It was a very special occasion for me.'

Despite still being hampered by his troublesome knee, Paul returned to City's colours in the summer of 2009 as part of the successful Central Masters-winning side.

# HOWARD RILEY

*Born:*  18 August 1938, Wigston, Leicestershire.

## Leicester City record:

*Appearances:*  League 193, FA Cup 24, League Cup 12, Other 4.
*Goals:*  League 38, FA Cup 5, League Cup 4, Other 0.
*Debut:*  22 August 1955 v Nottingham Forest (h) won 5–2.
*Also played for:*  Wigston Old Boys, Walsall, Atlanta Chiefs (USA), Barrow, Rugby Town, Burton Albion, Ibstock Penistone Rovers, Midland Athletic.

The outside-right in Leicester City's Cup Final sides of the early 1960s was home-grown talent Howard Riley. From a sporting background – both his father and grandfather played county cricket, and his two brothers were also keen footballers – Howard signed for the Foxes while still at school.

'I was only about 14 then and was in the reserves a year later', recalls Howard. 'I signed pro forms as soon as I could and was just a few days past my 17th birthday when I made my first-team debut. I remember feeling how brilliant it was to play alongside legends like Arthur Rowley and Johnny Morris.'

No sooner had the nippy winger begun to establish himself in the game when he was called upon for National Service with the Royal Leicestershire Regiment. 'I served alongside Colin Appleton and we played regular Army football together,' he says.

Back at Filbert Street, Howard's career began to blossom, and in the 1957–58 season he was called-up for the England Under-23 side, becoming the first City player to win a cap at that level.

Also that season Howard was given fresh responsibility as the club's penalty taker. 'I always remember the first time I was asked to take one. It was against Manchester City in an extraordinary game that we won 8–4. The great Bert Trautmann was in goal – fortunately I scored and became the regular penalty taker after that.'

Known affectionately as 'H' by teammates and fans alike, City's number seven played an integral part in the 1960–61 FA Cup run, scoring a couple of important goals along the way. The pen portraits in the Wembley programme for the Final listed Howard as 'the only local product in the side' and added, 'despite his lack of inches, he has terrific speed and a devastating shot.'

There was a shock for 'H', however, as one of the names listed in that programme was omitted from the starting line up.

'The team had been blending well together, but then we were hit with a bombshell when the manager announced at the last moment that Ken Leek had been left out of the team. I never did really find out the reason why, but there'd clearly been some sort of misunderstanding between the two of them.'

Whether the outcome could have been different will always be open to conjecture, but City suffered another set-back early in the contest. 'It was a shame that Len [Chalmers] got injured in the Final because it turned into a bit of a farce after that. Poor Len just went and hobbled out on the wing – but we were trying to play with just 10 men really. Individually I thought I played a pretty decent game, but there were obviously mixed emotions because we were all bitterly disappointed that we didn't win.'

That first piece of silverware remained elusive for City, but another opportunity soon came along with an appearance in the 1963 FA Cup Final, and Howard believes that one should have been won.

'Against Manchester United we were hot favourites. We'd beaten them 4–3 at home just a few weeks before in a match that produced hat-tricks for both Ken Keyworth and Denis Law. Only recently I read an article about that game that reminded me that all three of Ken's goals came inside a six-minute spell at the Filbert Street End and I crossed the ball for them all!'

Sadly, though, it was a different story when the two sides met beneath the Twin Towers. 'We were too relaxed, too confident, maybe even cocky – as it turned out we just didn't perform on the day.'

The following year City did, at last, win a major honour, defeating Stoke City in the two-legged Final. A 1–1 draw at the old Victoria Ground left the Foxes with home advantage for the return leg, and in a see-saw match it was Howard's late strike that clinched the victory 4–3 on aggregate.

'There was probably only about 10 minutes left – I cut in from the wing and let fly, left-footed, into the top corner. In terms of what it meant, it was probably the most important goal of my career.'

Shortly afterwards Howard began to look to the future by enrolling on a three-year full-time teaching course, meaning that his football had to take a back seat. 'Looking back, I should have carried on playing for another six or seven years. It's always been a bit of a regret that I didn't finish my football career properly and then go into teaching afterwards.'

'H' played a little more football, both in the United States and for a variety of non-League clubs, before concentrating on teaching both PE and History. He did complete all of his coaching badges and later returned to work at the Leicester City Academy, but he fondly remembers his playing days at the club.

'I was a traditional winger who played very close to the touchline and liked to get the ball and get a cross in. It was a good time to be playing, we had some amazing matches and I was just privileged to be a part of it.'

*'Against Manchester United we were hot favourites. We'd beaten them 4–3 at home just a few weeks before in a match that produced hat-tricks for both Ken Keyworth and Denis Law. Only recently I read an article about that game that reminded me that all three of Ken's goals came inside a six-minute spell at the Filbert Street End and I crossed the ball for them all!'*

# BOBBY ROBERTS

*Born:*        2 September 1940, Edinburgh.

## Leicester City record:
*Appearances:*    League 229, FA Cup 30, League Cup 22.
*Goals:*    League 26, FA Cup 4, League Cup 6.
*Debut:*    21 September 1963 v Fulham (h) lost 0–1.
*Also played for:*    Edinburgh Norton, Motherwell, Mansfield Town, Colchester United.
*Managed:*    Colchester United, Wrexham, Grimsby Town.

Bobby Roberts gave sterling service to the Foxes throughout the 1960s and was a member of the side that reached Wembley for the 1969 FA Cup Final.

Having caught the eye over five seasons with Motherwell, he was enticed south to become Leicester's record signing for a fee of £41,000. 'Ipswich were also keen', recalls Bobby. 'But I'd set my heart on Leicester and had a good friend there in Davie Gibson, whom I knew from our time in Edinburgh. I took a while to settle at the new club, primarily because I kept turning my ankle. It continued to be a problem until the end of the first season when the doctor knocked me out and manipulated it. I didn't have a problem again throughout my career.'

The Foxes won through to the 1964 League Cup Final, courtesy of a two-legged semi-final victory over West Ham United, with Bobby scoring in both matches. The home match was won in thrilling fashion 4–3, and the side travelled south full of confidence and won the match 2–0.

Despite scoring goals in both legs of the semi, Bobby did not play in the Final itself. 'You just accepted it back then. There weren't any substitutes then, so the manager just went with the XI he thought would do the job. It was around that time that I'd been having a few problems with my ankles in any case.'

The following year City again reached the Final, and Bobby remembers the tie with a wince. 'We'd lost 3–2 at Chelsea in the first leg, and then I was switched to play up front in the return. It's not true to say I didn't get a kick – because I finished the match black and blue, thanks to Chelsea's two uncompromising centre-halves, John Mortimore and Frank Upson! The match finished goalless, and I had to be content with a runners'-up tankard.'

Bobby was, by every definition, a central midfield player, but the manager would often call on his versatility. 'Ken Keyworth had a spell where he was quite prone to injury, and Matt Gillies kept asking me to play up front. I had a few self-doubts about it because I didn't really feel I was quick enough and always felt that I was just filling in. I did have a few successes, though, and I remember

*'It was 1–1 with about 10 or 12 minutes to go when Peter Shilton got injured and I took over in goal. I managed to emerge unscathed, although Bobby Charlton did blast one past me, but it was ruled out for offside – I always made out I could have saved it if necessary!'*

getting two goals against Everton at Christmas 1964. We beat them home and away inside three days!'

Bobby's versatility even stretched to the training ground, where he would occasionally go in goal towards the end of a session, a practice which put him in the firing line one day against Manchester United at Old Trafford.

'It was 1–1 with about 10 or 12 minutes to go when Peter Shilton got injured and I took over in goal. I managed to emerge unscathed, although Bobby Charlton did blast one past me, but it was ruled out for offside – I always made out I could have saved it if necessary!'

Bobby reveals that, like most young Scottish footballers, he had had a list of ambitions but always felt that playing at Wembley might be one that was never fulfilled. 'I'd played at Hampden Park for Motherwell in a losing Scottish Cup semi-final against Rangers but never really thought I'd get to play at Wembley. We'd come close in the FA Cup a couple of times before, losing to both Everton and Liverpool, but it was a bit of a surprise when we did get there in 1969.'

Leicester's League form that season was poor, so it was something of a surprise when they advanced to the Cup Final to meet Manchester City. 'We'd been tipped to get hammered, but on the day we created the better chances. Unfortunately none of them fell to Allan Clarke, who was in great form around that time and would have taken them, I'm sure.'

The Wembley programme that day highlighted the fact that Bobby liked to have a 'crack at goal'.

'It's true that a lot of people in the top tier of our Double Decker Stand were often in more danger than the goalkeeper, but I did like a shot from distance, and occasionally one would fly in.'

Of the 36 goals Bobby scored for City he has no hesitation in picking his favourite. 'Everton at home, I just leaned back and hit it from about 35 yards past 'keeper Gordon West and into the top corner.'

Bobby left Filbert Street for Mansfield Town in the summer of 1970 and then wound down his career before moving into coaching and management. He even returned to City for a three-year stint during the David Pleat reign.

Still a very respected scout these days, Bobby remains very passionate about the game but believes he played during a true golden period. 'It was marvellous to line up each week against some of the very best – Bremner, Giles, Charlton, Bell, Douglas, Clayton – every side seemed to have some real stars, but we coped and acquitted ourselves well, and we had a remarkable team spirit at Leicester.'

# IWAN ROBERTS

*Born:*           26 June 1968, Bangor, Gwynedd.

## Leicester City record:

*Appearances:*      League 100, FA Cup 5, League Cup 5, Other 1.

*Goals:*            League 41, FA Cup 2, League Cup 1, Other 0.

*Debut:*           27 November 1993 v Wolves (h) drew 2–2.

*Also played for:*   Watford, Huddersfield Town, Wolverhampton Wanderers, Norwich City, Gillingham, Cambridge United (loan), Wales (15 caps).

Iwan Roberts certainly brought his shooting boots with him to Filbert Street, but he admits that he was a bit concerned after playing his opening 45 minutes for the club.

'On my debut we were 2–0 down to Wolves at half-time, and we were booed off. I wondered, "What have I done signing for these?"' The turn-around was instant, however, as Iwan recalls. 'We came back to draw 2–2 in that match, and I got both goals but then missed the easiest chance of the lot for my hat-trick. I was just four yards out and put it over the bar – individually it was a great start for me though.'

They were the first two goals out of a tally of 41 that Iwan hit in exactly 100 League appearances for the Foxes. Among the haul in that first season was a home hat-trick against Derby County. In an amazing opening half, City again came back from two down to lead 3–2 and then go into the break level at 3–3.

'It was the first hat-trick of my career, so it was very special – I knew about the local rivalry and what it meant to the fans – so to score three in front of the Leicester fans was great. The second of the three was probably the best goal I scored in my career – a corner came out to me, and I just hit it sweetly from about 18 yards, and it flew into the net. It was a special moment in a really important game, and I've still got the matchball with all the lads' signatures on it.'

Having contributed 13 goals from just 26 appearances, Iwan's League campaign was brought to a premature end on 23 April 1994 – in an accidental collision with a future Foxes star. 'I broke my ribs in a game against Oxford United. I went up for a header with Matty Elliott and ran into his elbow – I've never felt pain like it!'

'Robbo's teammates did him proud by reaching the Play-off Final in his absence, and fortunately the injury healed in time. 'It was touch and go whether I would play or not, but when they saw our team sheet with myself, Walshy [Steve Walsh] and Sticks [Ian Ormondroyd] all included, there was only one way we were going to play, wasn't there?'

Leicester's direct approach was very much in evidence as they soon levelled Derby's opener, and Iwan admits that perhaps the goal was a touch fortunate. 'As the cross was coming in for Walshy to score I clattered into the 'keeper Martin Taylor, but thankfully the foul wasn't given.'

The jubilant scenes at the end of the match completed a fairytale first campaign at Filbert Street for Iwan. 'It was a great day – it really is the best way to get promoted. If the win was guaranteed I'd take that route every time!'

## 'It was a great day – it really is the best way to get promoted. If the win was guaranteed I'd take that route every time!'

Iwan's nine League goals during the following term confirmed that he was comfortable playing at the highest level, but City struggled throughout and lost their Premiership status at the first time of asking. 'It was a season of struggle really, and we didn't strengthen the squad as much as we should have done. We had our good days, but we had more that were "off" than "on".'

In his pomp Iwan was a fearsome sight – tall and strong with a good touch and powerful in the air, he was the complete centre-forward. The whole image was made to look even scarier by the famous toothless grin ('they were knocked out playing for Watford against Exeter when I was about 21'). The use of the term 'gap-toothed warrior' accompanied many a flattering press article about him.

Back in the Championship – and now under Martin O'Neill – the art of goalscoring was again made to look easy by the Welsh international, who converted 19 chances from just 37 games in the League – a total that included a goal in five consecutive games and also brought him another Leicester hat-trick – this time in a home win over Portsmouth.

Sadly, another end-of-season rib injury ruled Iwan out of another Play-off Final; although he had a big decision to make: 'I wanted to be involved, and I think Martin was considering putting me on the bench, but he asked me to be honest and admit that if one of our forwards was hurt in the first few minutes could I be confident of playing the rest of the match – I had to say no as I knew the injury wasn't up to it.'

'Robbo' moved on to Wolves during the next close season but regards his spell at Leicester as being one of the happiest of his career. 'I loved my time there – we had a great team spirit and used to go out and socialise together. We had terrific training facilities and the most passionate supporters around.'

A native Welsh language speaker, Iwan has now forged a successful media career as a popular and forthright pundit following the game in his homeland. He is also involved as a fundraiser for a number of charities, among them the Bobby Moore Research Fund.

# PETER RODRIGUES

*Born:*          21 January 1944, Cardiff, South Wales.

## Leicester City record:
*Appearances:*   League 140, FA Cup 19, League Cup 12.
*Goals:*         League 6, FA Cup 0, League Cup 0.
*Debut:*         1 January 1966 v Stoke City (h) won 1–0.
*Also played for:* Cardiff City, Southampton, Sheffield Wednesday, Wales (40 caps).

Roving right-back Peter Rodrigues played in Leicester City's 1969 FA Cup Final side and was an immensely popular figure in the game, who won 40 caps for Wales and went on to skipper Southampton to Wembley success.

He was a virtual ever-present for home-town club Cardiff City for three years after breaking into their first team as a 19-year-old. Although happy playing for the Bluebirds, Peter was ambitious to play in the top flight. 'At the start of their career every player aims to reach the very top of the game with luck – at Leicester I was given that opportunity.'

Despite the passing years, Peter can easily recall the exact date of his transfer. 'It all went through on New Year's Eve. 'I spent the night in a hotel in the city – I think it was The Grand – and I remember hearing the bells chime for midnight outside. Later that afternoon I made my debut for the club at home to Stoke, and we won 1–0 with Derek Dougan getting the goal. I was reasonably pleased with my debut and settled in quickly at Filbert Street. I found the manager, Matt Gillies, to be a really nice guy. In fact, everyone there was good to work with.

'I was an attacking full-back – similar, I suppose, to a modern-day wing-back. I liked to get forward – when I was fit and young it came naturally to me. Later in my career, when I was at Southampton, Lawrie McMenemy told me that he paid me to defend. I had to learn to do it at the right time, and I guess I improved as time went by.'

Peter also relished the opportunity of winning his own individual battle against an opposing winger. 'There was once that quote that I was quick enough to catch pigeons. My added strength was that I liked a sliding tackle and usually timed it right – I always felt it was my job not to allow them to get past me. I liked to slide in, and if I was beaten I could usually get up very quickly and then get at them again.'

Supporting the attack came naturally to the right-back, and he did chip in with a few vital strikes, but the City goal he remembers most came from the spot. 'We were awarded a penalty in a match against Burnley, and no one wanted to take it. I came forward quickly saying that I'd take it. I sensed that everyone was pretty nervous about me having it, but fortunately I managed to score!'

The stand-out moment of Peter's time at Filbert Street was the 1969 FA Cup run, and with defeat in the Final coming by the narrowest of margins it is inevitable that City fans wonder what might have been on that May afternoon in North London.

'People often comment on my miss that day', Peter smiles ruefully. 'For many years I told the story and always maintained that it was Lennie Glover who put the ball across. I'd never seen the match in all that time, but a couple of years ago a friend of mine told me that the match was now available on DVD and that he'd bought me a copy. I went round to watch it, and the pictures told a different story to my memory. We actually played very well on the day. We were underdogs, but on reflection we attacked them at every opportunity and weren't beaten out of sight. We had some good chances, and had mine fallen to one of the strikers I'm sure it would have been put away.'

'The first goal was vital, and my chance came just before they scored. Andy Lochhead put it in from wide on the left – I'd trundled into the box from the right-back position. It came in, and I initially missed it as I swung with my left – I turned as it hit the centre-half and came back towards me as I half scuffed it from five or six yards out, and it just trickled past the post. As I ran back to the halfway line I remember thinking "oh dear what a miss". It did haunt me for a while afterwards.'

Reflecting on his City career, it is clear that the Cup Final dominates Peter's thoughts, and he does have a couple of constant reminders of that day. 'I have a couple of photos on display– one is of me in line meeting Princess Anne before the game and the other one is of me on the goalline as the ball rifled into the net between me and Peter Shilton for their goal.'

Seven years later – at a different club and with a new nickname 'They called me "Pedro" at Southampton because of the facial hair I'd grown!' – Peter would belatedly have his big day at Wembley, captaining the Saints to their unexpected FA Cup triumph over Manchester United.

But for a change of manager Peter might have still been a Fox by that stage of his career. 'I didn't want to leave Leicester, but there was a clash of personality between myself and new manager Frank O'Farrell, and it was clear that I needed to leave in order to play first-team football. I really did enjoy my time there, though, and have always followed their fortunes ever since.'

*'I didn't want to leave Leicester, but there was a clash of personality between myself and new manager Frank O'Farrell, and it was clear that I needed to leave in order to play first-team football. I really did enjoy my time there, though, and have always followed their fortunes ever since.'*

# DENNIS ROFE

*Born:*         1 June 1950, Epping, Essex.

## Leicester City record:

*Appearances:*    League 290, FA Cup 22, League Cup 12.
*Goals:*          League 6, FA Cup 0, League Cup 0.
*Debut:*          26 August 1972 v Coventry City (h) drew 0–0.
*Also played for:*  Leyton Orient, Chelsea, Southampton.
*Managed:*       Bristol Rovers.

On more than 300 occasions during the 1970s, the City left-back berth belonged to the hugely-engaging Dennis Rofe. Brought to Filbert Street by his former boss Jimmy Bloomfield, he briefly broke a transfer record.

'For around the grand total of 24 hours I was Britain's most expensive full-back, says Dennis, when recalling the day of his move to Leicester. 'Then David Nish went to Derby County for around double my fee!'

He admits that at the time he was unsure how to negotiate a contract. 'I'd been on £30 a week at Orient, so I asked some of the senior guys there (the likes of Peter Brabrook, Mark Lazarus, Terry Mancini) about what to do. They told me to make sure I doubled my money but not to accept the first offer I was given. I remember driving up the M1 to Leicester in my Vauxhall Viva determined to ask for £70 but "not to take the first offer I was given". I arrived at Filbert Street, was shown into the boardroom, and Jimmy came in and said, "Don't beat about the bush, we're prepared to offer £100 a week." I said, 'Give me a pen quickly!'

Domestic arrangements were then put into full swing as Dennis adjusted to life in the East Midlands. 'I was put into the Holiday Inn – I was there for a few months and Frank Worthington was also there at the time. I tell people I was 22 when I went in and 34 when I came out!'

He did not manage to 'escape' until after he had got married, but even then his new bride had to spend time in the Inn. 'Sue and I brought our wedding forward to the November, and after the reception we drove up to Leicester, but I had to leave her at the hotel as I then had to go off with the team to play a match at Norwich the next day!'

A model of consistency, Dennis was a manager's dream. 'I was pretty quick and not afraid to put my foot in. I wouldn't profess to being the most skilful, but I didn't know when I was beaten – I was whole-hearted and used to be able to defend well.'

In a team that clearly bonded so well, Dennis was often tagged with being a bit of a 'character'. 'The truth is that part of the strength of our team was the camaraderie between us. We had a decent social life and tried to get out once a week as a group and tried to raise a few quid for charity if we could. We all got on and we pulled for one another. I was called the dressing-room joker, but really no-one could outdo Birch!'

Dennis was another who suddenly had to answer to another name, thanks to Mr Birchenall. 'He decided that I was to be called "Sid" as he reckoned that I resembled Sid James!'

'Sid' did not get too many goals in City's colours, but those he did get were memorable, particularly the timing of his first – against Birmingham City in August 1974. 'It was 3–3, late on, and I got the winner. They came out trying to catch us offside, but Jon Sammels chipped it over them and I just continued running from the left-back

*'I was pretty quick and not afraid to put my foot in. I wouldn't profess to being the most skilful, but I didn't know when I was beaten – I was whole-hearted and used to be able to defend well.'*

position. I went round 'keeper Dave Latchford and stuck it in. I didn't know what to do next or how to celebrate, but apparently I just "took off like a scalded cat"!'

A slightly more fortunate but equally important score came at home against Queen's Park Rangers. 'I took a free-kick from halfway line and don't know if the sun was in Phil Parkes' eyes or what, but he came for it and it just floated over him and into the net – I was elated but a bit embarrassed!'

Two spectacular strikes at Swansea top off Dennis' own 'favourite goals' collection. 'They were both left-footed from around 25 yards that flew in like rockets – I went in search of my hat-trick then!'

Although the City side of that era did not win the major silverware their creativity deserved, Dennis does have a lasting memento to look at. 'After we'd been beaten by Liverpool in the 1974 semis the FA made us play a third versus fourth-place match against Burnley, the other losing semi-finalists. All I remember was there weren't many people there and I've got a tankard which "commemorates" the occasion.' (City lost 1–0 to Burnley at Filbert Street on 9 May 1974, in front of 4,000 fans, and a third vs fourth place Play-off has never been played since!)

His other City treasure came after he had left the club for Chelsea in February 1980. 'I received a call from Jock Wallace to come back and "collect something". He told me he'd been presented with a Championship medal but wanted me to have it. That was a typical gesture from a magnificent man – I remember him saying, "I've got something for you, wee man"– it was the only time I understood him!'

Dennis confirms that he will never be able to forget his time with City. 'Our two sons, Daniel and then Marcus, were both born in the Leicester Royal Infirmary, and the younger one still supports the Foxes! I loved my time there – they were the happiest days of my career.'

# ARTHUR ROWLEY

*Born:*        21 April 1926, Wolverhampton.

*Died:*        18 December 2002, Shrewsbury, Shropshire.

## Leicester City record:

*Appearances:*    League 303, FA Cup 18.

*Goals:*          League 251, FA Cup 14.

*Debut:*          19 August 1950 v Bury (a) won 3–2.

*Also played for:*   Blackhall St Lukes, Wolverhampton Wanderers, West Bromwich Albion, Fulham, Shrewsbury Town.

*Managed:*      Shrewsbury Town, Sheffield United, Southend United, Oswestry Town.

No one has scored more goals in the Football League than one-time City striker Arthur Rowley. The Wolverhampton-born forward scored a grand total of 434 goals from 619 appearances, made over the course of 19 years. Eight of those years were spent at Filbert Street, where he contributed 251 League goals, 44 of them coming in the 1956–57 campaign – a seasonal best for a Foxes player.

To say Arthur came from a footballing background is like mentioning that Tiger Woods is 'a bit handy at golf'. His father had kept goal for Walsall and elder brother Jack went on to play for Manchester United and England.

Incredibly, full international honours always eluded Arthur; although he did make a solitary appearance for the B team, scoring once in a 4–1 win over Switzerland, and he also led the line for the Football League in a match against the Irish League. Both of those games were played during 1956, by which time Arthur was at the very peak of his powers. To mention his prowess purely in statistical terms would not do the Black Countryman justice. He was a rough, tough, battering ram of a forward and was just as lethal in the air as on the ground. His shot was venomous, particularly with his favoured left foot, and his accuracy was unerring. Goals were his business and defenders cherished the full-time whistle, hoping that they had not been embarrassed by their shortcomings against him.

Incredibly, Arthur may have had an even richer final tally of goals because he may have lost a season or two to the war. He made his early wartime appearances for Manchester United, alongside his brother, aged just 15, and he 'guested' for several other clubs during the conflict, as well as serving his country in both Germany and Palestine.

He joined West Brom after the war (in February 1948 he even played in goal for them for an hour against Leicester City), but it was after joining Fulham that he began to hit the net with increasing regularity and powered them to promotion.

*Twenty-eight League goals in his first season with the Foxes (after scoring on his debut against Bury) were followed by 38 and then 39 as the 100-goal mark was passed in just 122 appearances*

A transfer to Filbert Street for £12,000 soon followed and there began an amazing sequence of consistency which mere statistics, although impressive, will never fully do justice. Twenty-eight League goals in his first season with the Foxes (after scoring on his debut against Bury) were followed by 38 and then 39 as the 100-goal mark was passed in just 122 appearances – one of many club records Arthur would go on to hold.

Nicknamed 'The Gunner', he had raced to that target helped by a scoring streak that saw him net in seven consecutive matches in the late autumn of 1951, and during the 1956–57 promotion campaign Arthur repeated this feat!

A season later Arthur put his old club, Fulham, to the sword, netting four against them at home and then another three at Craven Cottage – both matches falling within a 10-day period.

Individual brilliance, even by someone of Arthur's stature, rarely succeeds in a team sport, and Leicester were still unable to get out of the second tier, but that was put right in 1953–54 when they lifted the title. An ever-present in the number-10 jersey, Arthur scored 36 goals, 30 of them in the League, including three on Christmas Day at home to Rotherham United. He remains the last Fox to score a hat-trick on 25 December (and is always now likely to remain so).

Leicester's stay in the top flight was restricted to just one campaign and it took two more years to get back there again. The 1956–57 promotion year was Arthur's finest as he scored 44 League goals, another City record. Among the avalanche of net-busters were hat-tricks against Bury, Notts County, Blackburn Rovers and West Ham United – the final four of the 16 he hit for the club.

A total of 20 Division One goals in 1957–58 ensured that City stayed up this time and completed a sequence of eight years running that Arthur had reached that landmark.

Realising that he could not go on forever – and accepting that Arthur had managerial ambitions – City accepted a modest bid from Shrewsbury Town to allow their most prized asset to move to Gay Meadow as player-manager. With a total of 265 first-team goals for the Foxes, 'The Gunner' had not quite overtaken Arthur Chandler's haul of 273 – but he had played in 98 fewer matches!

Showing that he was far from finished, Arthur banged in 38 goals in his first season and led the Shrews to an unexpected promotion. He continued playing until he was 40 and he also enjoyed a spot of Cup giant-killing when leading his side to victory over Everton on the way to the League Cup semi-finals.

He later managed both Sheffield United and Southend United with mixed success before returning to live in Shropshire, where he managed both Oswestry Town and then Knighton in Powys.

After leaving the game Arthur worked for Vernons Pools until his retirement and was a regular spectator at Shrewsbury matches until his death in 2002.

Purely in terms of League goals, Arthur Rowley will always remain the game's number one!

# JON SAMMELS

*Born:*          23 July 1945, Ipswich, Suffolk.

**Leicester City record:**

*Appearances:*    League 236, FA Cup 17, League Cup 12, Other 1.
*Goals:*           League 21, FA Cup 1, League Cup 3, Other 0.
*Debut:*          14 August 1971 v Huddersfield Town (a) drew 2–2.
*Also played for:*  Arsenal, Vancouver Whitecaps (Canada), Nuneaton Borough, Trowbridge Town.

Jon Sammels was a key component of an era in City's history when they were hailed for their attractive and attack-minded style of play. Curiously, however, despite notching up more than 250 first-team outings for the club, the only silverware he won came at the end of his debut! 'My first match for the club was the Charity Shield – as Division Two winners City were asked to play against the League Champions that year, and we beat Liverpool 1–0.'

Eight years with Arsenal had brought more highs than lows for the midfielder. He had played in two League Cup Finals and scored the winning goal in a European Final (the 1970 Fairs Cup win over Anderlecht), as well as winning a Championship medal during the Gunners' double-winning season.

Apart from the healthy competition for places at Highbury, Jon admits he fancied a new challenge, and he thus became Jimmy Bloomfield's first signing at City. 'The main reason I chose Leicester was because of Jimmy. I'd known him as a player at Arsenal and liked his approach to the game and knew what sort of football he would want to play.'

> **'The main reason I chose Leicester was because of Jimmy. I'd known him as a player at Arsenal and liked his approach to the game and knew what sort of football he would want to play.'**

Over the next few seasons it became apparent what sort of style that would be. 'We entertained – yes, we were inconsistent and didn't win all our games, but we entertained. Jimmy didn't over-complicate things or blind us with science but would leave us to go out and express ourselves.'

There were some drawbacks with that system, however, as Jon recalls. 'In many ways we were naïve – we liked to play and make it an open game as we had skilful players, but we did not know how to close a game out once we'd got in front.'

Those 'skilful' players included the likes of Worthington, Weller, Birchenall and Jon himself. 'I was labelled as being "an elegant midfielder", but I was never sure what they meant by it. Sure, I could pass a ball, but I always felt that was something that all professional footballers should be able to do – other attributes are important, but the 10 outfield players should be able to pass accurately.'

'Sammy', as he was known, also contributed some vital goals to the City cause, and he remembers the occasion of his 50th career goal very well. 'There'd been something in the press about me being on 49 goals and then we played Queen's Park Rangers. I shot and it hit the underside of the bar and came down – it looked well behind the line but the ref didn't give it. The *Mercury* printed a picture of it, showing the ball a good couple of feet over the line. In the next match – against Burnley – I struck a half-volley with my left foot from a long way out and it flew into the net. Jimmy said it was the best goal he'd ever seen!'

Praise was often being directed towards City, but the nearest they came to toppling the game's elite was in the FA Cup run of 1974, when they advanced to the semi-finals. 'The last four were Liverpool, Burnley, Newcastle United and ourselves. We knew we could beat the other two so it was frustrating to be drawn out to face Liverpool. At Old Trafford we managed a 0–0, but they were all over us – Shilton was quite brilliant that day and he kept us in it.'

The tie went to a replay at Villa Park. Lennie Glover cancelled out Liverpool's opener, and then came what Jon believes was the decisive moment. 'At 1–1 Keith Weller got through one on one against Ray Clemence – in that situation I'd back Keith every time but "Clem" made a brilliant save. The way the momentum had swung I'm sure we'd have won it if that had gone in. Then Keegan scored a brilliant volley after the ball dropped over his head and they got a late third with us chasing the game.'

Another FA Cup tie, this time against non-League Leatherhead, also provides a stirring memory. 'They'd been in the press saying what they were going to do to us and they did it! They went 2–0 up and it would have been three except for a brilliant goalline clearance by Malcolm Munro. I was captain that day, and at half-time I thought I'd better say something so pointed out a few home truths. Fortunately I then managed to score right at the start of the half and we went on to win – or that could have been very embarrassing!'

After almost seven years at Filbert Street Jon was ready for a new challenge and entered into negotiations to join Vancouver Whitecaps. 'I hadn't signed anything but had agreed the move then got a call from Frank McLintock saying he'd just got the City job and would I stay awhile to help him get sorted. I agreed to put back my move to Canada, but it was a shame how it worked out, and it wasn't very nice knowing that they were struggling and I was going to leave shortly anyway.'

Much more than just an elegant midfielder, Jon left Leicester City in 1978, but he will always be remembered as one of 'the great entertainers'.

# ROBBIE SAVAGE

*Born:*          18 October 1974, Wrexham.

## Leicester City record:

*Appearances:*   League 172, FA Cup 12, League Cup 17, Other 3.
*Goals:*         League 8, FA Cup 1, League Cup 0, Other 0.
*Debut:*         9 August 1997 v Aston Villa (h) won 1–0.
*Also played for:*   Manchester United (trainee), Crewe Alexandra, Birmingham City, Blackburn Rovers, Brighton and Hove Albion (loan), Derby County, Wales (39 caps).

If any one player typified Leicester City during the Martin O'Neill era then it would probably be Robbie Savage. The combative, tough-tackling midfielder was the footballing equivalent of Marmite – you either love him or hate him – and the City fans took him to their hearts from the moment he signed for the club.

Robbie admits he was left sweating for a while before he was able to join the Foxes. 'I knew that I was leaving Crewe, and I'd got talking to John Robertson at Leicester. John explained that Martin O'Neill was away on holiday but that he'd get him to call me. He rang me at my mum's, but I was out and missed the call so I was left hoping that he'd get back to me, but thankfully he did, and once I'd spoken to him there was no doubting where I wanted to go.'

It was clear from the start that the Welsh international was a hard worker who liked to keep things simple – win it and give it – qualities and commitment that were evidently appreciated by both teammates and fans.

The 1999 League Cup Final defeat to Tottenham Hotspur saw Robbie's image take something of a battering as a result of an incident in which Spurs' Justin Edinburgh had been sent off. 'That defeat was one of the biggest disappointments of my time at Leicester, but it was the game that made me what I am today because the London press slaughtered me afterwards. They were very biased in their coverage and you could tell that it was along the lines of "little old Leicester, little old Robbie Savage", as if we shouldn't be behaving like that. The player raised his hands to me – there wasn't much contact, but he had to go and the media projected an image of me because of that incident.'

Robbie's flowing blonde locks made it difficult for him to hide from the terrace boo-boys, but that did not concern him in the slightest. 'Nobody knew me before that game but everyone did afterwards – I became the pantomime villain, but it's a role I've loved and used to my advantage. It gets me going. The more they boo me the more I love it!'

*'I had a great five years at Leicester and always enjoyed a good relationship with the fans – but I gave them absolutely everything I'd got in every game I played for them – I'd like to think they remember me for that.'*

The personal and overriding regret of Wembley 1999 would have been the failure to win a major domestic honour but that was put right 12 months later with the League Cup Final win over Tranmere Rovers.

'There were some really difficult games just to get to Wembley', he recalls. 'We had to go to penalties to beat Leeds and Fulham, and then there was just one goal in it in the semi-final against Aston Villa.'

Robbie came up with a few important goals for the Foxes, and they were usually collector's items. 'I enjoyed one at Southampton when I beat my international teammate Paul Jones from outside the box, but my favourite was at home to West Ham when on the spur of the moment I jumped into the crowd at the Filbert Street End!'

Controversy was not usually too far away when Robbie was around, and a couple of incidents continue to stand the test of time. Brought down by Danny Higginbotham in the last minute of a fiery encounter with Derby County, the City number eight was surrounded and berated for his actions. 'People are still going on about it – but Danny put his leg in and I went over it. It was a penalty.'

Robbie again made the headlines in April 2002 in an incident that became known as 'Poogate'. Prior to a home game against Aston Villa, the midfielder used the toilet in the dressing room of the match officials. Referee Graham Poll included the incident in his match report, and 'Sav' was 'hauled over the coals' for it.

'It was absolutely ridiculous', says Robbie. 'I had stomach cramps and there was nowhere else available – in this day and age to get vilified for using a toilet is a nonsense. My club didn't fine me, but the FA did – to the tune of £10,000 pounds!'

'Sav' to friends – and 'Lily' to the fans – Robbie had to endure the nickname 'Pelican Head' from Alan Birchenall. Their relationship – and friendship – became legendary, with 'the Birch' sometimes meeting his match! 'We used to go to the gym together – I don't know why he bothered because he was about 95 then. Afterwards he would get the chef to do him a nice dinner to take home. It would be covered with foil so I'd nick the key to his office, go in and remove the dinner and leave him something else under the foil. He'd get home and go potty!'

As Robbie admits, moving clubs can sometimes emphasise the fickle nature of supporters, but he hopes he'll be remembered for his commitment above all else. 'I had a great five years at Leicester and always enjoyed a good relationship with the fans – but I gave them absolutely everything I'd got in every game I played for them – I'd like to think they remember me for that.'

# PETER SHILTON

*Born:*  18 September 1949, Leicester.

## Leicester City record:

*Appearances:*  League 286, FA Cup 33, League Cup 20, Other 1.
*Goals:*  League 1.
*Debut:*  4 May 1966 v Everton (h) won 3–0.
*Also played for:*  Stoke City, Nottingham Forest, Southampton, Derby County, Plymouth Argyle, Bolton Wanderers, Leyton Orient, England (125 caps).

Cold statistics can sometimes be misleading when applied to footballers, but when they confirm that a player has survived at the top of his profession for three decades and played in more League matches and made more international appearances than anyone else then they truly add weight to the claim that Peter Shilton is among the very best goalkeepers the world has ever seen.

Leicester-born – and associated with his local League club from an early age – Peter knew there was an almighty obstacle barring his path to the Foxes first-team. 'Gordon Banks was the England goalkeeper and wasn't going to be easily dislodged from his position. I had opportunities to go to other clubs as an apprentice but chose not to go down that route. My parents felt it would be better for me to live at home at that time, and I was more than happy to stay at Leicester and learn my trade there.'

Peter's development was rapid, and manager Matt Gillies had no hesitation in blooding the youngster while he was still only 16 years of age. 'My debut was pretty unique really', recalls 'Shilts'. 'Because in those days you didn't postpone League matches when there was an international going on, and Gordon was away with England. Anyway, I managed to keep a clean sheet in that match, and it has to be one of the best memories of my career.'

It seemed like Leicester were going to be forced into a decision, with two outstanding 'keepers on their books, and Peter recalls that he was the one whose performances were suddenly placed

*'I had a great time there and am so proud to have completed the full set of international appearances while at my local club – playing for England Schoolboys, Youth, Under-23 and the full side as a Leicester player was a very big thing for me.'*

under scrutiny. 'I'd had a few first-team outings, and after one outing – I think it was against West Brom – then there were some bits in the paper that one or two clubs were sniffing around after me. I didn't really want to sit in the reserves for another two or three years and would have been quite happy to leave, but then Gordon moved to Stoke, and people miss the part of it where I suddenly was the one under the most pressure.'

Ironically, almost immediately Peter sustained an ankle injury and was out for several weeks, but when back in the first-team fold his impressive displays were complimented with a real collector's item when, away at Southampton in October 1967 he became the first City 'keeper to score a goal – but he didn't even realise it at the time!

'We were 4–1 up in the last minute of the match, and I hit a long ball downfield and thought Mike Stringfellow had got a touch before it bounced into the goal. We'd gone down there by train and were booked back on the 5 o'clock departure, so it was such a rush afterwards that there wasn't even time for a shower. I remember us pushing the skip back up the road and asking people to hold the train for us. On the journey back a few of the lads made reference to me scoring, but I thought they were taking the mickey, but it wasn't until I got home and saw it on television that I realised what had happened.'

The Foxes had, of course, developed a reputation in the early 1960s for doing well in the FA Cup, and there was a feeling that a return to the Twin Towers was within their grasp as the decade drew to a close. That feeling intensified after a fifth-round replay win away at Liverpool, with Peter playing a starring role, saving a penalty from Tommy Smith in front of the Anfield Kop. 'All penalties involve a little bit of guesswork. He hit it well, I went to my left and was able to get across and knock it away.'

After further progress was made through the sixth round and semi-final, the Foxes came up short on the big day, losing 1–0 at Wembley against Manchester City.

'That was a weird Cup run – we were lucky in nearly every game but seemed to win them 1–0. Then the Final was the one game we really did deserve to win but ended up losing. Perhaps we'd used up all of our luck in the other rounds – we had some really good chances on the day though!'

The disappointment was intensified just a few days later. 'In those days a Cup run became the focus for a club – it wasn't a circus, that's not the right word – but the whole business became so big, and we took our eyes off the League results and ended up being relegated.'

Peter played a starring role though, keeping 23 clean sheets to help the club bounce back at the end of the 1970–71 season.

Despite winning a succession of major domestic and European honours, totting up more than 1,000 League matches, 125 England appearances and being awarded the MBE for his services to the game, Peter remembers his time at Filbert Street for the very best of reasons. 'I had a great time there and am so proud to have completed the full set of international appearances while at my local club – playing for England Schoolboys, Youth, Under-23 and the full side as a Leicester player was a very big thing for me.'

# JOHN SJOBERG

*Born:*        12 July 1941, Aberdeen, Scotland.

*Died:*        2 October 2008, Leicester.

## Leicester City record:

*Appearances:*   League 334, FA Cup 44, League Cup 34.

*Goals:*        League 15, FA Cup 1, League Cup 3.

*Debut:*        28 October 1960 v Cardiff City (a) lost 1–2.

*Also played for:*  Banks O'Dee, Rotherham United.

John Sjoberg was a defensive rock for Leicester City who spent almost 15 years at Filbert Street, appearing in more than 400 first-team matches and three domestic Cup Finals.

Tempted to pursue his footballing dreams by City boss Dave Halliday, John ventured from his Aberdonian roots and settled into a routine which enabled him to continue his accountancy studies during the daytime and to train in the evenings.

City's strong Scottish contingent helped John settle in quickly, but he had to learn his craft and bide his time before succeeding Lennie Chalmers in the right-back berth.

The 1960–61 season saw him make an overdue debut, but it was not for another couple of years that he nailed down a regular position in the side, playing in every round as the club progressed to their second FA Cup Final within the space of a couple of years. Like so many of his teammates, John did not look back on the Wembley defeat to Manchester United with any great fondness; although the preceding semi-final success over Liverpool remained one of his sweeter memories in a City jersey.

He did pick up a winners' medal one year later as the Foxes overcame Stoke City in the two-legged League Cup Final. Indeed, there was almost a repeat, but Chelsea denied Matt Gillies's side the chance of back-to-back wins in the 1964–65 Final. John's semi-final goal at Home Park had been the deciding moment that saw off Plymouth Argyle.

Although fiercely proud of his Scottish ancestry, the dressing room banter dictated that 'The Swede' would suffice as a suitable nickname for John; though his surname was always believed to have been of Danish extraction!

Quietly spoken and immensely likeable off the pitch, John was a craggy, no-nonsense bull of a defender on it. He could power a defensive header further than most mortals could kick it, and his hard-as-nails approach earned the respect it was meant to. He neither asked for nor gave any favours once he'd crossed the white lines.

It was a case of being in the right place at the wrong time though in a League game against West Bromwich Albion at The Hawthorns in April 1966. John's valiant attempts to clear his lines twice went awry as he became the first City player to score two own-goals in the same match. A sorry afternoon for all ended in a 5–1 pounding.

That same year the capture of Welsh international full-back Peter Rodrigues had prompted a defensive re-shuffle, with John moving inside to partner Graham Cross at the heart of the back-line. Aside from injuries, the two became the mainstays of City's defence for the next six campaigns.

In 1969 City reached their third FA Cup Final of the decade. The season had been one of utter frustration for John, who had repeatedly suffered from a groin tear, initially sustained playing against Darlington in the League Cup.

*Quietly spoken and immensely likeable off the pitch, John was a craggy, no-nonsense bull of a defender on it. He could power a defensive header further than most mortals could kick it, and his hard-as-nails approach earned the respect it was meant to. He neither asked for nor gave any favours once he'd crossed the white lines.*

He had managed to play in each round on the road to Wembley, but the injury hoodoo struck again, and a hastily arranged friendly against Brentford confirmed that 'the Swede' would be ruled out of the showpiece game, with Alan Woollett getting his opportunity in the number-five jersey.

The relegation that followed plunged the club into despair, but it was solid defensive foundations that provided the impetus for a Second Division title campaign in 1970–71. Only 30 goals were conceded throughout the entire League programme, with the defensive unit of Shilton, Whitworth (who had replaced the departed Rodrigues), Sjoberg, Cross and Nish performing shut out after shut out and missing a total of only nine matches between the five of them.

Shortly after confirming their promotion and collecting the silverware, City played Derby County in a testimonial match for John, and a crowd of 24,000 turned up; although the player always maintained 'they came to look at the trophy'!

In later years John would always say that the title-winning side was the best he had played in – and there was further confirmation of how good it was when City hosted the Charity Shield match against Liverpool, and the reigning Football League Champions were beaten 1–0.

Between 1966 and 1972 a football-themed general knowledge quiz show was a popular television treat, and on each of the three occasions that Leicester City took part John was one of the team members, starring alongside fellow players such as Derek Dougan, Graham Cross and Mike Stringfellow – as well as guest supporting personalities Nicholas Parsons, Lady Isobel Barnett and broadcaster Sam Leitch.

A persistent knee injury eventually brought the curtains down on John's days as a Fox, and he moved for a brief and unsuccessful stint at Rotherham United before returning to Leicester to run his own printing business.

Actively involved with City's Former Players' Association, John regularly attended home matches at both Filbert Street and the Walkers Stadium right up until his untimely death in 2008.

# ALAN SMITH

*Born:*          21 November 1962, Hollywood, Birmingham.

## Leicester City record:

*Appearances:*    League 200, FA Cup 8, League Cup 9.
*Goals:*           League 76, FA Cup 4, League Cup 4.
*Debut:*          28 August 1982 v Charlton Athletic (h) lost 1–2.
*Also played for:*   Alvechurch, Arsenal, England (13 caps).

Jock Wallace's final act for Leicester City was to sign a young non-League striker who immediately took the professional game in his stride before going on to become a much-vaunted top-flight goalscorer.

Alan Smith had joined the Foxes from Alvechurch but had only been at the club for a matter of days when Wallace left his post. 'It was all a bit strange at the time', recalls Alan. 'But it worked out very well in the end because Jock had warned me that I would be spending a couple of years in the reserves, learning my trade.'

New manager Gordon Milne quickly got down to assessing the strengths of his squad and that included a surprise opportunity for Alan. 'Towards the end of pre-season training there was a first-team friendly going on against Northampton. Gordon put me on for the second half and I got a hat-trick. That obviously put me into his thoughts, and he started with me on the opening day of the season.'

*'We thought we'd done enough when we drew against Burnley in our last match but then heard that the Derby v Fulham game had finished early because of a pitch invasion. It took some time before it was confirmed that we were up.'*

A week later Alan was celebrating a first League goal. 'It was away at Rotherham, and I remember anticipating a back pass and getting there to volley it left-footed past the 'keeper. After the game Emlyn Hughes, who was their player-manager, came across and said, "well done" to me, which I appreciated.'

Promotion at the end of his first full season completed a fairytale start in the game for Alan; although there was much confusion on the final afternoon as City awaited the outcome of their nearest rivals. 'We thought we'd done enough when we drew against Burnley in our last match but then heard that the Derby v Fulham game had finished early because of a pitch invasion. It took some time before it was confirmed that we were up.'

With Gary Lineker as his regular strike partner Alan scored 14 goals in a campaign that illustrated how well the pair's styles complemented each other. 'I could lead the line but I preferred to play with my back to goal and bring others into the game. I think my partnership with Gary worked so well because it was natural – he was always there if I flicked it on.'

In his debut season in the top flight Alan had a couple of very eventful afternoons – the first was a hat-trick, against Wolves. 'I was very pleased with that as it was on the box – on *Star Soccer*, I think – and there were a couple of decent long-range efforts among the goals.'

One other abiding memory is less pleasant – a kick in the teeth from a man who was later to become a teammate and close friend. 'We were playing Stoke, and I controlled the ball on my chest and it popped up, and Steve Bould's lanky legs smashed into my face. I remember seeing their winger, Mark Chamberlain, picking things up and handing them to the ref. They were three of my teeth. Fortunately they'd come out with the roots, and when I went to Leicester hospital they were able to put them back in.'

There were concerns of a different kind a year later when the FA ordered that a Cup match against Burton Albion would have to be replayed after a crowd disturbance. 'We'd won the match 6–1, Gary had scored a hat-trick and I'd scored two, and the first thing we asked was if the goals would still stand and the FA agreed they would!'

Alan's all-round game continued to improve and, with the departure of his strike partner to Everton, he had to shoulder the burden of even more responsibility. 'We missed Gary when he left, but it meant that I found myself in areas that he would normally have occupied,' he says.

Thirty-nine goals over the course of the next two seasons, including a run of eight from six matches during November and December 1985, ensured that he was being monitored by the scouts. In March 1987 he signed for Arsenal, but a compromise deal was arranged whereby he could see out the remainder of the season by staying on loan at City. 'The arrangement suited both clubs.' he explains. 'Arsenal had secured my signature before the summer and Leicester had me around for their fight against relegation. It did get a little awkward though when we went to Highbury. I asked to be left out, but Gordon Milne insisted on picking me. I remember having to wave to both sets of fans as they were all singing my name. We lost 4–1, but I nearly scored with a header – only to be denied as it cannoned off 'keeper Rhys Wilmott.'

Some time after his move south, another Arsenal star learned of Alan's Filbert Street nickname. 'The Leicester fans seem to call all Smiths "Smeggy". I went with Tony Adams to watch Watford play Leicester and the City fans were all chanting at me, "Smeggy, Smeggy, give us a wave". Tony had never heard it before, and he called me it from then on!'

'Smeggy' picked up 13 England caps, and an assortment of League, Cup and European medals during his time with the Gunners before finally bowing out of the game in 2005.

Since hanging up his boots Alan has become one of the game's most widely respected commentators and pundits on Sky Sports, and a forthright and entertaining columnist with the *Daily Telegraph*.

# BOBBY SMITH

*Born:*            21 December 1953, Dalkeith, Midlothian.

*Died:*            22 February 2010.

## Leicester City record:

*Appearances:*    League 181, FA Cup 10, League Cup 9.

*Goals:*            League 21, FA Cup 1, League Cup 0.

*Debut:*           1 January 1979 v Oldham Athletic (h) won 2–0.

*Also played for:*   Hibernian, Peterborough United (loan), Dunfermline Athletic, Partick Thistle, Berwick Rangers.

Bobby Smith had already made his mark in Scottish football and could have been playing in Old Firm tussles before eventually choosing to leave Hibs for the East Midlands.

'During his time as manager of Rangers Jock Wallace had been chasing me and trying to get me to go to Ibrox,' recalls Bobby, 'but when he went to Leicester, and he heard I was available then he came in and persuaded me to join him there.'

The new acquisition made his debut on New Year's Day 1979 at home to Oldham Athletic – and scored. It was the same day that City also fielded two other debutants, Gary Lineker and 16-year-old David Buchanan.

'It's a little strange now to reflect that it was myself and David who both scored that day and not Gary! A ball was played into the box and the 'keeper punched it out to me, around 25 yards out. I hit it with my right, which was usually my weaker foot, and it just flew in!'

It had been another turbulent few months at Filbert Street, with very little funding available to strengthen the side. 'When I joined, the club was regarded to be in something of a crisis, and we only just avoided relegation, but Jock had the knack of getting players playing for him. Most people thought he was physically intimidating, but the good thing about Jock was he never bore a grudge against anyone – if you committed a crime or crossed him, quite rightly he'd punish you, but then he'd forget all about it and the slate was wiped clean. The players certainly all respected him.'

Having re-grouped as a much stronger unit, City stormed to the Second Division title during the 1979–80 season, with Bobby finishing as second top scorer with 12 in the League. 'I'd taken over as penalty taker that year, and although I later missed one or two I generally had a pretty good record from the spot.'

The euphoria of promotion helped to dilute the embarrassment of City's FA Cup exit to non-League minnows Harlow Town. 'We'd slaughtered them in the first match at home. We hit the bar and the post several times, and the 'keeper had one of those days, but then they got a late equaliser to force a replay. I remember we went down there and it was raining – a really horrible night – and somehow they beat us 1–0. Afterwards it was the first time I'd ever known Jock to be utterly speechless.'

Bobby became known as a 'utility player' and admits he had to become used to playing in a few different positions. 'When I first signed for Hibs I was a centre-forward and had top-scored for them one year, but then they realised I'd got a good left foot so started playing me on the left side of midfield. I was used in the middle of the park when I first went to Leicester and then, primarily due to injuries, I eventually played in both full-back positions.'

City's stay in the top flight was brief, and back in the second tier Bobby had a season to forget. 'I had an injury and ended up having a bone graft on the side of my knee. As I was coming back to fitness Jock asked me if I'd start playing at left-back for him. At that time I didn't really want to – because before the injury I'd been playing in midfield and was doing really well there. Because I didn't fancy it he left me out altogether, and to get some games in I had to go out on loan to Peterborough. Typically, that was the period when the side enjoyed their FA Cup run all the way to the semi-finals and I missed out!'

The experience stood Bobby in good stead. 'Later on, under Gordon Milne, I went to left-back when I was asked and he rewarded me with the club captaincy!'

As with many Foxes of that era a nickname had to be found for Bobby, with teammate Eddie Kelly the man responsible. 'He found out that my middle name is Nisbet and began calling me "Nissie". It stuck, and I'm still called it to this day.'

Assessing his own qualities as a player, 'Nissie' says, 'I had a good engine and absolutely loved training and keeping fit – that served me well because I carried on playing until I was 37. I was a good passer of the ball and always likely to come up with a goal.'

He has two favourite scores from his days in a Foxes jersey, 'One was against Charlton at home – a left-foot shot into the top corner, and the other was against Spurs. A cross from Alan Young came in, and I went horizontal to beat Ray Clemence with a diving header.'

After exactly 200 games for City, another loan spell – to Hibs – preceded a permanent move back to his first club, but Bobby retains special memories from his time at Filbert Street. 'I made a lot of good friends at Leicester and try to get back two or three times a year. I always seemed to enjoy a great rapport for the fans, and I'll always thank them for that.'

(Bobby Smith was interviewed for this book in August 2009, six months prior to his death from cancer.)

*'I had a good engine and absolutely loved training and keeping fit – that served me well because I carried on playing until I was 37. I was a good passer of the ball and always likely to come up with a goal.'*

# SEP SMITH

*Born:*          13 March 1912, Whitburn, County Durham.

*Died:*          28 July 2006, Leicester.

## Leicester City record:

*Appearances:*  League 350, FA Cup 35, Other (wartime) 213.

*Goals:*          League 23, FA Cup 2, Other (wartime) 48.

*Debut:*         31 August 1929 v Huddersfield Town (a) lost 2–3.

*Also played for:*  Whitburn, England (1 cap).

Many elder statesmen still put forward a convincing argument that Leicester City's finest-ever all-round player was Sep Smith.

Football was clearly in his blood. The seventh son of a football-mad north-eastern family, Septimus Smith became the fifth brother to play League football: Tom had played in 81 first-team games for the Foxes between 1919 and 1924, Joe played for Leicester's reserves before joining Watford, while Jack and Willie made their names playing for Portsmouth.

Sep joined the club at 16, having shone to prominence with the England Schoolboys side (the North versus South trial match which earned him that selection was played at Filbert Street in March 1926). Two decades later he was still proudly representing the Foxes, his only senior club.

The bulk of his career was spent playing in the right-half position; although Sep's early League outings – including his debut at just 17 on the opening day of the 1929–30 season – were at inside-forward.

*Septimus Smith became the fifth brother to play League football: Tom had played in 81 first-team games for the Foxes between 1919 and 1924, Joe played for Leicester's reserves before joining Watford, while Jack and Willie made their names playing for Portsmouth.*

His first League goal arrived in October 1930 in a 4–1 home win over Aston Villa (with Ernie Hine getting the other three). Over the course of the next couple of seasons he began to cement his place in the side, his measured passing being a feature of his play, coupled with a keen eye for goal. He found the net 11 times in top-fight matches in the 1931–32 season – the best output of his career.

City were frequent occupiers of the lower positions in Division One and finished 19th in consecutive campaigns, but while the 1933–34 season again produced poor League form, it contrasted sharply with their progression in the FA Cup. Wins over Lincoln

City, Millwall, Birmingham City and Preston North End took the Foxes through to a semi-final meeting with Portsmouth.

Despite Sep being City's best player on the day, his side were comfortably beaten, and it was no consolation that his two brothers had the satisfaction of going through to play in a Wembley Cup Final.

Consistency in the League had been a problem for a number of years, and the Foxes finally paid the penalty by dropping out of the top flight at the end of the 1934–35 season – what a way to celebrate the club's 50th anniversary!

Relegation had been by a single point, with Middlesbrough the fortunate survivors, but City's inability to win any of their final six matches effectively sealed their own fate.

Despite this body-blow for the club, Sep's own profile continued to rise, and proof that he had caught the eye of the selectors came with a second-half substitute appearance for England against Scotland in a special Jubilee Fund Match in August 1935. Undoubtedly he was being applauded as one of the finest wing-halves in the land, and a full cap soon followed in a 3–1 win against Ireland in Belfast. Disappointingly – and probably because he was no longer playing his football in the top flight – Sep was then overlooked, and this turned out to be his only international appearance; although he was also called upon to play for the Football League against the Scottish League.

The Foxes finished sixth in their first season back in Division Two but, with Sep appointed as the new skipper, they stormed to the title in 1936–37, finishing ahead of runners-up Blackpool. If the fans had hoped that this was to be a new dawn for the club it was short-lived because within two seasons City were again relegated. League football was then suspended due to the outbreak of war, although Sep was able to turn out for the club for a large percentage of their wartime fixtures, clocking up another 213 appearances.

He was 34 when League Football resumed and continued to perform outstandingly for another couple of seasons; although he was denied a fairytale ending to his career by not making the starting XI for the 1949 FA Cup Final.

Sep's final match for the club was away at Cardiff on 7 May 1949, a game that City needed to get at least a point from in order to avoid relegation to the Third Division. Jack Lee's late leveller brought about a 1–1 draw – and safety.

Briefly Sep joining the club's coaching staff and remained a loyal follower of the Foxes for the rest of his days. He was the guest of honour at the last-ever game to be played at Filbert Street in April 2002, a 2–1 win over Spurs, and was afforded a generous and well-deserved standing ovation by the Leicester supporters.

Sep was 94 when he died in Leicester in 2006, and there was a minute's silence held in his honour at City's subsequent home game against Burnley. Matchday visitors to the Walkers Stadium can enjoy pre-match hospitality in the Sep Smith Lounge – a fitting tribute to one of the club's true legends.

# MIKE STRINGFELLOW

*Born:*          27 January 1943, Nuncargate, Nottinghamshire.

## Leicester City record:

*Appearances:*    League 315, FA Cup 28, League Cup 27.
*Goals:*           League 82, FA Cup 7, League Cup 8.
*Debut:*          20 January 1962 v Everton (a) lost 2–3.
*Also played for:*  Mansfield Town, Nuneaton Borough.

Mike Stringfellow became a firm favourite with Leicester City fans but remembers that the first time he played at Filbert Street he had a stinker and got dropped. 'I played there for Mansfield in the first season that the League Cup competition was held and we got hammered 4–0. At half-time the manager Raich Carter came into the dressing room and gave me a right rollicking – our skipper Sid Watson told me later that it was my own fault – whoever sat nearest to the door tended to get it in the neck when Raich wasn't happy!'

The winger was only 17 at the time but was already earning rave reviews, which ultimately led to his move to City. But the swiftness of that deal remained a mystery until 2009. 'It wasn't until I went to pay my respects at Bert Johnson's funeral that I discovered, from his son, that Bert had come to see play in a Monday night match and had spotted a Manchester United scout there who appeared to be taking an interest in me. Bert had told Matt Gillies to act quickly, and the next day I was summoned to go and see the Mansfield chairman and the deal was completed!'

Although he made a handful of outings the previous term, it was not until the start of the 1962–63 campaign that Mike really cemented his place in the Foxes side.

A goal at Fulham was the first in a sequence of five from the opening four matches of the campaign for the youngster, but his most important strike came seven months later – the FA Cup semi-final winner against Liverpool. 'It was a free-kick in from Howard Riley, and three or four of us jumped for it together. Sometimes there's a little bit of luck involved in who times their jump the best, but I managed to steer the ball down and into the corner.'

Through to Wembley for their second Final in three years, City were favoured to defeat Manchester United but did not perform to the best of their abilities. 'Our form had actually fallen away in the month leading up to the Final, but collectively we all had a bad day at Wembley. It was the only time I played there and should have been something we'd want to remember, but I think most of us have put it to the back of our minds ever since.'

A domestic trophy was claimed the following season with City lifting the League Cup, and Mike was among the second-leg scorers in the victory over Stoke City and feels the Cup would have been retained the following year but for an outstanding contribution from Chelsea's Eddie McCreadie. 'It was a wonder goal – he ran from one end of the pitch to the other.'

For six consecutive seasons Mike reached double figures in the League, with a best of 17 coming during that first full term. 'Teams did tend to score more goals in those days than they do nowadays, but it was still hard to do – especially when I played most of my matches out wide, with just occasionally a few appearances down the middle.'

Mike is modest in assessing his own worth to the team, however: 'I was quick and brave and pretty good at finishing, though I didn't have a tremendous shot on me – I only ever scored three or four from outside the box. I just had the happy knack of being in the right place at the right time.'

The Wembley match programme for the 1963 FA Cup Final had tipped Mike to be a future England international, but that prophecy was not realised, largely due to the succession of injuries that beset the second part of his career.

'I first felt it against Bolton – when I was loosening up doing a few sprints I felt a twinge in my hamstring. I played but I didn't feel right, it felt really stiff and tight, but I got it strapped up and played. Then Davie Gibson hit a ball over the top which I went after but pulled up in pain with a tight hamstring.'

'Then I began to have tendon and knee trouble – it was the unhappiest part of my life – I had one cartilage out, but after the first injury the knee just kept giving way and I had to have another op, but to be honest it was never the same again. I could never properly flex my knee as it couldn't really stand the strain.'

Although most City fans readily recall Mike's semi-final winner at Hillsborough, his own favourite goal came on the same ground against Sheffield Wednesday. 'It was a night game, I got the ball on the left, went by about three players and slipped it past Ron Springett to give us a 2–1 victory.'

Mike later ran a pub and then became a newsagent, but in his retirement he reflects on some wonderful memories from his days at Filbert Street. 'All I wanted to be was a footballer – I'd probably have played for nothing, but to get paid for doing it was brilliant. I just really enjoyed being a regular first-team player, and overall I had nine or 10 really good years.'

*'All I wanted to be was a footballer – I'd probably have played for nothing, but to get paid for doing it was brilliant. I just really enjoyed being a regular first-team player, and overall I had nine or 10 really good years.'*

# TOM SWEENIE

*Born:*             15 July 1945, Paisley, Renfrewshire.

**Leicester City record:**

*Appearances:*      League 51, FA Cup 1, League Cup 4.

*Goals:*            League 11, FA Cup 1, League Cup 0.

*Debut:*            27 November 1963 v Gillingham (h) won 3–1.

*Also played for:*  Johnstone Burgh, York City, Burton Albion.

But for a crippling knee injury, Tom Sweenie could have gone on to be one of the best players of his generation. As it was, he will be remembered as a Filbert Street youngster who had immense potential, scored some wonder goals and left his legacy as City's first-ever scoring substitute.

Tom's route to the East Midlands was almost intercepted by one of the greats of the game, as he explains. 'I was in the Highlands of Scotland and the management of my local club had a connection with Leicester City, but halfway through training one day I was told that I had a phone call. I'd hardly ever used a phone before, but on the other end was Bill Shankly. He said, "I know you are going to Leicester, but don't do anything until you've come and had a look at Liverpool first." Soon afterwards my mind was made up when Leicester reached the Cup Final against Manchester United. They invited myself and my father down to the game as their guests and we went to the reception in the Dorchester afterwards. At that age I usually ate beans on toast so it was a bit of a culture shock seeing all that cutlery and wine glasses on the table!'

Within three months of joining, Tom made his City debut in a League Cup tie against Gillingham and impressed sufficiently to be handed a starting berth in the League side to face Blackpool away.

'I scored twice that day to earn us a draw after being 3–1 down and could have had a hat-trick as our other goal came from the penalty spot after I'd been brought down. I learned later that my family back in Scotland had heard Eamonn Andrews on the radio giving all the scores out and saying that 18-year-old Tom Sweenie had got two of the goals!'

## 'There was something in the media comparing me to the great Hungarian star Puskas – I suppose I was of a similar build and had a decent left foot.'

Tom's rapid development and eye-catching performances were creating some bizarre headlines in the local press. 'There was something in the media comparing me to the great Hungarian star Puskas – I suppose I was of a similar build and had a decent left foot.' Laughing, Tom says that a more appropriate likeness has emerged in recent times. 'I was strong, with good energy and a good engine – a bit like Ryan Giggs, I suppose!'

Nominally an inside-forward, manager Matt Gillies even experimented by trying his teenage prodigy out up front. 'I preferred being in midfield, but occasionally I would play up front with Derek Dougan. I did all his running for him while he talked to the crowd!'

Dougan made a huge impact on the young Scot. 'He was the biggest character at the club and had the gift of the gab. We had plenty of Scots who would always try and pull his leg, but the big Irishman always managed to have the last word. I used to hang my gear up next to him, and he always used to tease, "Write to your mum and tell her that I talk to you".'

Just a year after pondering over which spoon to use for his soup, Tom was himself playing in a domestic Cup Final. 'I was roped in to play in the second leg of the League Cup Final against Stoke City. I think that night I played solely on adrenalin and covered every blade of grass. I remember that after the game most of the players were all for going out celebrating, but I'd got blisters on my blisters so just went back to my digs to rest.'

His winners' tankard had a companion 12 months later – albeit a runners'-up one, with Tom playing in the first leg of the losing Final against Chelsea. That same season he scored a couple of goals which he can still proudly reflect upon. 'Against Sheffield United I had the ball and was impeded just as I released it – I moaned to the ref, but the ball came straight back to me and I just struck it into the top right-hand corner from about 35 yards.'

Another wonder goal came at Sunderland as he ran the length of the field to score. 'We stayed there overnight and went to a night club,' he says. 'There were a few of us around a table and a bottle of champagne was brought to us, with the compliments of Charlie Hurley, who was known as "The King of Sunderland" at that time. I went over to thank him and said that I couldn't believe how much space I'd been given for the goal – he said he'd given me that space because he thought I was too exhausted to go any further!'

On 12 April 1966 Tom created a minor piece of Foxes footballing trivia when he became the first substitute to score for the club, after coming on to replace Mike Stringfellow in a home match against Blackburn Rovers.

Tom's rapid elevation within the game was brought to a crashing and painful halt in a League match against Nottingham Forest in February 1967 when he was clattered into after releasing the ball. 'There had been some speculation in the media beforehand that I was on the verge of being picked for Scotland, and it's clear Forest thought, "Stop this guy, he's on a roll."'

Although operations on his knee allowed Tom to make one or two attempts at a comeback, his promising career had been effectively cut short before his 22nd birthday.

# GERRY TAGGART

*Born:*        18 October 1970, Belfast, Northern Ireland.

## Leicester City record:

*Appearances:*        League 117, FA Cup 9, League Cup 14, Other 2.
*Goals:*        League 9, FA Cup 0, League Cup 2, Other 1.
*Debut:*        15 August 1998 v Manchester United (a) drew 2–2.
*Caretaker manager:* 25 October 2007–22 November 2007.
*Also played for:*  Manchester City, Barnsley, Stoke City, Northern Ireland (51 caps).

Strong as an ox – and twice as menacing – Gerry Taggart was a no-nonsense central-defender who played for City in two League Cup Finals at Wembley and later had a brief taste of life in the gaffer's hot seat when he stood in as caretaker manager for a month.

Gerry was already an established Northern Ireland international when he joined the Foxes in the summer of 1998, but he suffered an early set-back. 'I made my debut on the opening day of the season, coming on as a sub at Manchester United, and then I started in the next match but broke a toe. Although I carried on playing, I couldn't train for a couple of weeks and couldn't find either fitness or form early on. I think people were starting to think "Who is this guy?", but then I began to have a decent run, and from then on the fans were brilliant towards me.'

Helping Gerry settle in to his new surrounds was a very familiar face. 'I'd first met Neil Lennon when we were both about 10, playing for Lurgan Celtic Boys' Club. Then we were at Manchester City together and finally Leicester. He's remained one of my best friends in the game – in fact, we're more like brothers than just friends.'

Like most players to enter the City dressing room over the years, Gerry had to answer to a variety of innovative nicknames. Apart from the self-explanatory 'Tags', there was another which would be understood by keen cinema buffs. 'They called me "The Kurgan", after the towering monster of a man in the *Highlander* film!'

The highlight of Tags' Foxes career was the Wembley triumph over Tranmere Rovers in February 2000. 'To walk up those hallowed steps to receive the trophy is something I'll never forget. It was even sweeter having been beaten there in the Final the previous year.'

Although Spurs ruined Gerry's first appearance beneath the Twin Towers, he did get a modicum of revenge against them when the sides met again in the League six months later at White Hart Lane. 'We'd got back to 2–2, and then I went up for a corner. They cleared it but only to Muzzy Izzet, who squared it into my path. From just outside the area I hit it low, left-footed into the bottom corner. Ian Walker was in goal, and I took great pleasure in reminding him when he came to join us at Leicester.'

Another memorable goal came against Red Star Belgrade in the UEFA Cup. 'It was my first taste of European club football, and they scored after about 30 seconds, but we got back into it with a set piece. I was being marked tightly, in fact he had a piece of my shirt, but I managed to shrug the defender off by yanking his arm away and was then able to send a loopy header into the top corner of the net.'

Utterly reliable, Gerry embraced the very definition of an all-round defender. 'I was an aggressive player really. I liked to attack the ball in the air, and think I could read the game well – I was a good organiser and a pretty good tackler – and I like to think I could pass the ball as well.'

Gerry recalls the afternoon he felt at the very peak of his powers – a 2–0 win over Liverpool in March 2001. 'I thought this is as good as it gets. I felt sharp, my reading of the game was spot on, I felt I had strength, power and fitness, but it all started to go wrong for me straight after then.'

> *'To walk up those hallowed steps to receive the trophy is something I'll never forget. It was even sweeter having been beaten there in the Final the previous year.'*

A persistent knee injury ruled him out for almost the entire 2001–02 season, clearly a contributory factor in City's relegation that campaign. 'The injury started in my patella tendon, and I had a cyst on my knee which prevented me from training for a long time.'

Although Gerry eventually returned to full fitness and wound down his League career with Stoke City, he soon found himself back on familiar territory. 'I'd had a spell as player-coach at Tamworth and got a call saying that Gary Megson was going to be made manager at Leicester. I'd known him from ours days at Manchester City, and we talked and the chance came to come back to Leicester. Gary would watch the first half from the stands, and I would be on the touchlines doing the shouting and bawling, then suddenly he'd gone and Frank Burrows and I were put in caretaker charge.'

It turned out to be a four-week stint before Ian Holloway was appointed into the manager's position, and Gerry says it whetted his appetite for the future.

'Although I thoroughly enjoyed it – really it came too quickly in my career. Given the opportunity I'd love to manage Leicester one day. I've had a brief taste of what it's like, and you just hope that someday somebody will give you the opportunity to prove what you can do.'

In June 2010 'Togs' accepted an invitation to become assistant manager of Oldham Athletic, working under former teammate Paul Dickov.

# STEVE THOMPSON

*Born:*          2 November 1964, Oldham, Lancashire.

## Leicester City record:

*Appearances:*   League 127, FA Cup 8, League Cup 6, Other 14.
*Goals:*         League 18, FA Cup 1, League Cup 2, Other 4.
*Debut:*         26 October 1991 v Oxford United (a) won 2–1.
*Also played for:* Poulton Victoria, Bolton Wanderers, Luton Town, Burnley, Rotherham United, Halifax Town, Leigh Genesis.

Providing energy and impetus, as well as some important goals from midfield, Steve Thompson was a Wembley scorer during the club's Play-off trilogy in the 1990s. Evidence of his impact and popularity came with a couple of Player of the Year awards as well.

Having served Bolton Wanderers with great distinction for an 11-year stretch which included visits to the national stadium for the Freight Rover Final, the Sherpa Van Final and a Play-off Final, Steve unexpectedly made a decision to sign for Luton Town. 'I thought I'd test myself in a higher division, but it just didn't feel right there. Thankfully I'd only been at the club for five and a half weeks when the manager David Pleat asked me to go and see him as Leicester were interested in signing me. I went and spoke to Brian Little, and everything felt right – it only took about 10–15 minutes to sort things out, and it must have been one of the quickest transfers ever. Straight away it felt like a breath of fresh air, and I hadn't felt that at Luton.'

There was early evidence of Steve's ability to influence the course of a game. For his first match at his new club he came on as a half-time substitute in an away game at Oxford United and scored an absolute peach of a goal to secure victory. 'I remember that debut well, he says. 'We won it 2–1 in the end and I bent it into the top corner, right-footed from outside the box. It was the dream start for me really.'

That first season with the Foxes saw 'Thommo' make yet another return to Wembley, only for it to turn sour with the contentious award of Blackburn Rovers' winning penalty-kick.

Towards the end of August 1992 Steve scored his favourite goal in City colours, a last-minute winner from a beautifully curled free-kick to defeat Derby County 3–2 at home. Beating your local rivals in such dramatic fashion is sure to keep the fans happy. They were not so amused by a 7–1 humiliation at Newcastle at the end of the season, however; although Steve remembers the 'dark humour' of his involvement: 'It was a bit of a windy day, and I remember "Walshy" in the dressing room beforehand asking what I'd do if I won the toss. I told him to "kick against the wind and we'd try and hold them in the first half" – we were 6–0 down at the break! At half-time Brian Little went mad at us, and I remember "Walshy" thanking me for the advice but adding, "I wasn't banking on us having to get six in the second half!"'

Having re-grouped and made their way back for yet another Play-off Final, City again suffered a devastating anticlimax to their campaign. 'At Wembley we went through every emotion that day – we went from 3–0 down to get it back level at 3–3, then we were hit with the sucker punch.'

City's fightback had been completed by 'Thommo' himself, the grateful converter of the dramatic equaliser. 'Mickey Whitlow ran threequarters of the length of the pitch and pulled it back. Somehow I'd kept up with him, and when he pulled it back to the edge of the 18-yard box I took it on and across the centre-half before rolling it in with the outside of the right foot.'

The momentum of the match had swung dramatically, as Steve recalls, 'We were rampant. We had our tails up and looked certain to go on to win it but then were hit by them being awarded a debatable penalty. For the second year running we were left devastated.'

It says much for City's team spirit that they were able to make it back to Wembley for a third consecutive season, but Steve had missed a huge chunk of that campaign through injury, as he explains: 'That season I changed my boots supplier to another brand, and it was a big mistake – I had to have an Achilles operation to sort it out. It was a long and frustrating time getting back, but fortunately the manager put me on the bench for the Final and then brought me on. I was still feeling it a little, but it was great to be part of a winning side at Wembley. It's true what they say, it's the best place to win a match – but it's also the worst place if you get beaten.'

'Thommo' had been City's penalty taker for much of his time at Filbert Street, but in the Premiership – under a new boss – he was taken off them. 'I had a pretty good record from the spot with Leicester, scoring something like nine on the trot, then I missed a couple in succession and Mark McGhee took me off them. I was disappointed, as every taker has spells of missing them, but the manager has the final say!

Now a successful coach working under Ian Holloway at Blackpool, Steve believes his time at City was the most enjoyable of his career. 'Leicester means a great deal to my family. My son Curtis was born there and along with my wife Viv, and daughters Stephanie and Maisie, we were really settled and made to feel very welcome.'

> *'At Wembley we went through every emotion that day – we went from 3–0 down to get it back level at 3–3, then we were hit with the sucker punch.'*

# JOCK WALLACE

*Born:*          6 September 1935, Wallyford, Scotland.
*Died:*          24 July 1996, Fuengerola, Spain.

## Leicester City record:

*Manager:*       June 1978–July 1982.
*Also managed:*  Berwick Rangers, Glasgow Rangers, Motherwell (all Scotland), Sevilla (Spain), Colchester United.
*Played for:*    Workington, Berwick Rangers, Ashton United, Airdrieonians, West Bromwich Albion, Bedford Town, Hereford United.

Life was far from dull at Filbert Street during the four-year managerial reign of Jock Wallace. 'Big Jock', as he was known, led City into the top flight, and then following immediate relegation he brought joy of a different kind to the club's faithful followers by leading his troops to an FA Cup semi-final.

John Martin Bokas Wallace came from good footballing stock – his father, John 'Jock' Wallace senior, was also a goalkeeper, who represented Raith Rovers, Blackpool and Derby County.

Jock junior followed in his father's footsteps as a fellow 'keeper, and after being freed by his first club Blackpool he was given an opportunity by Workington. He served in both Northern Ireland and Malaya while completing his National Service with the King's Own Scottish Borders and resumed his football career with Berwick Rangers.

His travels took in a number of other clubs before he returned for a second stint at Berwick as player-manager, where he played in the most high-profile and memorable game of his career – a famous 1–0 giant-killing victory over Glasgow Rangers.

That same season, 1966–67, Jock achieved a notable first by becoming the only player to participate in the English, Welsh and Scottish Cups in the same season, having already represented Hereford United in the other two knockout competitions.

He joined Hearts as coach in 1968 before taking a similar role two years later at Rangers, serving under manager Willie Waddell. The duo masterminded the Gers' 1972 European Cup-Winners' Cup victory before Waddell moved 'upstairs' at Ibrox, leaving Jock to take over in the hot seat.

The Scottish Cup was lifted in his first season in charge, and he then ended Celtic's nine-in-a-row stretch as champions. 'Big Jock' was to take his place alongside Rangers' greatest-ever managers with the capture of all three domestic trophies in both 1975–76 and 1977–78.

At the peak of his success Jock unexpectedly resigned, believed to be due to a disagreement with the board, but his return to the game was swift; however, both in terms of distance and recent form, his next appointment was miles away from the success he had been experiencing at Ibrox Stadium.

*The new gaffer set about the club with relish – and the fist-pumping hard-talking Scot was soon being hailed as a great motivator. His passion for the game shone through, and the fans loved him. Tougher training regimes were introduced, and youngsters, including Gary Lineker, were given their opportunity and direction returned to the club.*

In June 1978 'Big Jock' was unveiled as manager of Second Division Leicester City. At that time the Foxes were in crisis – on and off the park. Financially, they were on 'their uppers' and the squad was hugely under-strength.

The new gaffer set about the club with relish – and the fist-pumping hard-talking Scot was soon being hailed as a great motivator. His passion for the game shone through, and the fans loved him. Tougher training regimes were introduced, and youngsters, including Gary Lineker, were given their opportunity and direction returned to the club.

In terms of League placings, Jock's first season at Filbert Street was not anything to write home about, but the first shoots of improvement were beginning to show and in May 1980 City confirmed their return to the top flight as Second Division champions.

A failure by the board to invest made a nonsense of Jock's pre-season prediction that his club would take the First Division by storm, and they finished in 21st place, only to go straight back down again.

The season did have its 'highs', of course, including a home and away double over Liverpool. City's 2–1 win at Anfield in January 1981 was the first home defeat suffered by the Merseyside club in 85 outings– and it came against a side who were on their way to clinching a third European Cup four months later.

Relegation to the second tier failed to bring the promotion charge that the fans craved for, but they were rewarded with an FA Cup run as Jock's side reached the semi-finals, only to lose to Spurs at Villa Park.

An eighth-placed finish in the League campaign was hugely disappointing, however, and the season ended in acrimony when Jock announced that he was resigning from his position to take over at Motherwell.

City's directors initially refused to accept his resignation but eventually – and reluctantly – they had little choice but to let him go, although they had vigorously pursued a compensation claim with the Fir Park club.

Although it is true that City were in the same division as when Wallace had taken over, he left the club in a more positive frame that it had been in for years, and the supporters, at least, had enjoyed a four-year stint which had been far from dull and had been moderately successful.

Jock returned to Glasgow Rangers for a second spell in charge between 1983–86 but could not deliver anything other than two League Cups to the expectant trophy room and was uncharitably relieved from his post as a result. Shorts spells at Sevilla, in Spain, and then Colchester United were the final ports of call for Big Jock, who was then diagnosed with Parkinson's Disease in early 1990.

Jock's final years were spent living in Fuengerola, Spain, and football mourned his untimely passing in July 1996.

# MARK WALLINGTON

*Born:*        17 September 1952, Sleaford, Lincolnshire.

## Leicester City record:

*Appearances:*     League 412, FA Cup 25, League Cup 23.
*Debut:*        11 March 1972 v West Ham United (h) won 2–0.
*Also played for:*  Heckington United, Walsall, Derby County, Lincoln City, Grantham Town.

Extending City's succession of truly great goalkeepers was Mark Wallington, a consistent, reliable performer who went on to establish a club record run of 331 consecutive appearances in the Foxes goal.

Mark had already played for England Schoolboys and was qualifying as a teacher when an unlikely opportunity came his way. 'Eric Houghton was a director of Walsall, and he lived just a few miles from me at Heckington,' he says. 'He came to present a trophy at our club and invited me to come down to Walsall during the summer for a trial.'

When Mark arrived he discovered it was to be a behind-closed-doors friendly against Leicester City. The game was at Fellows Park and Mark immediately recognised a few of the faces among the opposition ranks. 'When I got there I saw people like Shilton, Nish, Cross and Sammels, and I believe it was Jimmy Bloomfield's first game in charge after taking over. They put me on for the second half, and I saved a penalty from David Nish! I was then invited on to Walsall's pre-season tour and began my League career with them, but Leicester had obviously kept tabs on me. After I moved to Filbert Street I knew I had a lot of catching up to do as I'd not done an apprenticeship, but I learned quickly, working with Peter Shilton every day. His training regimes were notoriously hard, and that work ethic was perfect for me.'

The advice passed on from one great England goalkeeper supplemented what Mark had observed himself from his boyhood hero. 'I'd been and watched Gordon Banks play and noticed that everything went into his chest – straight into his body. That wasn't just good fortune or poor shooting, it was superb positional goalkeeping. He was rock solid and that's what I always tried to be.'

Shilton's eventual departure to Stoke City allowed Mark the opportunity to stake a claim for a permanent berth in the Foxes goal – with emphasis on the 'p' word.

Between 4 January 1975 and 6 March 1982 Mark played in every single City first-team game – a run of 294 League matches, 22 FA Cup ties and 15 appearances in the League Cup. He also played in every match in 1982–83 as well, the seventh time he had been an ever-present.

Mark admits that there were times when maybe his place should have come under scrutiny for fitness reasons. 'There were occasions when maybe I shouldn't have played, and towards the end of that run I was suffering with a back injury, but as a 'keeper you are either in or out, and whether it's the professional thing to do or not I always wanted to play if I could.'

The run was eventually broken after an injury sustained in a collision with Shrewsbury's Chic Bates in a memorable FA Cup quarter-final clash. 'They took a free-kick which clipped the wall and looped up – I started to go and threw myself at him and had to spread myself, but his foot was four or five feet in the air and he punctured my thigh with a stud.'

The injury necessitated a few stitches and Mark had to leave the action, but the incident also marked an enforced absence of six games. 'I returned to the side and typically the first game was again against Shrewsbury. I knew full well that the first loose ball that came my way he would be hitting me again, and I wasn't disappointed.'

*Between 4 January 1975 and 6 March 1982 Mark played in every single City first-team game – a run of 294 League matches, 22 FA Cup ties and 15 appearances in the League Cup.*

Mark had grown used to teammates calling him 'Wally', but another nickname was thrust upon him, courtesy of the club's leading mischief-maker. 'Alan Birchenall started calling me "The Duke" – as in The Duke of Wellington.'

Playing down his own strengths as being 'a good organiser – though not spectacular', Mark highlights the importance of gaining a psychological advantage over opposition strikers. 'In one on ones don't commit early – make the forward have to make his mind up – stand your ground.'

A particularly favourite save came at Anfield after Liverpool had come back from two goals down to draw level at 2–2. Mark recalls the drama of the final minute. 'Bruce Grobbelaar launched a long ball downfield and it bounced towards Ian Rush. I came out to the edge of my box and rose to take it. I heard the whistle go and thought it was a free-kick to us – but I was amazed when I realised the ref had awarded a penalty against me for coming out with my foot up. Graeme Souness came forward to take it but I got down to my bottom right to get a hand to it to keep it out. To seal a draw in front of the Kop was a pretty special moment for me.'

Mark's time at Leicester drew to an eventual close but not from his choosing. 'I would have stopped for ever, but as so often happens after a change of manager – there is a clash of personality and players come and go. The new manager wanted his own team, and clearly I didn't fit in with his plans.'

After eventually winding down his playing career Mark put his earlier qualifications to good use. 'I took a fresher and became a PE Teacher at Sleaford – I just tell people that I took a 20 year sabbatical!'

# JIMMY WALSH

*Born:*         3 December 1930, Glasgow, Scotland.

## Leicester City record:

*Appearances:*    League 176, FA Cup 18, League Cup 4, Other 1.
*Goals:*          League 79, FA Cup 5, League Cup 5, Other 2.
*Debut:*          23 March 1957 v Fulham (h) lost 1–3.
*Also played for:*  Valleyfield Colliery, Bo'ness United, Glasgow Celtic, Rugby Town.


Jimmy Walsh had enjoyed something of a cult-hero status as a home-town player with Glasgow Celtic before trying his luck south of the border with Leicester City.

Although he twice became top-scorer during his seven years in the East Midlands, his proudest moment was leading the Foxes ahead of the 1961 FA Cup Final.

Prior to arriving at Filbert Street, Jimmy had played in front of some huge crowds and had shown himself to be a man for the big occasion. In 1953 a special competition was arranged to celebrate the coronation of Her Majesty Queen Elizabeth II. Four leading English and four of the top Scottish clubs were invited to participate in the event, and the Final, at Hampden Park, in front of 117,000 spectators, saw Celtic defeat Hibs to win the Coronation Cup and become unofficial champions of Britain. Jimmy Walsh had scored the first goal in the Hoops' 2–0 win.

He was on the mark again two years later – scoring in the Scottish Cup Final against Clyde (att. 106,234) and a year later he was in the Celtic side which defeated Partick Thistle to win the Scottish League Cup.

A lone Under-23 cap had already come his way, so there was no doubting the pedigree of the player that David Halliday forked out £6,000 to sign in November 1956; although Jimmy was still forced to wait nearly four months for his English debut.

Although Celtic had occasionally used him on the flank, Jimmy's best position was as an inside-forward, where he could make stealthy surges into the opposition box. A good distributor of the ball and with pace to spare, he was a good link-up man with a keen eye for goal.

He had failed to get on the scoresheet in any of his first six outings for his new club but was clearly saving them up for a scoring spree that ran from Boxing Day 1957 to the beginning of April. During that 12-match burst he had netted on 13 occasions – with the biggest contribution coming in a remarkable encounter on 22 February 1958.

That afternoon at Filbert Street, Leicester City defeated Manchester City 8–4, with Jimmy scoring four times for the home side. Derek Hines was to achieve a similar feat in the same calendar year, but no other player would repeat the feat for the club during the next half century.

At the start of the 1960–61 campaign Jimmy took over the club captaincy, a position he would hold until Boxing Day 1962. His reign oversaw the birth of a new competition, the Football League

Cup. Opposing City in the first round of this new event were Mansfield Town, who came to Filbert Street on 12 October 1960.

Albert Cheeseborough scored the club's initial goal that night, but then Jimmy went on to score the next three – not only sealing a 4–0 victory and a place in the next round (where the Foxes lost to eventual finalists Rotherham United), but he also left his mark for all-time as it was the first League Cup hat-trick recorded across the country.

January 1961 saw City make advances with home victories in the FA Cup competition with Jimmy scoring once against non-Leaguers Oxford United and twice against Bristol City (after the original tie was postponed at half-time after a heavy downpour).

Further progress was then made as both Birmingham City and Barnsley were knocked out and the Twin Towers were almost in sight when the semi-final draw paired Matt Gillies's side with Sheffield United.

Eventually, after two goalless matches, it was Jimmy's 24th-minute header which set up a 2–0 victory in the third match at St Andrew's and sent the Foxes through to their first Cup Final since 1949.

The match will always be remembered differently – depending on your allegiances. Tottenham and their fans were able to celebrate the 2–0 victory which sealed the double for them, while supporters from a little closer to the River Soar look back only in regret and wonder what would have happened had City not suffered an early injury and had to play most of the game effectively a man light.

If there were any meagre crumbs of comfort from the defeat it was that the FA permitted City to become England's representatives in the Cup-Winners' Cup – their first adventure into major European competition.

The first-round pairing did not involve too many difficult travel arrangements as the Foxes were paired with Glenavon of Northern Ireland, with the first leg to be played at Filbert Street. Jimmy again sealed his place in the club's history books by scoring the first goal on this new adventure (and later added a second) as the Division One side won the game 4–1, before going on to take the tie 7–2 on aggregate.

Jimmy's sharpness in front of goal began to diminish and a run of injuries – plus issues with his sight that saw him become one of the first footballers to wear contact lenses during a game – gradually limited his opportunities, so by the time City had returned to Wembley in 1963 he was very much on the fringes of the squad.

After a brief stint in the non-League game Jimmy hung up his boots and became a popular stopping-off point for City fans at his newsagents in Leicester.

*Jimmy again sealed his place in the club's history books by scoring the first goal on this new adventure (and later added a second) as the Division One side won the game 4–1, before going on to take the tie 7–2 on aggregate.*

# STEVE WALSH

*Born:*              3 November 1964, Fulwood, Lancashire.

## Leicester City record:

*Appearances:*     League 369, FA Cup 17, League Cup 40, Other 24.

*Goals:*           League 53, FA Cup 1, League Cup 4, Other 4.

*Debut:*           23 August 1986 v Luton Town (h) drew 1–1.

*Also played for:* Wigan Athletic, Norwich City, Tamworth, Coventry City.

When BBC's popular Saturday lunchtime show *Football Focus* ran a poll in 2004 to find out who the fans regarded as their 'Cult Heroes' at each club, it was not the greatest surprise to discover that Steve Walsh topped the Leicester voting.

After joining from Wigan Athletic in 1986, Steve gave his absolute all for the club, as skipper, central-defender and even in attack, and he says that he knew from the off that it was the right move for him.

'Once I'd joined Leicester I realised what a big club it was. The leap up the divisions, the stadium and the history of the club was pretty special and I immediately knew I'd done the right thing. Wigan was, and still is, predominantly a rugby town, but Leicester's supporters grabbed me right away and I knew it was the place for me.'

In his early days at Filbert Street there were a few too many red cards and some notable bust-ups, particularly with the likes of Wolves' striker Steve Bull and David Geddis of Shrewsbury.

'I've always been competitive and I still am now. I absolutely hate to lose and I'll always give my all to win. In the case of Steve Bull, we actually got on well but we were determined to do well for our teams, which led to the clashes. The David Geddis incident is the biggest regret of my career, but I'd received absolutely no protection from the referee and it was just a case of retaliation gone wrong.'

In the first of City's trio of Play-off Finals, the penalty decision, won by Blackburn's David Speedie, sparked another classic grudge match – heightened by 'Speedo's later move to Filbert Street. 'I wasn't about to let him forget it when he joined City but having said that, I was a professional and David became an integral part of what Brian Little was trying to achieve.'

The dramatic Swindon encounter in 1993 had the Wembley fans on the edge of their seats, but it was another day that ended in disappointment for Steve, even though he got on the score sheet. 'We were incredible that day and I still can't believe that we didn't end up winning. My goal was nothing to write home about but it meant a lot to me to score at the Twin Towers. Not as much as the next year though.'

At the third time of asking City finally won a Play-off Final, defeating old adversaries Derby County in 1994, and in a personal triumph it was Steve who scored both of the Foxes' goals. 'I clearly wasn't fit for the game but I'd told Brian that I could play. No one could have stopped me from being involved to be fair! It's hard to describe exactly how you feel when you've won at Wembley, especially after the heartache of the two years before – but I was so drained both physically and emotionally. It has to be the greatest day of my career, though.'

If Steve and the Blue Army thought they had seen the back of the Play-offs for a while, they were mistaken with yet another trip there in 1996 and a dramatic last-gasp victory.

'As soon as Stevie Claridge crashed home the winner we knew we'd made it. I grabbed hold of Martin [O'Neill] on the bench and I can barely remember what we said to each other (I doubt it would be repeatable anyway!) but the euphoria was something else.'

A year later there was further success – and a proud moment for Steve as he lifted the League Cup aloft. 'We achieved so much that season, having been tipped for relegation, but to finish in the top half of the table and win a major trophy showed that the team and myself had confounded our critics.'

Two further League Cup Finals brought contrasting emotions – after defeat to Spurs in '99 there was a victory to savour the following year. 'We showed our resilience by returning and beating Tranmere to win the last-ever League Cup at the old stadium. I felt so happy for Tony Cottee, who had wanted that Wembley win so much and must have felt that the Spurs game the year before had been his last chance.'

Many old-fashioned central-defenders had often found themselves thrown forward in must-win situations, but Steve was so good up-front that he was often selected as a striker.

'I often trained as a striker under Brian Little and he obviously liked what he saw. I think in all honesty he wanted to keep me out of trouble, as I'd been picking up way too many yellow and red cards in defence. The move allowed me the freedom to still have an impact on the team, without getting into trouble with the ref. Everyone loves playing up front, but to be honest I was a defender and that was the position I loved the most.'

The club's 'No.1 Cult Hero' maintains the closest of links with the Foxes – both at the Walkers Stadium and as a feature writer for the *Leicester Mercury*.

'I'm delighted to still be in Leicester and be involved with the club. I'm a host in the 125 Lounge on matchdays, which is a real honour – and the *Mercury* column is great as it allows me to speak directly to the fans, the people that I cared about so much during my time as a player.'

> '*As soon as Stevie Claridge crashed home the winner we knew we'd made it. I grabbed hold of Martin [O'Neill] on the bench and I can barely remember what we said to each other (I doubt it would be repeatable anyway!) but the euphoria was something else.*'

193

# KEITH WELLER

*Born:*          11 June 1946, Islington, North London.

*Died:*          13 November 2004, Seattle, USA.

## Leicester City record:

*Appearances:*    League 262, FA Cup 24, League Cup 11.

*Goals:*          League 37, FA Cup 3, League Cup 3.

*Debut:*         2 October 1971 v Crystal Palace (h) drew 0–0.

*Also played for:*   Tottenham Hotspur, Millwall, Chelsea, New England Tea Men
                 (USA), Fort Lauderdale Strikers (USA), Fort Lauderdale Sun
                 (USA), England (4 caps).

*Managed:*       Fort Lauderdale Sun, Houston Dynamo, Dallas Sidekicks, San
                 Diego Sockers, Tacoma Stars, Sacramento Knights (all USA).

From a period in Leicester City's history when entertainment was paramount and when characters were in abundance, the creativity and artistry of Keith Weller complimented everything that was good about the game.

Not only did he epitomise City during the Jimmy Bloomfield era, but his individual quality and stunning strikes would comfortably elevate him into an exclusive bracket of players that could be classed as the finest-ever to grace the Filbert Street turf.

Keith's early dreams of making a career out of football were shattered when trials at Arsenal failed to earn him an apprenticeship. Although he began working as a floor layer, he persevered with the game and was taken on by Spurs – eventually earning a professional contract in January 1964.

His League debut 14 months later was a remarkable affair, with the North London side running out 7–4 winners over Wolves. With competition for places fierce at White Hart Lane the young midfielder then joined Millwall.

An FA XI tour of New Zealand and the Far East followed in 1969, and a year later he was sold to Chelsea for £100,000. He played in the side that defeated Real Madrid to lift the Cup-Winners' Cup in May 1971 and then, four months later, he joined Leicester City.

Some players are idolised almost immediately at new clubs, and 'King Keith' was one of them. His elegant touch, crisp passing and accurate shooting brought the best out of those around him as City's free-flowing style brought gasps of admiration from all true footballing fans.

Indeed, supporters from all clubs in the land were clamouring to back City as their 'second favourite' side. Keith's own stock rose sharply when a stunning hat-trick against Liverpool in August 1972 turned a 0–2 deficit into a 3–2 victory.

His goal output from midfield was more than respectable in the League, but the curly-permed Londoner saved some of his best City goals for the FA Cup competition. In February 1973 the Foxes

# 'Over the course of the next few years City were one of the dominant forces in the land, twice finishing in the top three positions, with

tore Luton Town to shreds with a masterful display of attacking football that brought a convincing 4–0 victory.

The television cameras were on hand at Kenilworth Road to witness a stunning effort from Keith that deservedly won the Goal of the Season award. Receiving a pass from Steve Whitworth 30 yards out, he completed a 360-degree pirouette to shake off a couple of markers, before going on a mazy dribble which left three more defenders in his wake, all unable to stop him dragging the ball onto his left foot and rifling it home from just inside the box.

Two years later – although not as spectacular – Keith scored a close-range winner from a Frank Worthington knock-down that saved his side from ending up with egg on their faces. They had again trailed by two goals before overturning the deficit – this time against plucky non-Leaguers Leatherhead.

Inexplicably, by that stage of his career Keith's international days were already over. He had gained four caps for England (all in May 1974), which included a rare headed goal that had been enough to defeat Northern Ireland at Wembley.

Perhaps his actions in refusing to take the field for the second half of a match against Ipswich Town in December 1974 had not helped – Keith had been frustrated at having a transfer request turned down. His 'strike' saw him put on the transfer list and fined two weeks' wages, but his differences with the club were soon rectified, and he returned to give of his best for a further four years.

Keith's final goal for the Foxes was another that will remain in the memory bank of all those who saw it. Playing against Norwich in another FA Cup tie, he skipped away down the right, beat a couple of defenders and cleverly wrong-footed the 'keeper before beating him at his near post. Any nerve that was involved in converting the score was more than matched by his attire. On a bitterly cold afternoon Keith was resplendent in white tights.

With knee injuries taking their toll, Keith wound down his League career and moved to the United States, where he continued to play before switching to coaching. He settled in the Seattle area but continued to follow the fortunes of his former club through his long-term friendship with former teammate Alan Birchenall.

Keith's life was rocked when he was diagnosed with a rare form of cancer, and through the generosity of 'The Birch's annual charity run, as well as other forms of sponsorship, City fans helped fund his treatment and also raised awareness into the illness.

Sadly, 'King Keith' lost his greatest battle in November 2004 and, paying tribute to his great pal, 'Birch' said at the time, 'For me he was one of the five greatest-ever players to pull on a Leicester shirt. His death is a tragic loss not just for Leicester but for the whole of English football.'

# MIKE WHITLOW

*Born:*        13 January 1968, Northwich, Cheshire.

## Leicester City record:
*Appearances:*    League 147, FA Cup 6, League Cup 12, Other 15.
*Goals:*           League 8, League Cup 1, League Cup 0, Other 0.
*Debut:*           1 April 1992 v Middlesbrough (h) won 2–1.
*Also played for:*  Witton Albion, Leeds United, Bolton Wanderers, Sheffield United, Notts County.

During Mike Whitlow's seven-and-a-half year stay at Leicester City he could perhaps be forgiven for feeling that every season ended with a big day out at Wembley Stadium. During the 1990s he completed the full set of playing in all four Play Off Finals, as well as the League Cup Final and replay.

Mike came to City from Leeds United towards the end of the 1991–92 season, where he had found himself on the fringes of the squad after Tony Dorigo's arrival, but he had played enough matches to qualify for a League Championship medal that same campaign.

His arrival at Filbert Street was timely, coinciding with City's push for a Play-off place – and a berth in the side that played against Blackburn Rovers in the Final. 'I had always wanted to play at Wembley, and I'd dreamt of it so many times as a kid, but 20 minutes into the match I was shattered with the sheer adrenalin of the occasion. I was fit, I could run all day – couldn't kick it straight but I could run – but I just found the occasion to be too much the first time around, and then we all felt massively hard done by with the penalty decision we felt wasn't justified.'

A year later it was Swindon Town who took the spoils in a Wembley epic. 'Glenn Hoddle was awesome for them to begin with, and then we got back into it. When Thommo [Steve Thompson] made it 3–3 I felt we had the momentum, but then in the blink of an eye they'd gone up the other end and they got their penalty and we were back where we were.'

*'Against Derby we were just too strong, and we battered them physically. They had good players on paper, but we were too physically overpowering for them.'*

196

Mike believes it was the spirit at the club that enabled City to persevere with a promotion push for a third successive year. 'We had a great group of lads – we really did. They were all hard-working, and every single one of them that had tasted the Wembley atmosphere wanted to have another bash at it. We'd got there before and left disappointed and wanted to get back.'

The third opportunity to claim a place in the top fight was successful, as Mike recalls. 'Against Derby we were just too strong, and we battered them physically. They had good players on paper, but we were too physically overpowering for them.'

The top-flight season brought one special moment for Mike that he's never likely to forget. 'Growing up I'd gone to watch whichever Manchester team was at home – I'd go to United one week and City the next. When we played at Old Trafford all my mates were behind the goal – in Row 11, in fact! We had a corner at that end, Gary Walsh dropped it and I side-footed it in from about a yard out. It was so simple it wasn't even worth shouting about, but my mates still haven't forgiven me! In many ways that remains my fondest moment in football!'

Mike remembers City's fourth Wembley trip with the Foxes as the day when Steve Claridge got some long-overdue plaudits. 'I thought it was going to penalties then Steve clipped one in off his shin pad! He became a cult hero off the back of that goal, and I felt chuffed to bits for him. He had this scruffy demeanour, with his socks rolled down and shin pads showing – and he's daft as a brush – but he's one of those blokes that it's really nice when something good happens to them because he never gets the credit for the way he gave absolutely everything for us.'

It was another City teammate who took the eye in the 1997 League Cup Final against Middlesbrough. 'Pontus Kaamark was brilliant – definitely our Man of the Match. Juninho was the key player for them, and the plan was to nullify him and Pontus did it superbly. Middlesbrough were so deflated after the Wembley game because they thought they'd won it, but we knew what they were about and knew we'd win the replay – but I couldn't have dream how it would finish and that it would be Claridge who came up with the goal again!'

Martin O'Neill had brought Steve Guppy to Leicester in early 1997 and began to deploy him in a left wing-back role, causing Mike to look at his options, and his days at Leicester came to an end when Bolton made an enquiry about his services. 'I'd played left-back since joining Witton Albion at the start of my career, but with Steve being used in that system I wasn't always sure of a game any more. Sam Allardyce wanted me to go to Bolton and join the "Head it, Give it, Kick It" brigade, and as I'd got family in that part of the country I decided to go.'

Mike spent six seasons at Bolton, before winding down his playing career with brief stints at Sheffield United and Notts County. Turning to coaching, he began the 2009–10 season as head of youth development at Mansfield Town – with the youngsters certain to be hearing abut all those trips to Wembley!

# STEVE WHITWORTH

*Born:*          20 March 1952, Ellistown, Leicestershire.

## Leicester City record:

*Appearances:*    League 353, FA Cup 29, League Cup 18, Other 1.

*Goals:*            Other 1.

*Debut:*           2 September 1970 v Bristol City (h) won 4–0.

*Also played for:*  Sunderland, Bolton Wanderers, Mansfield Town, Barnet, England (7 caps).

For a player that made his name as one of the finest overlapping full-backs of his generation, it remains one of the great mysteries of the game as to why Steve Whitworth did not manage to score a single League goal during his 353 appearances for Leicester City during the 1970s. That his solitary strike in the City colours was enough to clinch a major trophy is perhaps compensation enough though!

Attached to City from an early age, Steve had earned England School and Youth representative honours before getting a chance to step into the senior side following an injury – and subsequent departure – of the regular right-back Peter Rodrigues. Such was the impression made by the youngster that he retained his place for the rest of the season, helping his side to the Second Division title.

That same season Arsenal had completed the double of First Division champions and FA Cup winners, but they elected not to participate in the annual Charity Shield match, with invitations instead going to Liverpool, the beaten Cup Finalists, and Leicester City as Division Two champions.

The sides met at Filbert Street on 7 August 1971 in front of 25,104 fans, and the only goal came in the first period when Steve got forward to slide the ball beyond the reach of Liverpool 'keeper Ray Clemence.

Winning the Shield for the first (and so far only) time in City's history had been a fine way for new manager Jimmy Bloomfield's reign to begin. Over the course of the next few seasons the Foxes were branded as the 'most entertaining' side in the land, but at the base of the club's attacking flair and creativity was a solid defensive unit – patrolled on the right by Steve, who remained remarkably consistent and was an ever-present on four occasions. At one stage he was able to compile a run of 198 consecutive matches in the side.

Liverpool gained revenge for their Charity Shield defeat by halting Leicester's dream of a place in the FA Cup Final in a semi-final replay in 1974, the nearest Steve and his teammates would come to appearing on that showpiece occasion.

Having collected six caps at Under-23 level, his first call-up for the full international side duly followed, and in March 1975 he made his England debut at Wembley against the reigning world champions West Germany.

Six more caps followed (all during the same calendar year), but he was denied the opportunity of making an even greater impression for the Three Lions by the healthy competition for the number-two jersey. Dave Clement, Paul Madeley, Trevor Cherry and Colin Todd were all tried out there before the emergence of Liverpool's Phil Neal.

Steve's main attributes were his tackling ability, his great pace and his 'sixth sense' of being in the right place at the right time – the presence of mind to be able to spot danger long before it occurred.

After a total of 401 first-team outings for the Foxes (400 League and Cup, plus the Charity Shield match), Steve signed for Sunderland for a fee of £125,000 in March 1979. To commemorate his decade of sterling service to City he was granted a testimonial match, and in November 1979 he returned to face a Coventry City XI at Filbert Street, the Foxes winning it by three goals to one.

*'Over the course of the next few seasons the Foxes were branded as the 'most entertaining' side in the land, but at the base of the club's attacking flair and creativity was a solid defensive unit – patrolled on the right by Steve, who remained remarkably consistent and was an ever-present on four occasions. At one stage he was able to compile a run of 198 consecutive matches in the side.'*

That same season Steve helped the Wearsiders to win promotion; however, ironically they finished as runners-up behind his former club! After two and a half years at Roker Park the full-back moved on again, this time to Bolton Wanderers, with whom he spent two seasons before he returned to the Midlands to join Mansfield Town, where he finally fulfilled an ambition by scoring a League goal.

Fourteen and a half years after his debut – and in his 570th game – he slotted home a penalty in March 1985 against Hereford United. Incredibly, a fortnight later, also at Field Mill, he converted another one, this time against Exeter City.

Those two goals brought the curtain down on an outstanding League career, and he joined Barnet – then of the Conference – initially as player-coach but later as assistant manager to Barry Fry.

It may be a while before the Foxes lift the Charity Shield again, but at least that ensures that Steve Whitworth's 1971 winner will never be forgotten!

# TOMMY WILLIAMS

*Born:*            18 December 1957, Winchburgh, West Lothian.

## Leicester City record:
*Appearances:*     League 241, FA Cup 18, League Cup 12.
*Goals:*           League 10, FA Cup 0, League Cup 0.
*Debut:*           5 October 1977 v Chelsea (a) drew 0–0.
*Also played for:* Birmingham City, Grimsby Town.


Tommy Williams was a wonderfully versatile servant to Leicester City who played in over 250 first-team matches, but somewhat ironically he is perhaps best remembered for an unfortunate leg break sustained in the biggest match of his career.

He had had an early taste of success at Leicester City, when he was part of the youth team that reached Wembley. 'There was a national six-a-side competition, and we won through to play Arsenal, prior to the 1976 Charity Shield match.'

The club's record beneath the Twin Towers was not good then anyway, but Tommy and his teammates found a novel way to lose the match. 'The scoring system for the tournament was four points for a goal and one point for every corner you got. We lost 13–12 – so we missed out by one corner!'

Just over a year later and Tommy was celebrating his introduction to the first team and becoming yet another to graduate through the club's successful junior ranks. 'From the age of 12 or 13 I started going to the youngsters' coaching, every Tuesday and Thursday evenings. I played in a variety of positions even then – either full-back or in midfield usually – but I did prefer to play alongside the centre-back.'

In his first season of League football Tommy made 35 appearances and even chipped in with a few goals. 'One against Arsenal was pretty special, as it was against Pat Jennings – one of the game's really great goalkeepers. I was playing in midfield, and a long diagonal ball went to the far post. Billy Hughes headed it back to the edge of the box, and I hit it cleanly on the volley and it flew in. How it didn't make the *Top 100 Goals* video I'll never know!'

Tommy's debut season had gone well for him personally, but it was a pretty miserable campaign for the club as a whole and relegation from the top flight ensued.

It took a couple of years to get back, and Tommy enjoyed the celebrations that marked the Foxes' return to the top tier. 'We won the Championship title under big Jock Wallace with a team that had a lot of good home-grown talent in it. To me it was very was special from that point of view as you don't seem to get it so much nowadays.'

# 'Everyone seems to remember the 5–2 win over Shrewsbury, but obviously I have reasons for remembering the semi even more!'

City were being tagged a yo-yo club because they promptly went and finished in the drop zone yet again, despite doing the double over Liverpool, as Tommy fondly recalls. 'We'd beaten them at home and then went to Anfield, where they were on a long undefeated run – something like 85 matches I think – but we went and won 2–1.'

A year on and despite the agony of failing to mount a promotion bid City supporters did have an FA Cup run to enthuse over. 'Everyone seems to remember the 5–2 win over Shrewsbury, but obviously I have reasons for remembering the semi even more!'

Tottenham Hotspur were City's opponents at Villa Park, and it was a match that was to leave a lasting impression on Tommy. 'Spurs were a top team at the time and were miles too good for us really. We went 1–0 down and then the ball was played up to Tony Galvin. I did a half tackle from behind, but my ankle caught the rear of his heel and boot. 999 times out of 1,000 it would have been just a bruising, but as I tackled him my ankle went. I could tell straight away that it was a break. The doc made an emergency splint out of shin pads and I was taken back on the team bus before going off to hospital. It wasn't the way I'd dreamed of spending semi-final day!'

Months of recovery and hard work saw Tommy regain his first-team status, but having only just returned to the side fate played another nasty trick. 'I'd played four matches and we were in the gym at Belvoir Drive, playing five-a-side. I had a shot and caught a youth-team player on the follow through and the leg went again. It was maybe worse second time round because I knew what to expect and knew what I had to go through.'

Once again he recovered to return to the first team, even playing some of his best football as City again graced the highest division. 'At last I was deployed as a central-defender and thoroughly enjoyed it.'

In July 1986 Tommy signed for Birmingham City but was soon back at Filbert Street after the club awarded him a thoroughly deserved Testimonial. 'That was a really special night,' he says. 'Gary Lineker flew back from Barcelona to play, and there was a cracking turn-out from the fans which I really appreciated.'

After a couple of years at St Andrew's and slightly less at Grimsby, Tommy joined the Leicestershire Constabulary – occasionally having to police some of City's matches. 'It was a little strange at first, but it was good to go back and see many of the good people I've met over the years,' he says.

# IAN WILSON

*Born:*            27 March 1958, Aberdeen, Scotland.

## Leicester City record:

*Appearances:*      League 276, FA Cup 15, League Cup 18.
*Goals:*            League 17, FA Cup 1, League Cup 1.
*Debut:*            11 August 1978 v Rotherham United (h) lost 1–2.
*Also played for:*  Aberdeen, Dundee, Elgin City, Everton, Besiktas (Turkey), Derby
                   County, Bury, Wigan Athletic, Scotland (5 caps).
*Managed:*          Peterhead.

Despite playing in over 300 first-team games for Leicester City, Ian Wilson believes he is still mostly remembered from his time at Filbert Street by two goals – one he scored that helped secure promotion and one at the other end in an FA Cup semi-final.

City fans, however, will quite rightly point out that his consistent midfield performances and tireless, energetic running over an eight-year period was worth much more than a couple of mentions on the score sheet.

Ian had a brief taste of the professional game at a young age 'I'd had a bit of a run with both Aberdeen and Dundee but didn't make my mark before joining Elgin City, who were still playing in the Highland League at that stage. Elgin really is the very edge of civilization' he laughs. 'But I became physically stronger and more aware of what the game was about there. Out of the blue I heard that a couple of people were looking at me, and among them was Ian MacFarlane, Jock Wallace's assistant.'

'Wils', as he became known at City, was determined to make the grade in League football: 'I'd been playing semi-pro for Elgin and had just finished a business course, so the opportunity came at just the right time and there were lots of Scottish guys at Leicester who all helped me settle.'

Unfortunately, the timing of the transfer meant that Ian had to wait before pulling on the City jersey for the first time. 'I actually signed after the deadline day at the end of the 1978–79 season. Big Jock wanted to use me, but the League wouldn't let him.'

It was worth the wait, though, as Ian played his part in a hugely successful campaign. 'To win the Division Two Championship in my first full season was just unbelievable,' he says.

Regrettably, the next season did not go as well as was hoped, and City were relegated straight away, but there were some positives though, as Ian recalls, 'We did the double over Liverpool that year. They'd been on a long unbeaten run at Anfield, and we went there and won 2–1. It was a great win for us because they went on to win the European Cup that season!'

Back in the second tier City embarked on an FA Cup run that took them all the way to the semi-finals, where they faced Spurs at Villa Park. 'That was a disastrous day for us all – there's no doubt my own-goal sealed it. I don't think we played too badly, even after they went ahead, but then it all started to go wrong. Poor Tommy Williams broke his leg, and then I found myself running back as their winger Tony Galvin put in a cross – it came over everybody and was coming to me on the edge of the box – I thought I could quite comfortably play it back to Wally [Mark Wallington], but he'd come out and it might have taken a bobble or something but I managed to perfectly chip it over him. I still don't know how I did it! But it was hard to take afterwards.'

At the end of the 1982–83 season City regained their top-flight status and 'Wils' remembers the key game. 'At around Christmas we weren't anywhere near the top – then we started to have a long unbeaten run from around January until the end of the season, and the big match for us was against Fulham, another side challenging for promotion.

'Malcolm McDonald was their manager at the time, and I remember reading beforehand that he thought they were the best footballing side and were guaranteed promotion. That got me thinking how much I wanted to beat them. My chance came when I got the ball in midfield 25 yards out, let fly and hit it low into the corner.'

The win put the Foxes in the driving seat, but they could not relax as the promotion issue went right to the end of the season – and beyond. 'On the last day we played against Burnley – it was only a draw and we didn't play that well. Fulham were at Derby and were losing when the crowd spilled on thinking it was the final whistle – they couldn't get the game restarted, so there were all sorts of protests about if the match should be replayed or not. We went off on a club end-of-season trip to Torremolinos, and it was only while we were out there that we heard that we'd gone up!'

Ian's form was being closely monitored, but he acknowledges that his elevation into the international fold may have had a helping hand. 'Our goalkeeping coach Alan Hodgkinson also worked with the Scotland squad and I'm sure both he, and our manager Gordon Milne, had words with Andy Roxburgh and Craig Brown about taking a look at me. I got invited to play for the B team at Aberdeen against France and travelled up with Gary McAllister. On the back of that I was selected for the full side for matches against England and Brazil at Hampden Park. I felt so proud and also so grateful for everyone at Leicester who'd helped me to get that far in my career.'

*'We did the double over Liverpool that year. They'd been on a long unbeaten run at Anfield, and we went there and won 2–1. It was a great win for us because they went on to win the European Cup that season!'*

# ALAN WOOLETT

*Born:*  4 March 1947, Wigston, Leicestershire.

## Leicester City record:

*Appearances:*  League 213, FA Cup 15, League Cup 17.
*Debut:*  22 April 1967 v Sheffield United (h) drew 2–2.
*Also played for:*  Northampton Town, Corby Town.

Defender Alan Woollett gave great service to Leicester City, making 245 first-team outings over a 12-year period. Capable of filling in anywhere across the back line, he profited from an injury to a teammate to appear in the 1969 FA Cup Final.

Alan joined City as an apprentice straight from school and made his debut as a late substitute against Sheffield United. The following week, in April 1967, he made his first start. 'It was away at Stoke City and ironically it was the day that Gordon Banks, who'd just left us, made his debut in goal for them.'

The defender admits he took some time to win over the City supporters after an inauspicious start to their relationship. 'It stemmed from a Cup quarter-final against Everton, and I was put in at right-back to replace Peter Rodrigues. I was just a youngster and I couldn't handle it – I cracked up with the nerves of playing in such a big game in front of 40,000 people. I started badly and had a shocker. We lost 3–1 and the crowd blamed me for it, and I had a hell of a time with them for a while.'

Despite eventually winning round the fans, Alan was never certain of an extended run in the side, despite making 33 League appearances in the 1968–69 season. Even though he had played in the FA Cup semi-final win over West Bromwich Albion, the editors of the Cup Final programme omitted his name from the centre page team lists – John Sjoberg being listed alongside the number-five shirt.

'We'd gone down to Bisham Abbey in the lead-up to the Final, and a practice match was arranged to test the fitness of John and also Lennie Glover, who were both carrying knocks. John didn't come through it, and the gaffer [Matt Gillies] told me the day before the game that I was playing so there were a lot of calls home to tell people, and I could actually see my parents as our coach drove up Wembley Way.'

City's narrow loss to Manchester City is still a mystery to many who saw the game. 'I thought we should have won it – we had some great chances really.'

Alan had an unwanted view of Manchester City's winning goal. 'Mike Summerbee turned me and cut it back from the by-line – Graham Cross just missed it as I carried on trying to get back on the line, but Neil Young struck it really well and it hit the back of the net before I could get back there.'

The disappointment of defeat was tempered slightly by the realisation of what he had done. 'On reflection nobody could ever take away the fact that I'd played in an FA Cup Final.'

Once Alan Birchenall had joined City Alan was given a fairly obvious nickname which remained with him throughout. 'Birchy was the team clown – and he just called me "The Wool".'

It says much about Alan's loyalty to City that he remained there for so long, but he recalls one period when he would have moved on. 'I read in the *News of the World* that Birmingham City had made a bid for me – they wanted myself and Allan Hunter of Ipswich to shore up their defence. I would have gone, but Leicester wouldn't let me go. We were fighting relegation at the time, and Jimmy said it would look bad if they sold me and Birmingham stayed up and we went down.'

Despite 'The Wool's prowess as a defender, he did not make much of a mark at the other end of the park. 'I never scored for the first team, but it became so much of a joke that the one day I scored for the reserves I was given the matchball! It was against Cardiff City at Filbert Street, and I crossed from right-back and it went over the 'keeper and in!'

He did come close to breaking his first-team duck, however. 'I hit the bar once – against Burnley. I'd been told to man mark Ralph Coates – wherever he went I was to follow – so when he went back to defend a corner I went with him. The ball came in, Stringy stepped over it, and I lashed at it from about six yards and it bounced back off the crossbar.'

Man marking became something of a speciality of Alan's, and he was often utilised in that role whenever City faced a particularly difficult opponent.

'Whenever we faced Manchester United I always had the job of marking George Best, and to be honest I think I came out on top in our games with them. Kevin Keegan was different, he was possibly the hardest to mark. At his peak he was non-stop. The ball was played into him, he'd play it and be off again. I came in at half-time one day not having had a touch yet I was shattered – the gaffer was pleased though, he said I'd kept him facing away from our goal!'

Alan's loyalty to the Foxes was rewarded in 1977 when he was awarded a testimonial match at Filbert Street against Chelsea.

*'and the gaffer [Matt Gillies] told me the day before the game that I was playing so there were a lot of calls home to tell people, and I could actually see my parents as our coach drove up Wembley Way.'*

# FRANK WORTHINGTON

*Born:*         23 November 1948, Halifax, West Yorkshire.

## Leicester City record:

*Appearances:*    League 210, FA Cup 18, League Cup 11.

*Goals:*         League 72, FA Cup 4, League Cup 2.

*Debut:*         23 August 1972 v Manchester United (a) drew 1–1.

*Also played for:*    Huddersfield Town, Bolton Wanderers, Philadelphia Fury (USA), Birmingham City, Tampa Bay Rowdies (USA), Leeds United, Sunderland, Southampton, Brighton and Hove Albion, Tranmere Rovers, Preston North End, Stockport County, Cape Town Spurs (South Africa), Halifax Town, England (8 caps).

*Managed:*      Tranmere Rovers.

If goals are the most priceless commodity in football, then a sense of humour would be its equivalent in everyday life.

In Frank Worthington City had a rampaging centre-forward who provided both, and he is still widely regarded as being one of the very best players – as well as the most roguish – the club has ever had on its books.

Already in demand for his goalscoring exploits at Huddersfield Town, whom he helped into the top flight in 1970, Leicester enquired about his availability but it seemed he would be moving to Merseyside instead. 'Jimmy Bloomfield had been in for me before then – but then I was on my way to Liverpool, but the deal fell through because of my high blood pressure. Obviously the good living was catching up with me already! Then I went away on a tour with England Under-23s. When I came back there was Jimmy waiting for me at Heathrow – they say everything in life is down to timing, and that was perfect timing because he whipped me straight up to Leicester and I signed.'

Frank got off to the ideal start – with a goal on his debut against Manchester United. 'It wasn't spectacular or anything, it was a ball into the box, I got in front of the defender and clipped it in at the near post. It was just a good feeling to get off the mark for my new club.'

Over the course of the next few seasons City became branded as the 'entertainers' as flair players took centre stage at Filbert Street. 'Jimmy signed us, but it was the players that developed the style that made us so good to watch – playing with the likes of Weller, Birchenall, Glover, Sammels and so on really was enjoyable, and we became a sort of "stamp of approval" on the way Jimmy believed the game should be played. It's fair to say that most people enjoyed watching Leicester City play around that time.'

While City would usually do their best to put on a show, critics would point to a lack of silverware. 'We didn't win anything because we didn't really have a defensive plan – it was the one chink in Jimmy's armour. Don't get me wrong, we had some good players at the back, but collectively we didn't have the pace necessary – it was the one area we were vulnerable.'

The nearest Frank and his colleagues came to achieving a major breakthrough was in reaching the FA Cup semi-finals of 1974, where they lost in a replay to Liverpool. 'I was knocked out in three semi-finals in my career. People talk about losing a Final, but for me probably the hardest part of being in football is to lose in a semi-final – I've always believed the Cup Final is the greatest day in the football calendar.'

There was some compensation for Frank shortly afterwards when he was called into the senior England ranks for the first time, and he made his debut against Northern Ireland with City teammate Keith Weller scoring the only goal of the game. 'Wortho' himself notched two goals from his eight appearances, which all came between May and November 1974.

As the leader of the City line, Frank proved to be a handful for the most battle-hardened opponent. Predatory in the box but tireless out of it, his pace, strength and deft touches and flicks would compliment the most flowing of moves.

His fitness was key, too, and he did not miss a match in his first three years at the club. In fact, he was only absent on four occasions in his five years as a Fox. During his peak season at Leicester 1973–74 he registered 24 goals, with a hat-trick against Ipswich Town which included two from the spot. 'I loved taking penalties – I just enjoyed the pressure of the situation and always wanted to take them. I had my own technique: I'd decide left or right and stick to that decision, but I never looked at the goalkeeper, and then I'd hit it hard and low.'

Reflections from his Filbert Street days bring an inevitable smile nowadays, 'It really was a joy to go into training every day. You never knew what type of morning you'd have. The training would be a good, hard session, but there'd be plenty of laughs about as well – we believed in working hard and having fun.'

*'I loved taking penalties – I just enjoyed the pressure of the situation and always wanted to take them. I had my own technique: I'd decide left or right and stick to that decision, but I never looked at the goalkeeper, and then I'd hit it hard and low.'*

The laughs continued, whatever the outcome on the pitch. 'I was perhaps Elvis Presley's biggest fan and loved to dress a bit like the King of Rock and Roll. Birch was always calling me "Elvis", and we had some great sing-songs on the coach journeys home from away matches. I'll always remember Birch's brilliant rendition of Tony Bennett's *I Left my Heart in San Francisco*!

Frank was labelled as a 'footballing maverick' – but he was not only a character and a comedian, he was one of the very best forwards of his generation – and a true City Legend.